The Good Men Who Won the War

T0308097

The Good Men Who Won the War

Army of the Cumberland Veterans and Emancipation Memory

Robert Hunt

THE UNIVERSITY OF ALABAMA PRESS

Tuscaloosa

The University of Alabama Press
Tuscaloosa, Alabama 35487-0380
uapress.ua.edu

Hardcover edition published 2010.
Paperback edition published 2014.
eBook edition published 2010.

Inquiries about reproducing material from this work should be addressed to the University of Alabama Press.

Typeface: Caslon

Manufactured in the United States of America
Cover Illustration: Members of the U.S. Military telegraph construction corps hanging a telegraph wire, 1860s. Courtesy of the Library of Congress, L.C.-DIG-ppmsca-12583
Cover design: Todd Lape / Lape Designs

∞
The paper on which this book is printed meets the minimum requirements of American National Standard for Information Science–Permanence of Paper for Printed Library Materials, ANSI Z39.48-1984.

Paperback ISBN: 978-0-8173-5797-9

A previous edition of this book has been catalogued by the Library of Congress as follows:

Hunt, Robert Eno, 1952–
    The good men who won the war : Army of the Cumberland veterans and emancipation memory / Robert Hunt.
        p.   cm.
    Includes bibliographical references and index.
    ISBN 978-0-8173-1688-4 (cloth : alk. paper) — ISBN 978-0-8173-8352-7 (electronic)
    1. Soldiers—United States—Attitudes—History—19th century. 2. United States. Army of the Cumberland. 3. United States—History—Civil War, 1861–1865—Social aspects. 4. Slaves—Emancipation—United States—Public opinion—History—19th century. 5. Slavery—United States—Public opinion—History—19th century. 6. United States—History—Civil War, 1861–1865—Veterans. 7. United States—Race relations—History—19th century. 8. Public opinion—United States—History—19th century. I. Title.
    E607.H867 2010
    973.7'1—dc22

                                                                                        2009031955

Contents

Illustrations

Acknowledgments

This book has been a long time coming. What began as a Web page on the Tullahoma campaign has evolved into a full-fledged discussion of how Army of the Cumberland veterans remembered their involvement in the emancipation process. The last few years of researching and writing on this topic have led me on a fascinating journey.

Like other authors, I've had help at every step of the way. Middle Tennessee State University provided a noninstructional assignment and a research grant. Virgil Statom, my graduate student assistant for one semester, researched Joseph Warren Keifer. My conversations with him on the subject were, as always with Virgil, a discussion between colleagues rather than an interchange between student and professor. The anonymous readers for The University of Alabama Press provided excellent and detailed comments, and were nicer to me than they should have been. As I was beginning to work through the copyeditor's comments, I had a wonderful and encouraging set of conversations with Chandra Manning (I had asked her to be a speaker at an NEH workshop that I organized). If many hands did not make light work, they certainly made the job pleasant, rewarding, and more accurate.

I must also thank my partner in life, Deborah. She didn't type any of the manuscript, or copyedit it, or do any of those things that wives of professors used to do. She did read chapter drafts, however, and offered the kind of commentary one would expect from the former editor of a literary magazine. In any case, she is simply relieved that the thing is now done. So am I. Now we can celebrate.

Please note that any words italicized within a quotation are rendered this way because the author of the quote intended it. I have added no emphasis to any quotation.

The Good Men Who Won the War

Introduction

This study examines Army of the Cumberland regimental histories and personal memoirs in order to evaluate how the authors included emancipation in their interpretation of the North's victory in the Civil War. During the conflict the army had been instrumental in turning invasion into an act of liberation in Kentucky, Tennessee, and Georgia, and I wanted to see how Cumberland authors incorporated this fact into the war histories they wrote in later years—if they incorporated it at all.

While studying this question I found that the available historical literature on the subject took two very different directions. On the one hand, James McPherson has led the effort to turn the Civil War into an emancipation event—an interpretation made necessary by the civil rights generation, as Edward Ayers has rightly pointed out.[1] McPherson's work, in turn, has blended with the labor of those historians who have carved out the field of "soldier studies." By marrying military history to social history, these scholars have allowed us to see soldiers as thinking individuals and as important actors in policy making. Increasingly, these studies have also demonstrated that Union men willingly aided the process of emancipation during the war. The best of these works, Chandra Manning's *What This Cruel War Was Over*, even suggests that many of the Federal soldiers became converts to liberation as a genuine social revolution. In any case, if Manning is right, the Union soldiery was pragmatic and flexible in their ability and willingness to redirect the North's war toward the controversial objective of freedom.[2]

On the other hand, in contrast to this uplifting historiography, the narratives of Reconstruction and turn-of-the-century imperialism, respectively, paint a gloomy picture of racial failure, the rise of militarism, and political reaction. Parallel to this, students of Union Civil War memory have argued that the former Federal soldiery constructed a false recollection of the war. In Stuart McConnell's study of the Grand Army of the Republic (GAR), for example, the author insists that this veterans' organization created memories of "sentimental bivouac rather than a messy war." The GAR deliberately removed any "sense of tragedy" or references to the "shock of modern combat." The veterans simply did not allow the "real war" to be expressed in the collective memory. McConnell cites John W. DeForest and Ambrose Bierce as the exceptions.[3]

Such assessments of sentimentalist cover-up have opened the door for many scholars to dismiss Union war veterans and their memory, particularly on the matter of the emancipation legacy. According to David W. Blight's *Race and Reunion,* for example, veterans crafted a shallow and romantic recollection of the war, and this helped facilitate a national reconciliation movement that wrote African Americans out of the fight entirely. Union veterans, he insists, cooperated in creating a cult of common manhood blue and gray, leaving blacks to fend for themselves in segregated America. For her part, Cecelia O'Leary argues that the Grand Army of the Republic became openly reactionary, deploying their war memory to promote a culture of militarism in response to the labor, gender, and racial troubles of the turn of the century.[4]

This literature has been critiqued, of course. New studies have found that Union veterans were reluctant to abandon their former comrades in the United States Colored Troops (USCT), and were hardly eager to make common cause with their former Confederate enemies. In his excellent discussion of honoring the Union war dead, for example, John Neff asserts that most of the former soldiers did not support reconciliation but remained insistent in defending their triumph—their belief in the "Cause Victorious," as he styles it.[5] I certainly applaud this critical literature and hope that my effort gives it aid and comfort. For my part, I will critique the argument that Union veterans buried or distorted the "real war," because in the question of what counts as real lies the key to the Cumberland writers' memory of emancipation.

The authors of Cumberland regimental histories and memoirs were certainly part of late-Victorian culture and so it would be odd if sentimentalism did not run through their work in some form. This said, these authors did not use their narratives to indulge in literary escapism or romance. To the contrary, they constructed an argument. They used their histories to insist that the Union army had preserved the country's fundamental military traditions intact—particularly the ideal of the citizen-soldier—while adapting these traditions to the demands made by unprecedented war. According to the writers, the North's Civil War both sanctified and updated the country's way of war making, and this meant that the country could meet the challenges of the future. Cumberland authors did not write simply to tell of (or disguise) their experiences. They wrote to demonstrate that America would be a powerful nation in the new century. They argued that they had prepared the United States for a future on the world stage.

To be sure, Cumberland writers were crafting mythology when they made this assertion. Neff is right to argue that Union veterans forcibly *insisted* that they had won a victory. However, it is striking how accurate the authors often were. As will be seen in the chapters that follow, many writers were quite precise (even self-critical) about the nature of Sherman's hard war, the problems of mass-organized combat, or the shift in 1864 to a war of attrition. What Cumberland narrators actually did was blend their sense of the American citizen-soldier tradition with hard-headed war analysis. In any case, they did not smother the "real war" under false sentimentality.

Cumberlanders focused this blend of tradition and analysis on a fundamental problem: how to find true and lasting victory in what a later generation would describe as a modern, total war. This was a difficult issue. The North (and the South) organized incredible and unprecedented military power between 1861 and 1865. The region recruited men by the several thousands, developed efficient methods to support the armies, and eventually found a way to focus it all into an overwhelming destructive force. Compared to previous conflicts, the North's war was something close to a total mobilization—an American *levée en masse*. In addition, this mobilization was turned into a true total war by 1863. The Lincoln administration replaced the goal of restoring the Union with the idea that the Slave Power was a corruption of the American mission and that this social system had to be destroyed completely. Wartime victory would have to produce the most comprehensive kind of unconditional surrender.

However, all this mobilization and focused organization could not accomplish the intended object. First, although the North defeated the Confederate independence movement, the nation (or, better, the Republican party) never secured political control over the Southern states. Ironically, the more the Union organized its massive power, and the more it revolutionized its aims, the weaker it became. From 1863 on, the North was imagining a kind of total war that it did not have the capacity to win. Second, as the North learned to become more destructive in its war making—to create a true overwhelming force—the more this raised disturbing questions about violence. After all, the Civil War was not to be what white Americans defined as "Indian war," but a fight among equals kept within the boundaries of nineteenth-century civilization.[6] Once massive destructive force was unleashed, this raised the issue of whether the victors might lose their collective soul by winning. In the long and short of it, the embrace of modern, fully mobilized, total war produced an ironic mathematics: expanding power made victory more elusive.

Confronted with the need to make sense out of this total war in the years after Confederate surrender and Reconstruction, Cumberland writers responded by creating a kind of double picture. They happily described their own transformation from a collection of individual recruits to a massive, disciplined fighting and destroying machine. They celebrated the army, discussing in vivid detail its destructive capability, eager in the process to demonstrate how this capability had made America into a power. At the same time, few made reference to the Southern society that the army had supposedly conquered. To be sure, they wrote at length about dismantling the Army of Tennessee and ending the Confederate independence movement. However, outside of Albion Tourgee, who will be discussed in these pages, the writers left the enduring South alone.

Cumberland writers found their total victory elsewhere. The army had unleashed its massive destructive force on the enemy in the South. In the act of doing so, they said, they had protected and kept pristine the Midwest from which most of these men had been recruited. As they described it, war was indeed a horror of destruction, death, and degeneration. However, by entering a world of pure violence in the South they preserved a kind of innocence in the North. An innocence that wore many faces: the girl—or the wife and mother—left behind, the peaceful pursuits of industry, a society spared both militarization and destruction. Cumberland authors resolved the problem of elusive victory by constructing two contrasting images: a world of total war in a foreign land and a home world sheltered from the storm. In contrast to David Bell's portrait of Revolutionary France, where the population embraced a culture of militarism and pure war, Americans responded to the problem of total war by creating a dichotomy of separate spheres.[7]

The critical issue here is that Cumberland authors created in their memory of the Civil War what would become a foundation for later generations of Americans to understand and imagine their own total wars. Of course, the writers developed their themes within the context of the Victorian culture they knew, but the basic paradigm would outlive them. Indeed, later generations would not know of the Cumberland writers at all. The authors wrote their regimental histories and memoirs primarily for their comrades and their children. Only the occasional Tourgee or Wilbur Fisk Hinman (treated in chapter 4) achieved anything like notoriety. But the problem of massive power, millennial expectations, and elusive victory would hardly be limited to this small batch of Union veterans. The important point is that later generations would discover these same themes and rework them in their own way. Out of the urgency to come to grips with their own total war, Cumberland authors struck a taproot in American culture.

In this taproot, as well, lay the Cumberlanders' memory of emancipation. Without question, the writers provided no support for creating a revolution of race in the defeated Confederacy. As the following chapters will show, the Cumberland authors' attitudes toward African Americans, slavery, and postslavery were more complex and varied than the reunion and reaction school would admit, but there is no question that Cumberland writers side-stepped the issues raised by the failure of Reconstruction. Tourgee was the conspicuous exception. However, this hardly meant that the veterans "forgot" that blacks had been part of the war. Rather, they incorporated emancipation and its legacy into their war by absorbing it into their search for innocence. Specifically, the liberation of others became understood as a critical objective for which an American military fights. Cumberland authors turned emancipation into part of the comprehensive picture of American war making: a justification for American war in general. In this respect they absorbed African American liberation in a way similar to the cult image of Lincoln the Great Emancipator, as described by Kirk Savage.[8]

However, this did not mean that the Cumberland memory of emancipation was meaningless. Consider that the truth of Reconstruction politics was buried for years in the distorted memory of the "Tragic Era" until the civil rights generation revived it, while, by contrast, the issue of why an American military fights a modern, total war was a constant, enduring, and creative question. It was asked and answered in new ways and contexts from the early twentieth century up until our own time. The dawn of the Progressive Era inaugurated a century of American war, and so the issue of motive (and result) was a constant source of questioning—and social revolution. It is no accident that what we term the modern civil rights movement was a product of the Second World War. Cumberland authors had laid the groundwork for this fulfillment in the American way of war making that they had described at the turn of the century.

~

I chose to use Army of the Cumberland memoirs and regimental histories for this study because I know these men. Having worked in Middle Tennessee for several years, I have walked the army's battlegrounds and driven along the campaign trails. I have also tried to help preserve the army's few remaining historic sites. More than this, I chose to study Cumberland memory because the army viewed slavery at close range and from many angles. Created in its original form as Maj. Gen. Don Carlos Buell's Army of the Ohio, the army spent its first months organizing and training in Kentucky. From the first moments of deployment, the men dealt with slave refugees, accepting some of these individuals as camp cooks and teamsters. From this point the soldiery experienced all manner of tricky, muddled, or confusing situations: Unionist slave owners in Kentucky; Tennessee's exemption from the Emancipation Proclamation; the massive influx of contraband into Nashville and other Middle Tennessee garrison towns; the recruiting of the USCT and the use of black troops in formal combat at the Battle of Nashville. The Cumberlanders saw slavery and the disintegration of the institution in several contexts and situations. As well, these were Midwesterners and Kentuckians (there were fourteen numbered Kentucky infantry regiments in the force as of spring 1863)—hardly an army of idealistic or revolutionary New Englanders. In short, the Army of the Cumberland is an excellent source for studying the issues and ideologies involved in slavery's dismantling during the war, while the soldiers' regimental histories and memoirs provide a way to measure what was remembered of it later.

In putting this study together I used the Army of the Cumberland's order of battle as it appeared just before the Tullahoma campaign in June 1863. The army was complete at this point. By this juncture the original regiments that had formed Buell's Army of the Ohio in 1861 had been joined by reinforcements from Missouri and by units newly formed in 1862. In addition, a "Reserve Corps" under Gordon Granger—troops that had been stationed in Kentucky—were now incorporated into the main force. Fully fleshed out in this form, the Cumberland army would fight through the Tullahoma campaign and Chickamauga. After the latter engagement, the Army of the Cumberland would be reinforced by two corps from the Army of the Potomac that would operate under Maj. Gen. George H. Thomas's command during the Atlanta campaign. These new arrivals were eastern troops who had missed the early days in Kentucky and the long occupation of Middle Tennessee, and so I did not include these regiments in my study.

From this order of volunteer infantry regiments, artillery batteries, and cavalry squadrons I searched for every available regimental history or personal memoir published in 1880 or later.[9] I chose this year because the memory and reunion literature sees this point as the beginning of the Union veterans' decline in their commitment to emancipation. Thus arranged, the sources run from works published in 1880 up to the *Life Story of Captain Newton H. Kingman* released in 1928. I have used published works exclusively because it is the public presentation of the veterans' war memory that I want to explore. Regimental histories and personal memoirs were public monuments in words, and the fact that the authors would have polished the marble a bit is the very point of looking at these sources. Granted that most of the regimentals were published for "the boys" in the respective units, the authors still understood that they were writing for posterity. They were quite conscious that they were discussing and defending the army's reputation and memory.

As well, I worked entirely with regimental histories and complete personal memoirs. I avoided the large collection of articles in the Commandery Papers of the Military Order of the Loyal Legion of the United States, for example. These papers and like sources focus on individual battles, anecdotes, and incidents. I wanted to review those sources where the authors understood that they were writing about the war as a whole. To be sure, a regimental history focuses solely on one unit but the author had to cover the duration of service and make several choices about what to include. These were not simply battle and campaign studies. Authors discussed how their particular regiment was raised, the motivations for joining up, encounters with civilians during the long months of invasion, and a number of other subjects. Some even included long political discussions of the coming of the war. In each case, authorial choice was crucial and revealing. By selecting what to include and not include, these writers defined the meaning of the war. *Their* real war did get into the books and it is precisely this war that I want to evaluate.

As one might expect, the story varies from one source to the next. Among other things, these were histories written from 1880 to 1928 and they each represent idiosyncratic decisions about when to publish and what to include. Although authors of different histories would make textual references to one another, there was no concert of action. Thus, there is a huge range. Some are far too short. William A. Schmitt's *History of the Twenty-seventh Illinois Volunteers,* for example, is only ten pages. By contrast, Charles Partridge's study of the Ninety-sixth Illinois includes numerous anecdotes from a number of the men, along with rosters and the basic story line. It runs over a thousand pages. Likewise, ideology and focus varies. Marvin Butler's 1914 work, *My Story of the Civil War and the Under-ground Railroad,* is not a war study at all but an abolition romance about the liberation of Tennessee slaves during the war. By contrast, Charles Manderson's *Twin Seven-Shooters* is the one true reunion and reconciliation memoir in the batch. For his part, Judson W. Bishop of the Second Minnesota included a detailed list of recommendations for preparing America for the next war. Bishop had been the regiment's colonel and had risen to brigade command during the war, and so his thoughts about military organization came naturally.[10] In any case, the last thing one finds in these memoirs and regimentals is endless repetition of campaign, battle, and campfire stories devoid of politics or controversy. The tough interpretive task is to find the common ground.

In this regard it is quite a help that most of the authors were amateurs. Albion Tourgee, of course, certainly knew the ropes. Wilbur Fisk Hinman and J. Henry Haynie were also professional writers. However, most of the Cumberland narrators broke into literary history only at this one, solitary moment, and most called attention to their lack of skill. From the historian's perspective, it is a wonderfully advantageous amateurism. Because most writers sought to use everything pertinent to their regiment's service, particularly the juicy stories, they remained blissfully unaware or unconcerned about ideological or narrative consistency. The authors wanted to be inclusive, and if they were conscious of potential ironies or contradictions, they were happily uncaring. Their collective memory is all the more genuine and revealing for this.

A final word on these sources. I have avoided the memoirs of the major figures from the army, such as Philip Henry Sheridan. Civil War historians have explored the top leadership of the western armies at length, and so there is a large secondary literature available. I am looking at other veterans. If not always the ordinary soldier—Benjamin Franklin Scribner was a brigade commander, for example—I have focused on sources that no one but Civil War military historians (and western theater specialists at that) know about or ever use. Moreover, I have avoided the magnificent work of Ambrose Bierce. No American wrote about the war with such intensity and fundamental anger as this Army of the Cumberland veteran. There is an extensive secondary literature on Bierce and he is an obligatory reference in any memory study. However, to include him here would require a lengthy and special treatment, and I could say nothing that the hordes of Bierce students have not already said. More to the point, my study is not about the trauma of war. Unlike the Great War poets, the Cumberlanders did not produce a literature of disillusion.[11] They produced a literature of victory. For that reason, Albion Tourgee matters more than Bierce. Tourgee was the North's most brilliant Carpetbagger. His view of the war was bound up in Reconstruction and its failure, and so he is a vitally important counterpoint to the other Cumberland authors.

This study is divided into a prelude and four chapters. The prelude provides a brief overview of the Army of the Cumberland's organization, campaigns, battles, and invasion of the South. For those readers who are not practicing historians of the Civil War's western theater, this will be important backstory. Chapter 1 explores how the Cumberland veterans recalled and described their embrace of emancipation war. The war became a revolution under their feet. How did they describe and interpret this process later? Chapter 2 examines the Cumberlanders' understanding that they were citizen-soldiers who had entered a war beyond anything known in American history up to that point. It was out of this situation that they described this new and confusing "real war" and went on to define the victory they had won. Chapter 3 discusses how Cumberland writers incorporated African Americans and former Confederates into their war and into their definition of victory. In their collective memory the authors had to come to terms with the army's former allies and former enemies. Finally, chapter 4 focuses on two individuals, Wilbur Fisk Hinman and Joseph Warren Keifer. As the author of *Corporal Si Klegg and His "Pard,"* Hinman wrote a war novel that created a kind of master narrative of the Cumberland soldier's experience. Keifer, a Republican congressman after the war, wrote the most politically charged memoir of all the authors. More importantly, he took his memory of the war with him into a long congressional career. In two blocs of consecutive terms he served in the House up to the Wilson administration. These two authors represent the legacy of the Cumberland army's war. They are the bridge between the recorded experience of individual regiments and authors, and the enduring vision of an American way of war that would long outlast these former soldiers.

Prelude

The Army of the Cumberland's War, 1861–1865

> I am not an Abolitionist, ie., a *political* abolitionist. I have no affilia-
> tion with or sympathy for the *political* abolitionist, for they are a cant-
> ing hypocritical set of cowards, having courage only to support their
> peculiar opinions with their tongues; they can't be found in our armies
> now, but are at home, holding their tea party conventions, mourning
> over 'man's inhumanity to man' and adopting addresses to the Presi-
> dent entreating him to proclaim to the world that the negro is the
> equal of the white man, and that it is an abolition war. The fanatical
> fools! Can't they see, without conventions or proclamations, that it is
> an abolition war?
>
> You see I am a *practical* but not a *political* abolitionist.
> —James A. Connolly to his wife, November 22, 1863

In a journal he kept during the war and in several letters to his wife,
James Connolly, a major in the 123rd Illinois, chronicled the life of the
Union's Army of the Cumberland. What he discussed was not the glories or horrors of battle but the cruel reality of invasion, demonstrating in
his description how this invasion led to revolution. Connolly was a self-
proclaimed Democrat, and so was no friend of President Lincoln or the
congressional Radicals. Yet, as he discusses above, he became an abolitionist nonetheless. Connolly exemplified what Mark Grimsley refers to
as the Union's "hard war" mentality. Soldiers and officers came to believe
that they could destroy the rebellion by decimating Confederate property,
property in slaves included. In this sense, all Union soldiers would eventually become "practical abolitionists." Connolly made the point directly. In
the fall of 1862 he ranted to his wife that the army needed a general "who
sees nothing sacred in negro slavery . . . who will not guard rebel wells and
springs to keep our thirsty soldiers from slaking their thirst—one who will
hang every rebel guerilla in Kentucky, drive every cowardly sympathizer
out of the state and confiscate his property for the use of our soldiers."[1]

When writing their regimental histories and personal memoirs at the
turn of the century, Cumberland authors remembered the war that Con-

nolly described in 1862 and 1863. The narrators did not write exclusively about combat because their war had been about battle only in part. From the moment the army began its life in Kentucky, the soldiery embarked on the hazardous adventure of invasion. The men lived in the enemy's country, encountered hostile civilians and guerillas at every step, fought the ever-elusive Confederate cavalry, and dealt constantly with refugee slaves. When Cumberland authors sat down years later to put it all in print for the remaining veterans and their families, this would be the war they recalled. As the army first penetrated the upper South, and then worked its way deeper into enemy territory, the soldiers and officers had to learn how to prosecute a war of destruction, not simply engage in combat.

The army began its existence under Don Carlos Buell. Appointed to relieve a distracted William Tecumseh Sherman on November 9, 1861, Buell was given command of the various regiments then based or arriving in Kentucky. He took over the training camps and began to organize the men into brigades and divisions, titling the whole as the Army of the Ohio. Buell then spent the winter trying to discipline his sadly under-trained men.[2]

Buell was a soft-war man. Convinced as were many at the time that secession represented the conspiracy of an extremist political leadership, the general believed that keeping hands off the property of Southerners and hands off their slaves would persuade the majority to return to the Union. No friend of abolitionism, Buell wanted to ensure that his army showed no radical taint. Moreover, as a West Point career officer, he feared that licensed marauding would corrupt an army composed of volunteers. Buell had his reasons. He wanted to discipline his men and concentrate on defeating Confederate troops in battle. In so thinking, he would come to enrage individuals like Connolly, but his views were perfectly in harmony with War Department policy and with the ideas of his military superior, Maj. Gen. George B. McClellan.[3]

But the war would quickly outrun Buell. First, Kentucky's divided population made the common soldiers suspicious of the civilians who surrounded them. Then, when the army moved into Tennessee in spring 1862, the men hardened further, and for good reason. The Army of the Ohio occupied Nashville shortly after Ulysses S. Grant took forts Henry and Donelson in February. When the troops arrived in the city they found a defiant civilian population.

Nashville and Middle Tennessee had embraced secession with all the fervor of a convert. When the crisis of 1861 first opened, the area was Unionist. John Bell, after all, was from the area. However, when Sumter was fired upon and Lincoln called for troops, the counties of the mid-state switched sides, providing the swing vote necessary to allow Tennessee to secede. Having thus shifted their politics in response to the threat of direct coercion, Middle Tennessee residents were outraged when Union forces actually appeared. It hardly helped their mood that Nashville was the first Confederate state capital to fall to the Union.[4]

John Fitch recorded the Tennesseans' anger. In his 1863 *Annals of the Army of the Cumberland,* this officer—the army's judge advocate—stated that "in no city in the South had our army met with so bitter a reception as at Nashville." He continued that "the intense hatred of the Secessionists of Nashville for the Union troops displayed itself in the most contemptuous expressions and incidents." He then reprinted a message "written in a female hand" left in an abandoned house. "I hope that every officer who enters this house may depart this life in double-quick time; that they may suffer the torture of ten thousand deaths before they die. And paralyzed be the hand that would alleviate their sufferings; and may the tongue of him who would speak words of comfort cleave to the roof of his mouth. And as for the Yankee women who are hungry for the spoils, may—but cursed are they already. God bless the Southern cause! curse the Northern, and all that fight for it!"[5] To the rank and file of Buell's army, such sentiments did not suggest Southern hearts and minds eager to be won back to the old loyalties.

Within the next few weeks, the situation with Southern civilians got worse. A short time after his arrival in the Tennessee capital, Buell moved his army south and west toward a junction with Grant's forces at Pittsburg Landing. In addition, he sent a division under Brig. Gen. Ormsby M. Mitchel into northern Alabama and southern Tennessee. Mitchel split his force into its component brigades and regiments along the Memphis and Charleston rail line, which exposed the now-isolated units to Confederate raiding and civilian rage.

The enemy struck quickly. In a widely reported incident Southern irregulars sabotaged a railroad bridge on May 1 and burned a train. A Union lieutenant recorded that one of the bridge guards told him that the insurgents "'had surrounded the train and fired into it, wounding several of the soldiers and they would not allow the Negroes to help our men out and two of them were burned to death. Our troops swore vengeance.'"[6]

On the same day, several companies from the Eighteenth Ohio were surprised by Confederate cavalry and driven in panic from the little town of Athens, Alabama, where the troops had been stationed. Later, the Rebel commander boasted that "'my boys took few prisoners, their shots proving singularly fatal.'" To make matters worse, the fleeing soldiers "'received insults from the men and women of the town when they were driven out, being called 'G——d d——d Sons of Bitches' and the women spit on their faces.'"

These incidents prompted reprisals. Col. John Basil Turchin, the local brigade commander, occupied Athens a few days later. As he was establishing a defensive perimeter, at least two of the regiments under his command proceeded to loot the town's stores, the incident becoming known infamously as the "Sack of Athens." It did not help that Turchin was, in fact, Ivan Turchaninov, an émigré and a former officer in the army of the Czar. Remarks about Cossacks circulated widely.[7]

Clearly, the situation in northern Alabama was deteriorating rapidly. Buell's attempt to script a tender invasion was falling apart. In particular, the general was losing control not only of his men but also his subordinate officers. As the situation with Turchin demonstrated, brigade commanders were effectively determining war policy, and were doing so with something other than a spirit of charity toward the enemy. Buell tried to reassert control by arresting Turchin and impaneling a court-martial, but that body—composed largely of the Russian's fellow brigade commanders—refused to convict the officer. Worse yet, the War Department then promoted him.[8]

As spring turned to summer, northern Alabama degenerated into war to the knife. John Beatty, another brigade commander, had sat on Turchin's court-martial, but was hardly sympathetic to Buell's attempt to prosecute a gentleman's war. In reaction to a guerilla attack near Paint Rock, Alabama, Beatty warned the surrounding civilians that there would be reprisals. Describing it in his journal the commander noted that he had informed residents that "hereafter every time the telegraph wire was cut we would burn a house; every time a train was fired upon we should hang a man; and we would continue to do this until every house was burned and every man hanged between Decatur and Bridgeport."[9]

The local Rebel population gave as good as it got. Later in the summer another of the army's brigade commanders, Robert McCook, was assassinated in an ambulance. McCook was ill and unable either to command men or defend himself, and this only made him an easy target. The incident was infamous enough to be depicted on the cover of *Frank Leslie's*

Illustrated Newspaper. As Gerald Prokopowicz observes, the men of the Ninth Ohio, "McCook's original regiment, responded to the atrocity in kind, hanging civilians and burning houses for miles around."[10] Obviously, Buell was losing control of his army and his invasion policy.

After taking part in the Battle of Shiloh and in the capture of Corinth, Mississippi, Buell took the Army of the Ohio east along the Memphis and Charleston rail line to threaten Chattanooga. To counter this, Confederate general Braxton Bragg organized a sizable force and moved with it into Kentucky in an attempt to bring the Bluegrass State into the Southern republic. The move failed politically, but it forced the Union commander to backpedal all the way to Louisville. The two armies fought an inconclusive battle at Perryville on October 8. Though Bragg retreated, Buell's performance in the action was pointedly lackluster, while his pursuit produced a fatal disagreement with Lincoln and the War Department about his ultimate objective.[11] By November he was replaced by Maj. Gen. William S. Rosecrans.

The new general was in command but a short while before he saw action at Stones River on December 31, 1862, and January 2, 1863. Fought largely to solidify the Union army's hold on Nashville, the battle was a near thing, but it was Bragg who retreated (to Shelbyville and Tullahoma). The Federal army had a victory of sorts. As well, the combat marked the date on which the Emancipation Proclamation went into effect. Although Tennessee was expressly exempted from the directive, it was clear enough that as the army went further south it would take liberation with it.[12]

For the present, however, the army sat. Rosecrans wanted to rebuild and retrain his force—now officially the Army of the Cumberland. Operating out of Nashville and Murfreesboro, the army lay at the end of a long and tenuous supply line, and this line would only lengthen the further south Rosecrans went. The general insisted on building up his wagon transportation to operate in this situation. Moreover, he wanted to create a mounted arm able to handle the Confederacy's formidable horsemen. John Hunt Morgan, Nathan Bedford Forrest, and Joseph Wheeler had made a logistical and communications shambles of Buell's drive toward Chattanooga the previous year, and Rosecrans wanted no repeat performance. But creating such a buildup, particularly in horses and mules, took a tremendous amount of time. As a result, the Army of the Cumberland stationed itself in the Nashville-Murfreesboro area for six months.[13]

By default this made the army into a force of destruction by virtue of occupation. Even with supplies coming from the North, the Cumberlanders had to forage heavily on the local civilians and had to do so repeatedly, stripping the countryside bare. With this continual pressure on Tennessee citizens, Buell's original soft-war policy became nothing but a memory. Officers and men took a hard line with disloyal civilians and their property, if for no other reason than they had to do so to supply themselves.[14]

This hard line hardened further because the Cumberlanders' occupation took place as a civil war began to erupt among Tennesseeans. In March 1862 Andrew Johnson had been sent to Nashville with a brigadier general's commission and an appointment as the state's military governor. His regime quickly dissolved into factionalism as the state's Unionists divided into pro-emancipation and anti-emancipation wings, a split that roughly reflected a divide between Unionist refugees from East Tennessee and pro-slavery loyalists from the middle part of the state. These two factions, in turn, were attacked tooth and claw by swarms of Confederate Tennessee irregulars angered not only by Union occupation but by neighbors whom they saw as traitors. As Stephen Ash observes, Middle Tennessee became an ungovernable place.[15]

The irregulars focused their attention as much on their Tennessee neighbors as they did the Army of the Cumberland's troops. In Ash's description, guerillas combined terrorism with sabotage, creating a stream of refugees and making the countryside unsafe. The situation then became worse as guerillas degenerated into little more than bandit gangs. Middle Tennessee became less an occupied zone than a lawless "no-man's land." As Ash details, slow-moving Union infantry could provide little help. Anarchy ruled outside the garrison towns.[16]

This disintegration of the countryside opened the door to slavery's end in Tennessee. As Stephen Ash and John Cimprich have described, slavery's infrastructure disintegrated as the state drifted into disorder. When the countryside crumbled, bondpeople had no reason to stay on the farms or plantations, while no slave patrols were around to keep them there. They could flee to Nashville, or to other makeshift refugee settlements. Wherever the Army of the Cumberland established a garrison, blacks showed up, often in huge numbers. Despite Tennessee's exemption from the Emancipation Proclamation, slavery was falling apart anyway.[17]

And the army's commanders saw tremendous advantages to this situation. Despite the enormous refugee problem, contraband became a welcome source of labor to a nineteenth-century military force starved for workers. Indeed, the use of contraband had started early, when the Army of the Ohio had first entered Nashville.

In his *Annals,* Fitch described the chaotic scene when Buell had to backtrack into Kentucky to chase Braxton Bragg's Confederate invasion force. The Union commander was forced to uncover Nashville, prompting Johnson to insist that the city be defended. In response, Buell ordered his chief engineer, Capt. James St. Clair Morton, to build fortifications, the first of which would come to be known as Fort Negley. Morton set to work quickly, impressing all the black labor he could find in the immediate environs of Nashville. As Fitch admitted, the process was anything but liberating. "Every able-bodied negro in the city whom [Morton] could lay hands upon he 'pressed' and put upon the work. Barber-shops and kitchens were visited, and their inmates taken 'willy-nilly.' The Commercial Hotel was thus cleared of servants one morning: there was no dinner for many an expectant guest, and the house was closed."

Fitch went on to say that by these means "a force of two-thousand negroes were soon at work upon Fort Negley." Almost sheepishly, he added that "to the credit of the colored population be it said, they worked manfully and cheerfully, with hardly an exception, and yet lay out upon the works of nights under guard, without blankets, and eating only army-rations."[18] The Army of the Cumberland was hardly the most pleasant of employers.

But the slaves came anyway. Whether individual officers were high-handed or sympathetic, the Union army's continued occupation of Tennessee meant that bondpeople had a place to run. Not only did this fact create an enormous refugee problem, it rattled the state's slave system to its foundation. Maj. Gen. Lovell Rousseau, in command at Nashville, stated the point succinctly in a January 1864 report. "Slavery is virtually dead in Tennessee, although the State is excepted from the emancipation proclamation. Negroes leave their homes and stroll over the country uncontrolled. Hundreds of them are now supported by the Government who neither work nor are able to work. Many straggling negroes have arms obtained from soldiers, and by their insolence and threats greatly alarm and intimidate white families, who are not allowed to keep arms, or would generally be afraid to use [them] if they had them."

As his words indicate, Rousseau—a Kentucky-born officer—was no supporter of this process. In his eyes, the freedom to flee had produced not liberation from bondage but insolence of temper. "Negroes leave their homes to work for themselves," he complained, "boarding and lodging with their masters, defiantly asserting their right to do it." Completely misjudging the drift of policy in the Lincoln War Department, Rousseau whimpered that "this State being excepted from the emancipation proclamation, I supposed all [these] things are against good faith and the policy of the Government."

Thus did the soldiers of the Army of the Cumberland participate in a dramatic evolution toward destructive war. By 1864 invasion meant no quarter for suspected guerillas and their civilian supporters, along with a calculated stripping of the Southern countryside. The long occupation of Tennessee was nothing less than a war on civilians. Included in this was the destruction of slavery, whatever Lincoln's policy might be regarding exemption from the Emancipation Proclamation. As Major General Rousseau pointedly stated, "it is now and has been for some time the practice of soldiers to go to the country and bring in wagon-loads of negro women and children to this city, and I suppose to other posts."[19] Courtesy of their constant presence in Tennessee, Cumberland soldiers came readily to understand that the war of invasion was about dismantling the South, not simply fighting the enemy in formal combat.

~

But the Army of the Cumberland had its share of battle. In late June 1863, Major General Rosecrans finally yielded to War Department pressure and moved his force south in what came to be known as the Tullahoma campaign. The Union commander maneuvered General Bragg's Army of Tennessee out of the southern part of the state without a major battle, and in August prepared his army to perform a similar trick in northern Georgia. However, the Richmond government—alarmed at last—reinforced the Confederate general, enabling him to fight Rosecrans in the brutal two-day Battle of Chickamauga. It was a horrible and near thing. The Confederates chopped Rosecrans's army in half, routing one portion, while the rest made a magnificent stand on Snodgrass Hill, saving the situation. The men then retreated to Chattanooga, and once there found themselves under siege.[20]

Because of this disaster, Rosecrans was relieved and George H. Thomas—the soldiers' favorite—was placed in charge. This change made, the Cumberland army then lost its status as an independent command. To confront the Confederates besieging Chattanooga, the War Department brought in elements from the Army of the Potomac under Joseph Hooker and the Army of the Tennessee under William Tecumseh Sherman. In charge of the whole was U. S. Grant. Quickly enough he raised the siege of Chattanooga in a battle that included the Army of the Cumberland's spectacular charge straight up Missionary Ridge. After the battle Grant went east to assume overall command of the Union's military forces, leaving Sherman to take charge of the men at Chattanooga.

As part of this Chattanooga army group, the Army of the Cumberland became a full-fledged, full-time combat force. The Cumberlanders had spent most of the war's first three years fighting civilians, guerillas, and the vaunted Confederate cavalry. Full-scale battle had intruded brutally but only occasionally. Now the army became part of the combined forces that Sherman led south to Atlanta. From May to September 1864, the Cumberland brigades and divisions—along with Sherman's other units—knew nothing but constant maneuver and combat. Save for the garrison troops stationed in Tennessee, the Cumberland men had left occupation duty far behind. Invasion now meant the piece-by-piece destruction of the western Confederate army. This force was skillfully led by Joseph E. Johnston during that officer's tenure in command. His replacement, John Bell Hood, would bring the Confederates to grief.

With the fall of Atlanta in September came the Army of the Cumberland's last shift in mission. Strictly speaking, the army ceased to exist. It was split in half, the Fourth Corps going as part of Thomas's contingent back to Tennessee to protect Nashville from Confederate raiding, while the Fourteenth Corps, under Jefferson C. Davis, went with Sherman on his March to the Sea and his Carolina campaign.[21] Because the Fourth Corps participated in the Battle of Nashville, many of its regiments saw United States Colored Troops in action, and regimental historians would comment on the fact later. For its part, the Fourteenth Corps was part of Sherman's big raid, and so became part of that officer's legendary assault on Southern civilians. The fact of the matter, however, was that Cumberlanders had been engaged in the practice of hard war since the spring of 1862. Indeed, they had been more effective at it than Sherman, since they had remained a voracious presence in Middle Tennessee for several months.

In any case, the war effectively ended with Sherman's move into the Carolinas. Grant broke through Lee's Petersburg lines and then forced the sad remnants of the Army of Northern Virginia to surrender on April 9, 1865. Confronted with this fact, Confederate general Joseph E. Johnston took matters into his own hands and, defying his president, surrendered his own force to Sherman. This accomplished, the other Rebel forces gave up, leaving the Confederacy devoid of formal military power. Given this vacuum, the Southern republic effectively ended, not through any formal political capitulation but because the South's uniformed military leadership removed the possibility of further legitimate resistance. With this accomplished, Cumberland soldiers, and all the other Union forces, could return home.

~

Thus the Cumberland soldiers' war. When in later years the veterans sat down to write the history of their particular regiment, or of their individual careers, the authors certainly had plenty of important formal combat to discuss. In particular, survivors of Snodgrass Hill had at least a plausible claim that their brave stand on the little rise had saved the entire Union war effort from collapse. Cumberland men had certainly seen battle.

Yet formal combat was only a segment of their war. For the majority of their time, the soldiers had dealt with Confederate civilians, the various issues of occupation and invasion, and refugee slaves. It would be odd that veterans writing later would include nothing of this other war in their recollections, although with some authors this was in fact the case. But with many of the memoirs and regimentals, the Cumberlanders' real war did make it into the recorded collective memory. These authors sought to describe in some form the *complete* war they had experienced. The issue at hand is the way they conceived this war and the way they tried to find enduring victory.

1
Remembered War;
Forgotten Struggle

[We] were all anxious to leave the scenes of warfare and strife and go
back to God's country, to home and friends and loved ones; to lay aside
the uniform and the sword and take up the implements and avocations
of peace.

—Thomas Crofts, from his history of the Third Ohio Cavalry

At various times after 1880 individual authors (or committees) sat down
to write the history of a Cumberland army regiment or the story of a soldier's life. When they did so there was no agreed-upon pattern to follow.
Although a number of the authors read their compatriots' works (often
enough for the purpose of disagreeing about campaign details), no standard was ever set for what a regimental history or military autobiography
should contain. The writers composed their studies at different times
prompted by various circumstances. As a result, Cumberland narratives
are a hodge-podge. Some are richly textured, voluminous discussions of a
regiment's or an individual's service, while others are merely sketches.

Fortunately, the more elaborate Cumberland histories create nearly a
complete look at the army's war. This completeness does not represent the
particular writer's interpretive ambitions so much as the desire to include
all the experience that could be recalled or copied from journals and notes.
Cumberland narratives are excursive more than systematic or analytical.
But from the desire to tell it all, the authors fashioned something of a total picture. In addition to describing combat, the writers discussed camp
life, the enlistment process, the virtues of a citizen-soldiery, the politics of
secession, and, most important, the shift in the army's strategy from the
"rosewater" days of 1861 to the hard war that took hold beginning in early
1862. As part of this, the writers discussed slavery and emancipation, looking at how these elements were woven into the evolution of the war itself.
In this respect, the real war got into the books.

As a result, one can read the detailed memoirs and regimental histories as testimony to the Cumberland veterans' willingness to remember
emancipation and the larger Civil War. Far from removing or forgetting

this memory, the narratives provide a look at the process by which the men came to link the abolition of slavery to the war against the Confederacy. In particular, the memoirs and regimentals provide an important angle on the army's change of temper on this issue, because the stories are with few exceptions written chronologically. Not only did Cumberland authors make emancipation part of their remembered war, they retraced the process by which the soldiers came to support the idea. This chapter will detail this evolution as the narrators wrote it into the army's memory.

Importantly, Cumberland authors ended their tale with the Confederate surrender. If they were inclusive and expansive when describing events from Fort Sumter to Joe Johnston's capitulation, the narrators ever so conveniently ended things in summer 1865. The "problem" with the regimental histories and memoirs is not that they erased the African American presence in the larger war. Rather, it is that the authors, with but a couple of exceptions, chose to disconnect Reconstruction from the story.

Albion Winegar Tourgee, the famous Carpetbagger, illustrates why. An officer in the 105th Ohio, Tourgee had been part of the Army of the Cumberland until injury forced his resignation and return home in 1863. Years later he was enlisted to write *The Story of a Thousand,* the unit history of his regiment, which he completed in 1896. The book is of a piece with its fellow regimentals, which is to say that it is unlike Tourgee's other writings. In particular, it is unlike *A Fool's Errand,* a work in which the Ohioan produced a fascinating analysis of why the North could not reorder the South after the war. As will be discussed in this chapter, Tourgee argued forcefully and in detail that Reconstruction was a failure. Given such failure, what Cumberland narrators confronted at the turn of the century was not the need to rewrite the war but the necessity to be crafty about describing the peace. After all, the army's authors insisted that they had won an *enduring* victory. Such a triumph would have to be found elsewhere than in the Reconstruction that Tourgee portrayed as a political and ideological disaster.

The Unprovoked and Dastardly Attack

When Cumberland regimental historians sat down to write the history of their respective units, most began with the mobilizing of the men. At other points in their narrative authors provided context by describing the long sectional controversy of the antebellum period and the country's sad political collapse, but they began with recruitment. Of course, mobilization was an obvious place to begin a regimental history, but the authors were making a larger point. They intended their readers to find reassurance in what the authors defined as the country's military tradition of the citizen-soldier.

By invoking this tradition Cumberland authors blended accuracy with myth. On the one hand, by beginning the story with mobilization the authors correctly referenced the fact that the sectional debate and even secession itself had been confusing and divisive. The politics of Southern extremism did not galvanize the North for action so much as stir up doubt, partisanship, and anxiety.[1] It took Fort Sumter to change this. The unprovoked and dastardly attack ended the complicated, tortuous internal debate in the North, replacing it with a collective outrage over the assault on the flag. Charles C. Briant made the point in his 1891 history of the Sixth Indiana. When the news of the attack was received in Indianapolis, he noted, "the loyal people of the United States abandoned the field of argument, and ceased to discuss measures and plans for the peaceable restoration of the national authority." Loyal Indianans, he insisted, "accepted the issue of war," with a "singular unanimity and determination."[2]

Briant rightly captured the spirit of the moment. Sumter crystallized the situation. For a few months, resolution and singleness of purpose replaced divisiveness and partisanship. The Indianan wrote into the collective historical record what James McPherson describes as a *rage militaire* that followed Sumter. Intense, spontaneous, emotional outrage quickly outran political and ideological division, producing a primal urge to defend a national community under attack. Indeed, the Charleston incident spawned what became four separate military mobilizations—two each in 1861 and 1862, respectively. Furthermore, anger at the initial attack welded the enlistees into the army with a sense of determination strong enough to endure years of dramatic setbacks along with several changes in mission and commanders. Northerners who volunteered to fight or who supported the soldiery from the homefront found in Charleston harbor an event and symbol that sustained them through the worst war in the country's history. By beginning with the process of unit mobilization, Cumberland authors referenced this emotional and ideological breakpoint, and wrote it into their army's collective memory.[3]

But then the myth entered. If Cumberland authors correctly observed that Sumter marked a new departure for the North, they also used their discussion of mobilization to invoke the hallowed tradition of the American citizen-soldier. The writers described regimental recruiting using the sacred images of the Revolution.[4] Their description recalled 1775 and so interwove the dramatic events of 1861 and 1862 with the legend of the country's origins.

Cumberland authors referenced this tradition by combining two themes. They insisted, first, that military reverses only made a free people more determined, and, second, that voluntarism and the citizen-soldier were the proper foundations of an American army. Robert Kimberly and Ephraim Holloway of the Forty-first Ohio wrote about the men who signed up in late summer 1861. The defeat of Bull Run had struck their northern Ohio homeland with "a stunning shock." Among the residents, "incredulity and consternation were the contending emotions." However, the authors continued, the people "roused themselves" to "face the situation." It was now evident that the war would not be a "brief excursion," but would require the entire "military strength" of the "loyal States." John Beach of the Fortieth Ohio agreed. Writing in 1884, he recalled that Bull Run had "shattered the hopes of the North that a campaign of sixty days would end the war." The "extent and serious character of the undertaking" now became apparent to "the Northern mind."[5]

This serious undertaking demanded a sober response from the citizenry. Cumberland narrators argued insistently that the increasingly demanding situation brought out the North's best: the ordinary men who represented the virtuous productivity of the Midwest. With great pride David Bittle Floyd of the Seventy-fifth Indiana observed that the regiment's recruits left "comfortable homes and profitable professions, trades, and lines of business to volunteer their services to country and flag." On a more personal level, Spillard Horrall of the Forty-second Indiana stated that when he joined up he left his wife without a dollar. Her response was "'God bless you, and protect you!'" Judson Bishop of the Second Minnesota openly wondered "that so many could and would divest themselves of all impending business, social and family obligations and restraints, and commit themselves for three years to the then unknown hardships and perils of a soldier's life."[6]

This was traditional citizen-soldier imagery at its finest. From the days of the Revolution it had been important for Americans to believe that the country's military strength came from its citizenry, not a professional army, and that these amateur civilians-in-arms were made powerful not by some militaristic ethos but by their willingness to sacrifice property and home life for the country's cause. George Morris certainly emphasized the idea. There was "nothing of the soldier" in the Eighty-first Indiana's recruits, this regimental historian insisted. Indeed, they made "all sorts of blunders and funny mistakes." Nonetheless, these were "sturdy, resolute boys," who were "the best material for an American volunteer regiment." Although they were "raw, undisciplined country boys," they were "animated by a sincere love of country, and a desire to do their whole duty."[7]

In such opening passages Cumberland narrators focused attention on the character of the men rather than the character of the war. In grounding their description in the country's military tradition, they opened the master narrative by highlighting the moral qualities of the volunteers rather than the causes and consequences of the fight. As will be discussed in chapter 2, the Cumberland regimental historians and memoir writers had certain self-serving reasons to do this, but the larger effect and intent of such descriptions was to ground the origin and prosecution of the North's war on the solid foundation of the nation's sacred past. By focusing the lens on the recruits, the writers reaffirmed what most people considered to be basic American principles, sliding past the fact that the war had happened because the republic as an institution had collapsed. James Buchanan, the former president, was hardly alone in wondering how a partisan political democracy based on electoral consent could be saved by coercive war. As the old Jacksonian Democrat observed in his last message to Congress, secession marked the death of the Union whatever the constitutional technicalities of South Carolina's act.[8] In addition, when the war of coercion came to include emancipation, it connected the cause of the nation with what had been to that point the radical abolitionism of the John Brown variety. Northern soldiers did not save the Union, they conquered the Confederacy and stirred emancipation into the ashes.

As the Cumberland narrators worked their way through the story of their war, they would explain this destruction, conquest, and liberation. But not at the beginning of the tale. Rather, they saw it as more important to argue that the men "came not from the rabble," to use Frederick Keil's phrasing. For this historian of the Thirty-fifth Ohio, the critical point was that the recruits were not "the lawless; but were substantial men in every respect."

In this way Cumberland writers covered over *their* revolutionary war. Although they would describe the invasion of the Confederate South in their narratives, along with the vast reordering that attended it, the authors began the story with the country's mythic past. Cumberland soldiers were the Minutemen reborn. The vital memory was that the boys of '61 and '62 had mimicked the old yeomen with their Kentucky rifles on the mantle. Similar to the old farmer and artisan militia, the Cumberlanders had come "from the stores and counting rooms, from the colleges and country school houses, from village, town and city, from shop and farm." They had willingly abandoned "every prospect of future comfort for the hardships, danger and death that awaited them in their new lives as soldiers."[9]

Invading an Enemy's Country

Having described the recruits of '61 and '62 as worthy inheritors of America's military tradition, Cumberland authors now took up the prosecution of the war. When they did so they had to characterize their Confederate enemy and describe the process by which they had destroyed him. Of course, the writers happily discussed battle and campaign in this regard at length, glowing with pride particularly about Snodgrass Hill and Missionary Ridge. However, the good Cumberland men had won the war by invading and dismantling the South, not simply by fighting the soldiers in butternut. In their various regimental histories and memoirs, writers described this process of invasion, reproducing in reflection and anecdote the particulars of how the soldiery became an army of destruction and liberation.

In composing these descriptions, the authors recorded a memory with two dimensions. First, the narrators repeated the highly charged characterizations of the South that had been the staple of the North's ideological war during the antebellum period. In the heat of Fort Sumter and its aftermath, the recruits had to explain to themselves as well as others what sort of people could commit such treachery and why good Northern men had to respond to it. Years later, regimental authors and autobiographers restated these interpretations. In the process, they wrote into their historical record their sneering evaluation of the slave system that, in their eyes, had made the Old South corrupt. Second, the writers noted how they and their units had come to prosecute an actively emancipationist war. During the conflict, this had not been an easy transition. According to Chandra Manning, when the fight began the soldiers were more than ready to cite the peculiar institution as the explanation for Confederate corruption and treason, and this feeling helped lead them to support the conversion to emancipation. Yet, as Manning also discusses, the process had its complexities.[10] Writing about it all years later, many regimental historians recorded the moment of conversion in this regard, and were candid and detailed about the process.

~

According to Cumberland authors, Confederates did not simply attack a fort in April 1861. Rather, the assault revealed the depth and extent of the Old South's corruption. Whatever reunionist sympathies were percolating through American society at the turn of the twentieth century, Cumberland narrators wanted it understood that during the 1860s they had fought a just and necessary war against a perfidious enemy. Although Cumberlanders exercised a certain limited forgiveness toward uniformed Confederate soldiers, as will be discussed in chapter 3, they left no one in doubt about their view of Southern treason and its roots.

In general, Cumberland authors repeated in their histories and memoirs the sectionalist attitudes that had been developed during the 1840s and 1850s. As Susan-Mary Grant observes, antebellum Northerners had created a sense of particular nationhood and national destiny by turning the South into an "other." Northerners based this contrast on the ideals of free labor, an ideology that, according to Grant, appealed to a broad spectrum of Northerners, although the Republican party would attempt to make it their exclusive partisan property.[11] Decades later, Army of the Cumberland veterans employed free-labor imagery to explain to their readers why the war against the South had to be fought.

In his regimental history of the Fifty-ninth Illinois, George Washington Herr created one of the most elaborate and nuanced of these characterizations of a debased South. Though written in 1890 at a time when the agenda of sectional reconciliation was presumably sweeping all before it, Herr laid the responsibility for the Civil War at the door of a Southern "chivalry" so blinded by its belligerence and arrogance that it could never fathom either the North's resolve or the integrity and strength of Northern society. Herr blended this ideological smugness, in turn, with an often savvy and plausible analysis of the politics of breakdown.

As Herr discussed it, neither Lincoln's election nor South Carolina's dramatic secession produced war. According to him, the Southern radicals had not foreseen that the majority of people in both sections desired peace. In particular, the hotspurs miscalculated the strength of the Northern Democrats. This party, said Herr, represented "the proletariat of the towns and cities north of Mason and Dixon's line," and these people "were willing to defend the inherited rights of the slaveocracy" in order to preserve the Union. Quite accurately, Herr argued that the Democrats had always "been controlled by the South, and . . . [were] at all times *en rapport* with the slaveocracy of America." Moreover, he continued, many in the

South wanted nothing of war. Unionists like Alexander Stephens "could only see property and business depression or ultimate ruin in war and a change of government." Others were "ultra secessionists," but they hoped for peaceable separation. They "did not believe that war would come." Even the bulk of the Southern planter class wanted a bloodless victory. Although Herr characterized these men as "burning for war" because they were "members of the F.F.V.'s, the Southern gentry, the military class," they had presumed that secession and their aggressiveness would win the victory by bluff and bluster.[12]

In the middle of this confused situation a small but determined group of Southern militants maneuvered to bring on a fight. In Herr's characterization, these men were certainly driven by the desire to protect and extend slavery. In the author's description, this was a Slave Power war. However, deeper than this was the South's hatred and contempt for the North as a society of sturdy laboring people. Southerners of Herr's description harbored a ferocious loathing for a social order based on work. According to the author, the South's planter class saw Northerners as mere "mechanics and laborers, bent and grimed by the toil of field and foundry, mill and workshops." According to the author, Southern bluebloods saw the North's working population as an industrial peasantry "largely impoverished and forever absorbed in the never-ending struggle to obtain the common necessaries of life. How could an army composed of such material withstand the youth of the South, the chivalry of the Republic?" Northern youth "knew nothing of arms, of the saddle, of the field and flood and chase." Yankees were merely "laborers and mechanics." As Herr described them, Southerners believed that their opponents lacked "pride of caste, family individuality and martial spirit." In the author's estimation, the gentry were "full grown fed and fattened on the unrewarded sweat of black brows," and so "regarded the Northern representatives of labor with such withering yet honest contempt!"

In Herr's portrait, war came out of the need of this impetuous, arrogant people to triumph over what they saw as the degraded proletariat of the North. To this end, the hotspurs engineered Sumter. "To the mercurial and impulsive people of the South," the harbor attack was "an act at once sudden, bold, brave, chivalrous!" It never occurred to the bluebloods that this assault on the flag would fill Northerners with "a terrible earnestness."[13]

Thus Herr fixed responsibility for the war. He turned Southerners into moral cripples, tying their corruption to slavery. They had disdained the

North's "mechanics and laborers" because the gentry lived off the toil of their slaves. Having raised themselves above work, they could not fathom a society where the population gained both its energy and sense of civilization and legitimacy from labor. From the chivalry's resultant primal rage came militancy and political extremism, and from this came treason. Thus did Herr connect the dots. In his 1890 memory of the war he preserved the reasoning that had predisposed many Cumberland soldiers to turn against the peculiar institution when they came across it during the invasion. Years of sectional conflict had provided the means to believe that Confederate insurrection grew from the exotic system and culture of slave owning. Years later, the memory of this original sin held firm, even in the midst of a reunion crusade.

∼

As Cumberland narrators turned their attention toward describing the day-to-day progress of their invasion of the South, George Herr's context of a vast moral divide was blended with a more realistic and day-to-day assessment of how the soldiers had become liberators. When talking about campaigning and foraging in Kentucky and Tennessee, revealing anecdote and descriptions of incremental progress (or the lack of it) took over from glib generalization and simple moral contrasts. As the narrators moved into the details of invasion and occupation, their writing became more realistic, specific, and interesting.

In describing how the army converted to emancipation on the march, the authors emphasized two factors. First, the initial willingness to link slaveholding to treason was amplified by what the narrators described as the arrogant behavior of individual slave owners and the belligerent resistance of white Southerners generally. In a word, Southern behavior turned Northern soldiers against the peculiar institution. Second, Cumberland authors affirmed James Connolly's description of how he had become a practical abolitionist, noting that the army as a whole came to the obvious conclusion that emancipation was a means to destroy the rebellion.

In the master narrative, the progression toward liberation began as the various regiments moved from their Midwestern training camps into Kentucky. Although the state never formally seceded, Cumberland writers argued that the soldiers had looked at Bluegrass citizens suspiciously because their behavior toward the army was unpredictable. In certain situations and places, Kentuckians behaved like appreciative Unionists. When James Birney Shaw's Tenth Indiana crossed the Ohio River into Louisville in September 1861, Shaw reflected that the citizens "cheered us as we wended our way through the streets." Importantly, "the female sex was most ardent and effusive in their welcome, and nearly every man had a girl hanging from his arm." Frederick Keil, however, observed that his Thirty-fifth Ohio received a decidedly cold shoulder in Covington—an attitude of "go to h——l, you Yankee——."

Kentucky was tricky. Confederates openly recruited in the state. John Hunt Morgan and John C. Breckinridge were Rebel heroes. Early in the conflict, the state had declared its neutrality, but this "amounted to nothing," according to Robert Rogers of the 125th Illinois. "It was the opinion of us all," this author stated, "that for a neutral state, Kentucky held many bushwhackers, and guerillas, who, from behind trees and rocks, murdered our boys whenever opportunity offered." For Rogers, the state was nothing but "rebellion in ambush."[14]

In this atmosphere of distrust and defiance, slavery in Kentucky quickly became an issue. Writing about it years later, regimental historians and autobiographers made it a point to discuss the fact. Frederick Keil stated that his regiment began to see the "practical" (James Connolly's lovely word) side of the "negro question" the moment that this unit entered the state. Some of the officers had brought free black servants with them across the border, and this became a problem because, as he explained, "the delicate nerves of the great Commonwealth of Kentucky could not tolerate the presence of a free negro on its soil."[15]

Most narrators who discussed the issue focused on the problem of refugee slaves. Cumberland units faced the problem of runaways from the moment they entered the Bluegrass region. Fugitives from Kentucky's plantations and workshops wormed their way into army camps, and this put the soldiers directly in conflict with local slave owners and slave catchers. Several writers recorded specific incidents, confirming the arguments of William Freehling and Chandra Manning that slavery on the ground had great effect on the Union soldiers.[16] More to the point, Cumberland authors recounted these situations in vivid detail thirty and forty years later, suggesting not only the impression that had been made at the time but the intensity with which this became part of the soldiery's permanent memory.

In his 1905 memoir *Echoes Of The Civil War As I Hear Them*, Michael Fitch recorded such an incident when he discussed his Twenty-first Wisconsin's march toward what would be the Battle of Perryville in 1862. One evening three local farmers "came into camp seeking a negro," and were told by the regiment's colonel that "'we came down here to suppress a rebellion against the United States government and not to steal negroes, nor yet to be negro catchers. If your negro is in our camp, you can take him, but I shall give you no assistance in running after him.'" Fitch went on to say that the farmers quickly left camp and appealed to the division commander—Kentuckian Lovell Rousseau—who sent a staff officer conveying the general's orders to deliver the fugitive over. But, Fitch noted, that officer, "in passing out of camp stopped at a crowd of the Twenty-first Wisconsin men who were discussing the question of delivering slaves to slave masters, and entered into a controversy." The soldiers actually threw the man out bodily, causing Rousseau to respond with a dressing down. Fitch concluded his description by noting that "the slave in the meantime had escaped out of camp and the owner did not recover him."

John R. McBride told of a similar incident, wrapping the tale in an elaborate discussion of the issue. In his 1900 regimental history of the Thirty-third Indiana, he included a short section titled the "The Slave Question" that dealt with the Kentucky situation in detail, noting that Cumberland soldiers had little sympathy for slavery but no "undying love for the negro," either. Regardless, the various units took on fugitives, which brought them into conflict with Kentucky authorities and would-be claimants. Reviewing the problem, McBride insisted that the Washington government should have created a commission to adjudicate legitimate claims. However, the author then discussed a particularly violent episode from the fall of 1861 when a master had intruded into camp to capture an escaped slave, and then led the unfortunate individual away. The owner, mounted on horseback, pulled the slave along behind on foot with a rope tied around his neck. This was too much for the men in the First Ohio Battery (camped near McBride's unit), who witnessed it all. The artillerymen intervened, mocking the owner by asking the slave if he had had any breakfast. Then, they deliberately cut the rope, pulled the master off his horse, and "kicked [him] for his insolence and his barbarous treatment of his slave."[17]

Obviously, such events had affected the soldiers. Men claiming to be slave owners had ridden defiantly and arrogantly into various regimental camps demanding to be allowed to search the grounds. Often enough, these owners were brutal, as above. Often enough, they were not owners at all. They were simply "Negro-stealers," or spies. Even after thirty or forty years, the particulars remained fresh and exact in the written memory of several regiments. Moreover, the authors made a point of saying that such moments prompted the men to question slavery itself. As James Birney

Shaw observed after such a confrontation in his Tenth Indiana, the "episode caused a good deal of talk," among the men.[18]

Then, as Cumberland historians described it, the army moved from "neutral" Kentucky into Tennessee and things got worse. All the nastiness that John Fitch described in his *Annals of the Army of the Cumberland* came to pass, and regimental historians and authors of memoirs wrote anecdotes into the record years later.[19] They also made it a point to record that this atmosphere of hot conflict made further regimental converts to what was fast becoming a military version of emancipation.

Joseph G. Vale of the Seventh Pennsylvania cavalry wrote a particularly revealing account. Vale made it a point to say that "the political complexion of all [the regiment's] companies, except one, was that of decided Democrats, and but little antislavery sentiment was heard in the regiment." He made this remark in preface to recording an incident that happened soon after the Battle of Shiloh. A party of mounted men entered camp, insisting that they be allowed to search for "a certain colored man, claimed as the property of one of the party." The regiment's lieutenant colonel escorted these men. Suddenly in Company C's camp a black cook bolted from a tent. "'Stop, you d——d nigger!'" one of the intruders shouted. "'Stop, till we see who you are!' 'Stop, or I'll shoot.'" Vale continued that the intruders "dash[ed] after [the fugitive] on a gallop, and fir[ed] their pistols indiscriminately in the direction in which he was running." This firing in the regimental camp enraged "the soldiers, [who] as one man, flew to arms, surrounded the citizens, dismounted and disarmed them." Upon interrogation, the author continued, the captives revealed that they were actually enemy cavalry on a spying mission. Vale concluded: "the entire political sentiment of the regiment was changed by the incident, and, henceforth, it was one of the strongest anti-slavery regiments in the service."[20]

Thus did the pat ideology of writers like George Herr translate into concrete situations on the ground, and this not only in the experience of the individual regiments at the time but in the memory of the veterans who later wrote the stories into the record. Invasion had changed the soldiers' "entire political sentiment," independently of the politics of Lincoln and the Radicals. Anger at slave owners merged with disdain for the Confederate slave-owning society that fought against the Union, prodding the Cumberlanders during the war to free the captives of their enemy and later to make it an important part of the war of invasion that they remembered and described.

This memory of individual encounters also merged with a larger discussion of the army's conversion to "hard war." Protecting individual fugitives from the wrath of perverted slave catchers and spies blended with the all-too-obvious realization that four million bondpeople were both the strength and weakness of the Confederacy. Frederick Keil said as much. He repeated into the record an observation he had first made while marching across northern Alabama in 1862. Recalling that he had seen black women tending fields of corn, he noted that he had mused at the time that "from this it was plain that the confederate authorities could call out the full strength of the white men fit for military duty, and use colored men to do pioneer duty, repairing roads, build fortifications, etc., while the colored women did the farming." Judson Bishop of the Second Minnesota made the same point in a slightly different way. Describing his unit's stay near Gallatin, Tennessee, just after the Emancipation Proclamation went into effect, he noted that whatever the legal niceties of exempting the state from that document's provisions, it "hastened the complete desertion by the negroes in that vicinity, of their old homes and masters." Some of these individuals, Bishop continued, came to the Second Minnesota's camp with information about butchered hogs stored and hidden nearby awaiting delivery to the Confederate army. The soldiers located this store and "brought shovels, and the crowd of darkeys who had joined us, some from camp and some from neighboring farms, very willingly helped to resurrect the barrels which were buried side by side about two feet deep in the continuous graves."[21]

~

In this way Cumberland authors created a memory of the war that focused as much on the progress of invasion as on combat. Elaborate descriptions of battles at Chickamauga or Stones River were merged with recounting incidents involving fugitive slaves or foraging for pork and other commodities in cooperation with "the darkeys." The army's narrators were happy to recall the comprehensive nature of their war against the South. Yet, in the same spirit of completeness, Cumberland authors tempered these descriptions with the observation that it had sometimes been difficult to move the men from practical abolitionism to support for the politics of emancipation. Hiding refugees, removing black workers from Confederate fields, or facing down defiant planters was one thing, supporting War Department and presidential policy was something else. This is an intriguing honesty. Like most veterans, Cumberland narrators were more than eager to claim credit for every element of their victorious war. Hardly above self-congratulation, they wanted history to show them on the winning side in every sense of that term. Thus, thirty and forty years after the fact, it would have been perfectly understandable for the regimental authors to have placed their particular unit at the cutting edge in the great humanitarian cause of the age.[22] Yet, many Cumberland writers added qualifiers, suggesting that the authors really were trying to be accurate as well as inclusive in their descriptions of the war. Cumberland narrators were quite willing to admit that the decision to support the *politics* of liberation in 1862 and 1863 had not been easy.

In his 1887 history of the Ninety-sixth Illinois Charles Partridge discussed the turmoil caused by the fact that in early 1863 Midwestern Copperheads had begun sending letters to the men encouraging them to desert, the Democrats arguing that the Emancipation Proclamation was illegitimate. The author noted that there were desertions, particularly in Kentucky regiments. In response, the officers of his brigade met and drafted a series of resolutions. These denounced "that clique of miscreants in the loyal States," who were promoting what the officers defined as treason. In response, the resolutions stated that the brigade "fully and unequivocally indorse the policy of our civil rulers, in using all necessary means to strike decisive blows at the unholy rebellion, and to bring the war to a speedy, sure and glorious termination."

Partridge continued his description by stating that the men were formed in hollow square to hear the resolutions read. Then the ayes were requested. The ayes were a majority but it was not unanimous. Meetings and discussion followed that evening. Yet there was still considerable dissent. In the case of the Ninety-sixth, the regiment's colonel sent a copy of the resolutions to the local papers, noting that they had been adopted without a negative vote, which was true only in the sense that the nays had not been requested. "He dared not put the negative for fear the nays would be so numerous as not to look well for a Regiment from the State which was President Lincoln's home."[23]

While Cumberland narrators were eager to sanctify their cause, they produced no emancipation romance. In their wish to describe the whole of their particular regiment's experience (or their own), the authors were often remarkable for their forthrightness. As was Partridge here. Although the Cumberland army's writers readily claimed the laurels of winning a war that expanded freedom in America, they were also careful to point out the limits or qualifications on that freedom that had been part of the conflict.

The authors emphasized limits and qualifications as the master narrative proceeded through the complex chronology of the war. When in Kentucky, Tennessee, and northern Alabama, the Army of the Cumberland had been occupiers, constantly in contact with Southern civilians and local slaves. Between 1861 and mid-1863, the troops had been stationary much of the time, providing plenty of opportunity for runaways and necessitating constant foraging. Most of the comments in the narratives about fugitives and owners refer to this period. But then the army's mission changed. The Tullahoma campaign of June 1863 put the Cumberlanders on the road and in combat, and then Chickamauga, Chattanooga, and the Atlanta campaign followed. For a solid year the army's mission was battle and the veteran writers discussing it all later focused here. Then the army's mission changed again, as the Fourteenth Corps went with Sherman across Georgia and up into the Carolinas. As the troops moved into the Deep South, refugees became part of the army's war once more, and Cumberland writers thirty and forty years later accordingly returned them to the narrative. But the story had a harder edge now. At this juncture in the war fugitives were a problem to the army, and discussing this in hindsight was a delicate matter.

Particularly troublesome was whether or not to mention the incident at Ebenezer Creek. During Sherman's march toward Savannah, the army crossed this stream, and Maj. Gen. Jefferson C. Davis—the commander of the Fourteenth Corps—used the crossing as an opportunity to strand thousands of refugees who were trailing the Union forces. Under Davis's orders, the men quickly pulled up their pontoon bridges after the soldiers had crossed this very considerable creek, leaving the straggling bondpeople on the far shore. Refusing to be sacrificed to the Confederate cavalry and irregulars who were hovering about, refugees plunged into the water, trying to get across. Many drowned. Eighteen years later, in his history of the 125th Illinois, Robert Rogers felt compelled to comment, and did so forthrightly. "It seemed to be a cruel order, but it was necessary." He went on to say that this was the case even though guerillas and bushwhackers followed in the army's rear, "and it is to be feared that their usage of these unfortunate creatures, when they fell into their hands, was cruel in the extreme." In this new phase of the war, the fugitives had become expendable. In his 1882 regimental history, Rogers made this judgment honestly, if briefly.[24]

A Fool's Errand

Cumberland narrators provided ample testimony that the Civil War had been tricky and confusing as well as deadly. Judson Bishop of the Second Minnesota welcomed refugees from slavery when he dug up pork carcasses in Gallatin in 1863, but, according to Robert Rogers, the same kind of people became a problem a year later at Ebenezer Creek. During the war, it was often difficult to figure out the proper or effective thing to do at any given time and place, particularly regarding the black fugitives. Yet Cumberland authors made it clear that this war with its many twists and turns had been guided by a fundamental and consistent logic. The aim had been victory and victory could be measured. The Union had been out to destroy the Rebel armies and force the collapse of the Confederate national government, and the army did whatever it had to do to achieve triumph defined in these terms. Thus the Cumberlanders' larger context for emancipation war.

But it was an open question whether such a triumph was complete. Union cavalry captured Jefferson Davis in May 1865 and this personal embarrassment effectively ended Confederate political authority. For their part, Robert E. Lee and Joseph E. Johnston led the formal armies into the surrender process, and this, as Jay Winik rightly observes, proved to be the critical act.[25] When the uniformed Rebel forces capitulated, the substantive force behind Southern independence was thereby destroyed. But did this surrender create true and lasting victory?

Cumberland authors provided a ready answer to this question by refusing to ask it. The narrators recorded the wild swing of emotions when Lee's surrender, Lincoln's assassination, and Johnston's capitulation happened in quick succession. With this they ended the story. Some authors continued the tale through their respective unit's demobilization, while others discussed Sherman's victory parade (if they were a part of it). Still others described the individual mustering-out ceremonies in Peoria, Chicago, Indianapolis, or elsewhere. As will be seen in chapter 2, they also discussed postwar life in the North. But the authors stopped *the war* with military surrender and the return home to "God's country."

Alone among the Cumberlanders, Albion Winegar Tourgee went further. Unlike the overwhelming majority of his fellows, this former lieutenant did not go back to the Midwest to enjoy the fruits of triumph on the farm, or in a business. Tourgee went to North Carolina to help reform what he saw as the depraved and defeated South. When he did he ran headlong into one of the fundamental realities of modern war. Though it seems decisive, military victory has always been wrapped in circumstance and limit. Surrender on the battlefield has rarely produced anything like total triumph. Tourgee's mountain of troubles, as he recorded them in *A Fool's Errand,* is excellent testimony as to why Cumberland authors had every reason to declare victory in 1865, and then direct the reader's attention back to Indiana, Illinois, and Ohio.

~

In his 1884 narrative of the Seventh Pennsylvania cavalry, one of Tourgee's compatriots, Thomas Franklin Dornblaser, suggested the risks of describing too much beyond the stacking of arms and hometown welcoming speeches. Discussing the problems that his unit faced in Georgia as the war drew to a close, he noted that a Lieutenant Hayes became something of a temporary county-level administrator of occupation. In this capacity he issued an order to the local civilians, counseling "mutual forbearance" in creating new relations between the races. Complaints started coming from everywhere. "An old colored woman walked four miles one morning to report to the governor that her master had struck her over the head with a wooden-bucket, bruising her face badly." The lieutenant had the master arrested. The man "stated frankly that he had struck the old woman senseless . . . and that he would do it again, if she ever insulted his wife again." The prisoner clarified: "It was wash-day on that plantation, and the women had some sharp words; and in the midst of the quarrel, the black woman made this dreadful remark to her haughty mistress: 'I is just as free as you is!'" Dornblaser then commented that in thus staking her claim, the "defenceless black woman" had given the former "slave-driver" "too much" to take, and so he hit her. After reciting several such incidents, the author concluded that these were only some of "the many perplexing cases that were presented to the Lieutenant in the short space of three or four weeks."[26]

Without question, "perplexing case" described the defeated Confederacy in the days, months, and years following the war. Little had been decided beyond the Rebel armies' formal surrender and the disappearance of the Confederate national government. Enlisted to destroy rather than create, the Cumberland army's officers and men were hardly prepared in this situation to do much of anything beyond collecting weapons and paroling prisoners. Men like Albion Tourgee took the next step. Though he had moved back to Ohio in December 1863 after leaving the army (due to injury), he reentered the fray when he moved his family to North Carolina.

Although he did this in part for his health, he also wanted to help make the North's victory complete. While still in the service he had written a friend that he had no desire to restore "'the Union as it was.' I want & fight for the Union better than 'it was.' Before this is accomplished we must have a fundamental thorough and complete revolution & renovation." As good as his word, Tourgee became a political figure, judge, and a prominent and effective legal reformer. Even his Redeemer enemies credited his intelligence and savvy. Nonetheless, like all the Carpetbaggers, Tourgee was forced out eventually.[27]

In his 1879 political novel *A Fool's Errand,* Tourgee makes it clear that he had embarked on his mission armed with all of his region's ideological weapons. Like George Herr, he eagerly contrasted a virtuous, hard-working, democratic North with a benighted South. At one point, Tourgee has his main character, Comfort Servosse, explain in a letter to a Republican senator that "'the constitutions of the North had fostered individual independence, equal rights and power, and general intelligence among the masses.'" By contrast, the South kept both suffrage and jury duty "'guarded from the poor.'" In that region, "'wealth was a prerequisite of office eligibility. It was a republic in name, but an oligarchy in fact.'" In the same discussion, Servosse argued that this sectional contrast had been born in the colonial period, for the original Puritan settlements had created the "'township system,'" where offices were elected and the electorate was inclusive, and this had created the "'nursery of democratic freedom.'"[28]

Slavery, of course, was the foundation of this Southern oligarchy, and so, for Tourgee, the essential remedy for the problem was to shift the system to free labor. The author has one of Servosse's opponents assert that Southerners believed that "'niggers were made for slaves; and cotton, terbacker, sugar cane, an' rice, were made for them to raise.'" To answer this attitude Tourgee created the character of an ex-Confederate soldier, one Exum Davis, who came back home to a ruined farm. In a letter to Servosse, this individual described his plan to get back on his feet. I "'went to work, hired some niggers, and, when the crop was sold, we would divide.'" This worked. "'We made a splendid crop, and I divided right smart of money with them in the fall.'" The farmer then elaborated that in the next year "'some of them wanted to work crops on shares,'" so he agreed to sell them horses and mules in the bargain to increase their productivity. "'The spring opened, and I had the busiest farm and finest prospect I have ever seen. I was running a big force, and every nigger on the plantation had a full crop about half pitched.'"

Here was self-evident moral truth in action. In Tourgee's mind, the innate superiority of the North's labor and political system was no fictional device; it was the method to rebuild the South. As the author's character testified, it all made good business sense. However, Reconstruction was not about political democratization or intelligent economics. Just after his description about a full crop, the enterprising Mr. Davis observed that the Klan visited him and his workers. They insisted that he must "'stop selling horses to niggers and letting crop on shares.'" They "'had made up their minds that no nigger should straddle his own horse, or ride in his own cart, in this county.'"[29]

In this way Tourgee described both the promise of victory and the brutal reaction that snuffed it out. As the author's title suggests, *A Fool's Errand* is a tale of misplaced idealism. The victory for self-evident moral principle and free-labor economics succumbed to hard-bitten, near-fanatical resistance. It simply did not matter that any real-life farmer Davis (to say nothing of aspiring landowners among the former slaves) might have discovered a path to a big farm and a fine prospect. As Tourgee observed, the former Confederates had simply made up their collective mind that "no nigger should straddle his own horse."

In fixing the blame for this turn of events, Tourgee savagely attacked the national Republican party. In the author's estimation, the party leadership—the "Wise Men" in his sarcastic term—refused to impose direct political rule on the South, leaving policy initiatives up to the vulnerable, isolated Republican parties in each of the former Confederate states. The national leadership then "abandoned these parties like cocks in a pit, to fight out the question of predominance without the possibility of national interference. They said to the colored man . . . 'Root, hog, or die!'"[30] In this situation, Klan insurgents and Redeemers were able to subvert the process.

Yet Tourgee went deeper than this. When the author imagined that North and South represented two distinct cultures, he argued that while Northerners were democratic, Southerners believed in the triumph of the will. Tourgee has Servosse compose a long letter to a Dr. E. Martin, an old friend and tutor, explaining the fundamental problem. Reflecting on the Republican party's failure, Servosse muses that "'I begin seriously to fear that the North lacks virility.'" The North was a conqueror, and "'she must rule as a conqueror.'" Specifically, Tourgee's character argues that the Union should have reduced the former Confederacy to a "'thoroughly organized system of provincial government,'" but "'in this the North fails.

She hesitates, palters, shirks.'" Unfortunately, Servosse continues, the North was "'debauched by weak humanitarianisms, more anxious to avoid the appearance of offending its enemies than desirous of securing its own power or its own ends.'"

According to Servosse, Southerners suffered from no such handicap. The former Confederates were "'aggressives, who, having made up their minds to attain a certain end, adopt the means most likely to secure it.'" Such people were "'born rulers,'" who used the full measure the "'power, the intellect, the organizing capacity, the determined will.'" Given this situation, Servosse writes, Reconstruction "'will fail . . . as certain as the morrow's sunrise.'"[31]

As evidenced by *Fool's Errand*, Tourgee was fascinated by the extent and determination of the Confederate South's resistance. As the author saw it, the North's grand vision failed less because of particular policy mistakes than because the war's victors lacked the will to complete the triumph. Out of his frustration, Tourgee even grew to admire his opponents, criticizing Sherman's looting in his regimental history, *Story of a Thousand*, while adopting a kind of cultural relativism in *Fool's Errand*. Putting his vision of Northern superiority aside for the moment, the author observed that no people were "kindlier, more hospitable, or more religious" than these Southerners, "only they were kind according to *their notion*, as everybody else is; hospitable according to custom, like the rest of the world; and religious according to education and tradition, as are other people."[32] Clearly, Tourgee's Southern experience had made him wiser.

What the Ohioan had stumbled over was less a cultural divide than a fundamental fact of war. Former Confederates were inspired by their defeat, not subdued by it. Tourgee referred several times in his novel to the fact that the racism involved in slavery was made doubly intense by the South's subjection. As one sympathizer tells Servosse, the war has "'intensified . . . the pride, the arrogance, and the sectional rancor and malevolence of the southern people.'" The fact that Servosse was a Northerner meant that he represented the military power which took the South's "'property, liberty, and a right to control their own,'" and now he and other reformers were encouraging the former slaves "'to *buy and hold land* and to *ride their own horses*.'"[33] As Tourgee's italics indicate, the result of this was predictable. The author defined himself as a fool for good reason.

Out of this intense anger Southerners would make every effort to redefine the war and turn the story of the defeated Confederacy into the foundation of renewed resistance. Tourgee knew it and reported on it in his novel. In Servosse's letter to his friend, E. Martin, the character notes that "'Davis, Lee, and their compatriots have already won a distinction and eminence they could not have hoped for had they remained peaceful citizens of the Republic.'" The "'glory of the Confederate leader,'" Servosse continues, "'will hourly wax greater and brighter.'" The former Rebeldom was a place of "'pride, even in defeat,'" assuring any Redeemer that he could "'appeal with certainty of receiving an unshrinking response.'"[34]

With such a clear eye did Tourgee identify the fundamental problem of the North's Civil War. Reconstruction failed for a number of complicated reasons. Among other things, the original free-labor ethic grew increasingly irrelevant as industrialization emerged, while the national Democrats continually and effectively frustrated the Republicans' various strategies.[35] But what one could describe as the irony of the North's war figured into the calculation as well. Massive, unprecedented mobilization and destructive power had produced frustration rather than triumph. Confederate surrender seemed to empower the former enemy and weaken the victor.

This was a particularly odd point given the country's history up to that time. During the Jacksonian period, the United States had been a military weakling. The army was small, the officer corps decrepit, and the volunteer "system" amateurish. Yet, during this same period, imperial expansionism had been dramatic. Indeed, from the earliest days of the colonial period, Americans had developed a finely honed, deadly, and comprehensive vision of conquest and applied it to the North American continent with a vengeance. They took vast territory, recreated the landscape entirely in their image, and ejected the former inhabitants or reduced them to political nothingness. Americans did not build an empire, they went *beyond* empire by reordering and repeopling the conquered land, and then defined the process as "settling" the "wilderness."[36] Thus, Americans had created comprehensive control over most of a continent while the country's formal military force remained essentially comical.

Paradoxically, the North's Civil War produced the exact reverse of this formula. In response to Sumter, the Union organized a military power never before seen on the continent. An army of Napoleonic scale (with technological updates) was backed by experimentation in finance, transportation, and production that created the country's first experience with a modern military-industrial complex. Yet the victory brought complication and failure rather than comprehensive control over the enemy's former territory. As Wolfgang Schivelbusch has argued, modern war (to use his term) has never subdued the losers. Rather, as he argues it, surrender has inspired them. The prospect of humiliation has fueled defeated populations with a creativity and indomitable will to turn the tables.[37] In the case of the former Confederates, the defeated people had a large population base and owned all the local economic, political, and military institutions. With these tools, they could readily connive to win the peace. What Tourgee had run across in North Carolina was not a society defined by an outmoded political economy or an archaic culture, but an assertive order of former Confederates who insistently refused to accept defeat and had the resources to back up their defiance. The author said as much himself. Through the character of Servosse, Tourgee noted that "'the most reckless and unworthy of those who led in the war will again come to the front. Their success will make them the heroes of the people, and they will win place and honor thereby.'" Southerners had made sure that "'the road to honor, renown, fame, and power, . . . lies through the "Traitor's Gate."'"[38] Former Confederates remained openly treasonous because in this way they would reverse the verdict of the war. Tourgee came to respect and even admire their resourcefulness and energy, even as he deplored their politics of racial aristocracy. Though forever a Northern ideologue, Tourgee nonetheless understood that in important respects the former Confederates had gained more from their loss than Unionists had from their victory.

In any case, the Carpetbagger had no place to go but out. He retreated from North Carolina politics and took up the pen to describe the process by which the North's war became the North's defeat. For their part, Cumberland army comrades made their retreat through silence. As will be seen in chapter 3, there were some regimental historians, writing in the early 1880s, who in their commentary ventured briefly into the Reconstruction world that Tourgee had tried to conquer. Their weak efforts, along with Tourgee's openly admitted failure, suggest why most Cumberlanders made sure to end the war with Confederate surrender rather than with the politics of the Republicans' Southern adventure. Cumberland narrators insisted that they and the North had won a complete and enduring triumph in the war. However, as Tourgee's experience demonstrated, Northerners would not find it in North Carolina.

2
Victory in "God's Country"

Glorious News! How the hearts leaped for joy! ... Home, Home, Sweet
Home; Father, Mother, Wife and Babies: these words and thoughts
alone filled the mind of the few of us who were left, and for the first
time in our history we turn our back upon the enemy, and strike out
for *Home.* ... [W]hen the life of our Nation was in danger, and the
old Ship of State was about to sink, we dashed into the breakers, at
the risk of our own lives, and went to her rescue at the cost of our own
blood and trials and hardships untold. We brought her safely to shore,
with her colors proudly floating to the breeze, and to-day we see her
mistress of the oceans all over the civilized world.

—Charles Briant, Sixth Indiana (1891)

As Albion Tourgee discovered, the North could not remake the defeated
Confederacy in its own image. The Civil War was a different kind of conflict, unlike the long process of Native American removal or the brief fight
with Mexico. The Northern victors of '65 could not clear the landscape or
move in to civilize a metaphoric "frontier." Many Northerners might have
wanted to tame what they saw as the Southern moral "wilderness," but
they lacked the power. Union soldiers had destroyed the Confederate independence movement, but Confederate society remained intact and vibrant.

Awakening to this reality, Tourgee discovered the defects in the sim-
plistic formulations of the antebellum Benevolent Empire.[1] Just because
Northerners (or most of them) were persuaded that the Slave Power had
been corrupt did not mean that former Confederates happily abandoned
their presumed "sinfulness" once Union victory occurred. While living in
North Carolina, Tourgee ran into determined and expert resistance rather
than a people eager to admit their guilt. White Southerners faithful to the
old system did not pray to be redeemed from themselves. Ironically, Tourgee even came to admire them for their stubbornness.

But the intransigence of former Confederates left the matter of victory
in doubt. As Reconstruction faded from view, one could question what the
North had won. Those Southerners who created the Lost Cause certainly

did. Army of the Cumberland writers responded insistently. Whatever the individual authors might have believed about postwar Republican policy, they were unanimous and vocal in proclaiming victory. They simply insisted that this triumph was occurring in their homeland. This was no tactical retreat. To the contrary, Cumberland narrators combined a belief in the tradition of the citizen-soldier with a reverence for the Midwest present and future, and so found legitimate victory in the progress of their beloved "God's Country," and in the returning soldiers who had saved it. Cumberland authors claimed triumph because they saw the United States as an emerging world-class power and saw themselves as the model for how to protect it and live in it.

According to Cumberland writers, the foundation of this comprehensive victory was the belief that the soldiers had preserved the country's military tradition while winning an unprecedented war. Far from simply celebrating their campaigns and battles, the narrators closely evaluated the unanticipated demands that the Civil War had placed on the men at arms. In this examination, the authors measured how their understanding of the citizen-soldier ideal stacked up against the military realities of the 1860s, speculating as well about whether a civilian-based military could meet the demands of warfare in what everyone knew was a new kind of world. The writers did not produce a memory literature but a critical examination of how well the country's military tradition could adapt to profound change.

This examination of military competence led seamlessly into an exploration of moral worthiness. All the writers recognized that the Civil War had been unprecedented and that danger lurked in the novelty. The army and the war had produced a host of temptations, and it was vital to know whether the men had preserved themselves while destroying the enemy. Cumberland authors indulged in no fantasies of regeneration through violence. Rather, they worried about moral degeneration in the midst of a long and cruel war. This discussion, in turn, carried over into a look at the "God's Country" of the postwar period. Essential to the examination of worthiness was the part that the veterans were playing in the country's turn-of-the-century development. After all, the idea of the citizen-soldier meant that the fighting man must become a citizen again, and the return to the Midwest was a return to an industrializing society. When Cumberland writers found victory in themselves and in their homeland, they necessarily referenced the Chicago–New York City corridor, with all the dynamism, corporate spirit, and entrepreneurialism that William Cronon has so well described.[2] In coming home to "God's Country," Cumberlanders became builders of the engine that would drive twentieth-century America.

Hardy Men; Disciplined Men

When the original dream of a ninety-day war died at First Manassas, Union volunteers in all theaters began to understand that this would be a new kind of war. As recruiting efforts were restarted in the wake of Union disasters, mobilization into the uniformed armies reached levels unimaginable in previous American wars. Furthermore, the citizen volunteers were expected to gain the ability and discipline of Regulars. An army composed of raw civilians had to achieve a Napoleonic level of expertise, and face formal combat on a truly mass scale. Finally, and most importantly, Northern troops encountered an enemy equally well versed in the Napoleonic military tradition and one able to recruit its army from a large democratic base. After all, Southern whites shared the nation's citizen-soldier ideal in every particular. As the war deepened from weeks into months and years, it became clearer that Northerners (and Southerners) had engaged a kind of war that differed from anything they or any prior generation had known.

Looking back on it years later, Cumberland narrators insisted that they had met the challenge. In particular, they said that they had mastered the physical demands of long-term hard campaigning and learned a discipline in camp and combat that made them able to fight any army in the world. All this, they continued, while remaining true to the democratic ideals of citizenship. According to them, their experience proved that ordinary American citizens could gain the hardihood, discipline, and efficiency to fight a vast and professionalized war. As they saw it, their experience demonstrated that the country's military tradition still worked, providing America with a democratic method to exert credible power in the coming new world.

~

Cumberland authors were happy to admit that they had been unprepared for the demands of the Civil War. By this they meant many things, but they particularly had in mind the physical challenge of active campaigning. Because of its theater of operations, the Army of the Cumberland had been a marching force. It had moved from Kentucky to Tennessee to Alabama and back, then south again through the Volunteer state, northern Georgia, and the Carolinas (or Nashville and south Alabama). Cumberland soldiers had traveled a long way and this had meant learning endurance on the march, surviving with scanty or nonexistent rations, and being exposed to the elements and awful water. The authors noted that nothing about the recruiting or training process had prepared the men for these physical rigors. As a result, the writers insisted, the early months of active campaigning had been a Darwinian test of the survival of the fittest.

Robert Rogers argued that much of this attrition resulted from thoughtless enlistments. He condemned "the careless examination by the mustering officer" in his unit. No surgeon ever looked at the recruits in his 125th Illinois, he said. The individuals had only to advance three paces and show their teeth. Charles Briant agreed, commenting that his Sixth Indiana had lost 593 of its original 1,095 by the spring of 1864. The cause, he said, was that the volunteer army "was composed of men yet in their teens, while some were in their fifties. Young and old alike were placed side by side in the ranks, required to carry the same load and to march the same number of miles."

George Lewis of the 124th Ohio got to the heart of the issue. Civil War mobilization had aimed for the North's moral strength, ignoring the question of physical ability. Looking back in 1894, Lewis wanted to be gracious to those who had proved incapable. He observed that "patriotism brought to our ranks very many never calculated, either physically or mentally, to make soldiers. Their intentions were high and noble, and they failed by no fault of theirs; their final discharge was a mercy to them." Lewis then added insistently: "and a blessing to us."[3]

To such imperfect initial screening was added a training process that took no account of the physical demands that the soldiers would encounter. While all the narratives refer to drill, none discuss anything resembling a fitness program. Then, suddenly, as the men crossed over into Kentucky in 1861 or 1862, they found themselves marching several miles a day loaded down with heavy knapsacks. For their part, few officers had any understanding of proper rest halts or the problem of dehydration. Add to this the fact that few of the men knew how to cook, regiments were often sited in badly drained camps, and proper sanitation took time to learn. Several authors commented on the hardships of the march, the physical exposure, and sickness. All suggested that Lewis was right to discuss the attrition this caused.[4]

But the men who survived became something else. George Morris of the Eighty-first Indiana beamed that the men "in a few months became as tough as pine knots, and nothing hardly affected them afterward." In like spirit, Henry Aten described the nasty job of building roads in the sloppy winter of the Carolina campaign. It was "not unusual to be compelled to corduroy four or five miles of road" in a day's march, he noted. The author of the history of the Eighty-fifth Illinois then boasted that "in all that long march we found no mud deep enough, no hills steep enough, and no quicksands treacherous enough, to prevent the taking of our trains wherever the column was ordered to move."[5]

Pride was certainly talking in such remarks. The Cumberlanders' Civil War had been a test not simply of courage but of toughness and endurance. Clearly, the survivors of the early attrition basked in their accomplishment. But they also argued that the process had turned them into emblems of the power of a citizen-soldier army. In what has to stand as the most potent expression of this attitude, the authors of the history of the Eighty-sixth Indiana described chasing after Braxton Bragg during the Kentucky campaign of 1862. In their discussion they noted the tremendous difficulty in finding water. In a passage describing what happened when the men came across a pond with a dead mule in it, the authors took the opportunity to distinguish the good soldier from the unsuccessful. They began their discussion by highlighting those men who refused to drink the putrid water. The passage is worth quoting at length.

> Such men were already more than half beaten without the suspicion of the smell of gun-powder. Others, however, of firmer fibre, stauncher mold, and iron nerve, and a resolution that would never say "hold, enough," parted the thick green scum, filled the canteen, shut their eyes and drank deeply of the water as it washed back and over the festering animal matter, set in motion as it was by the dipping of many canteens. Such material makes invincible soldiers, as near, at least, as human beings can be called invincible. Of such material was the Army of the Cumberland composed. Father Abraham at Washington had no better, truer, soldiers than those of this old army after the chaff was winnowed out of it.[6]

Father Abraham had good men, indeed! The Cumberland soldiers had left farm, shop, or store and learned to survive the roughest of conditions. Or the better ones had at least. The men of "firmer fibre" rose above the rest and became "invincible soldiers." Out of the country's civilian base came men of a "stauncher mold," "iron nerve," and "resolution." They were men of a more solid character than the norm—more resolved, more determined, according to the authors' description. So these became a human

1. A typical image of a veteran: "Dr. Joseph B. Shawgo, Company G," from *History of the Eighty-Fifth Regiment, Illinois Volunteer Infantry*, Henry J. Aten.

"material" out of which the toughest kind of soldiery could be crafted. Victory in war depended on such good men.

While the early campaigning thus served to separate wheat from chaff, the Cumberland soldiers next faced a challenge to their democratic integrity. The fierce spirit of Jacksonian individualism would have to give. The populist revolution of the 1820s and 1830s had democratized political participation (for white males), and had done so in a way that created a near-obligatory suspicion of any structured hierarchy or domineering form of command. In such a populist climate, the West Point military academy certainly qualified as an enemy. Though created in 1802 by Thomas Jefferson as a brilliant way to reconcile the nation's need for a trained officer corps with the necessity to protect republican institutions, the school drew fire when the Jacksonian era changed the country's political culture. To many Americans of this new generation, the Point was an aristocratic institution, while the officers it produced were something akin to neo-monarchists. According to these same critics, the small regular army that served under such martinets could be composed only of destitute immigrants or men so devoid of character and ambition that nothing was left for them but to surrender to military slavery. Many Cumberland authors, writing years later, kept this contempt alive. Albion Tourgee, in his 1896 *Story of a Thousand,* described the military academy as nothing but a disgrace.[7]

As Richard Bruce Winders discusses, the Mexican War amplified the problem. In his description, the West Point cadre saw the conflict as a chance to redeem the academy and the army's reputation. A precisely engineered victory would demonstrate the worth of military professionalism, and as if to prove their point, West Point officers sneered at volunteer units as unworthy. For his part, Maj. Gen. Winfield Scott reinforced this attitude when he conducted his decisive Veracruz campaign, assigning the starring roles to his Regulars. Most of the civilian volunteers never saw action, or were assigned to auxiliary duty. These citizen-soldiers had reason to be angry. Then, as Amy S. Greenberg observes, the decade of the 1850s added another dimension to the issue by giving rise to a renewed filibustering spirit, an enthusiasm stimulated by the possibility of taking Cuba, among other Latin American states. As she describes it, military amateurism and downright rowdyism gained a new lease in the American imagination, despite the fact that any drive to the south brought up the controversy over slavery's expansion.[8]

Given these developments neither side was prepared for the kind of war that evolved after the summer of 1861 failed to produce an instant victory. West Point-like discipline was anathema to the men in the volunteer regiments, but after First Manassas it also became clear that this would be no "breakfast war," nor some fantasy adventure in an imaginary tropical republic. The conflict would be fought in formal, large-scale Napoleonic style, and so precise order on the march, in camp, and on the firing line was absolutely essential. What the Cumberland authors describe in detail is the difficult, contentious effort to combine the legitimate needs of command with the long-practiced antagonism to professionalism and the long-developed celebration of American military amateurism. This problem was complicated by the fact that it was well understood that West Point–trained officers would be recruited wherever possible.

First of all, Cumberland authors made it clear that they had asserted certain fundamental rights and ideals during the war no matter the claims of combat or chain of command. Writers who commented on the notorious career of Charles Gilbert made the case in point. A staff captain in the early days of Kentucky recruiting, he was promoted to the rank of major general of volunteers, but not through the normal process. Buell chose to recognize his rank, however, and made him a corps commander in the army's reorganization just before the Battle of Perryville. Despite an atrocious performance, he would command troops up until the spring of 1863. By all accounts Gilbert was the very embodiment of the petty tyrant, a characteristic no doubt amplified by the fact that his stars were never legitimate. The men simply detested him, and regimental historians were more than happy years later to write about various altercations with the general. Because he was such an extreme example, Gilbert represented a clear boundary of the citizen-soldier's tolerance for the pretentions of those who wore shoulder straps.

James Birney Shaw of the Tenth Indiana described a particular incident in which Gilbert demanded the regiment's colors because the men did not salute him after a night march. The color sergeant "gave [the general] a cursing and told him that if he polluted the colors by touching them he would kill him. Finally the boys began to get mad and thought they had enough of his insults." Shaw continued that the men drew bayonets and jabbed the general's horse until the animal withdrew. Shaw then concluded the scene. The men resolved to kill Gilbert at the first moment when they could disguise the act under a combat situation. Shaw cheerfully admitted this in his history, and then mused with complete disdain that there was "no danger of that." Gilbert, he stated, "was too big a coward to get near enough for any of our men or the enemy to get a crack at him."[9]

With the negative extreme thus established in the record, Cumberland authors went on to observe that the volunteers had understood perfectly well that they would have to adjust to a new kind of discipline. Their various anecdotal comments create a kind of profile of the key characteristics of officers good and bad, along with an inventory of the problems and complexities of commanding a citizen-based soldiery.

Robert Kimberly and Ephraim Holloway of the Forty-first Ohio—men who rose to high rank themselves—produced one of the most intricate of these discussions. They described the training regime of William B. Hazen, the regiment's first colonel, and an officer who would go on to win fame as one of the army's finest brigade commanders. Organizing the men in their training camp near Cleveland, Hazen, a former lieutenant in the Eighth Infantry U.S., was comprehensive and intense. "Drills, study, recitations, camp police duty, the cut of the hair and cleanliness of person, roll calls, meals, reveille and tattoo and taps, absence from camp or from any duty, sick calls . . . every minute detail of the daily routine and life . . . was specified and prescribed with the precision of a disciplinarian."

Hazen never let up. "The men began to wonder if two day's work was not crowded into the twelve-hour program." In a fascinating if mixed image, the authors describe the colonel as a "threshing machine" who thought his men were "thirty-day clocks," to wind up and run for a month without stopping. But Hazen had his reasons. He "knew, better than any other in the command, the tests to which the regiment would be put, and also that the time for preparation would be far too short, crowd it how he would." Hazen had no choice but to force things, even though his routine "benumbed the minds of many," to the point that "they went through prescribed motions like automatons."

Kimberly and Holloway then made a point of saying that Hazen had his reasonable and human side. This was no Charles Gilbert. "For lack of willing disposition [on the part of recruits], Hazen had no mercy," the authors reflected, "but to simple lack of adaptability he was widely charitable and considerate." Understanding coupled with a necessarily hard training program eventually worked its effect, and the soldiers became "practiced, alert and obedient." The authors then added the significant phrase: "with no loss of spirit."[10]

When trained with the determination of a Hazen, such "practiced, alert and obedient" men became proficient in the demanding art of Civil War formal combat. According to the Cumberland authors, this proficiency had a double nature. Though disciplined to fire and move in efficient formation, the men retained a certain distinctive responsibility and enterprise that not only marked them as American soldiers but served to make them more effective in a fight. In their descriptions of the men in combat, Cumberland writers insisted that while the men had learned the discipline of a mass army, they had retained this vital core of the citizen-soldier ideal.

Grit was certainly part of such a soldier's makeup. Writing with great pride about their regiment's part in the stand on Snodgrass Hill, the authors of the history of the Eighty-sixth Indiana noted that "the very fact that superior force was before them and that they had so little ammunition, was sufficient of itself to dismay the hearts of these Union troops on Snodgrass Hill. But not so. The Spartans of old had not more courageous troops than were these men, boys rather, who faced the foe in the closing hours of Sunday, September 20, 1863."

But these historians of the Eighty-sixth went beyond Sparta. Describing the unit's performance on the previous day, the authors reflected that "each man felt the terrible weight of responsibility that rested on him personally for the results that shall be achieved that day. It is this disregard of peril in the moment of greatest danger, this decision, this purpose and grand courage that comes only to the American citizen soldier, who voluntarily and with unselfish patriotism stands in defense of principle and country."[11] For these authors, the key point was that the men had stayed put because each soldier felt personally accountable. Training may have made these men efficient, and they may well have had the courage of the ancient Spartans, but their identity as responsible citizens had kept them steady.

This self-consciousness and sense of accountability was central. Cumberland authors acknowledged that tight discipline had been necessary to the army, but the regimentation had never destroyed the fundamental characteristics of the citizen-soldier. The spirit of defiance that badgered a Charles Gilbert was the same force that generated a profound personal responsibility. The men fought from a sense of duty that had been cultivated and reinforced in their civilian lives.

From this central characteristic blossomed intelligence and initiative on the battlefield. Belief in individual accountability kept the men steady in tight spots, but this same sensibility also inspired a willingness to transcend orders when the situation demanded. The Cumberland citizen-soldiers had proved tough in battle in part because they could act creatively on their own. They did not simply respond to commands from generals or other officers.

Cumberland authors turned the charge up Missionary Ridge at the Battle of Chattanooga into the preeminent example of this trait. The action was one of the army's crowning glories in any case, but the writers made it exemplary for its demonstration of soldierly enterprise. After all, at that moment in the battle, the troops assaulted the Confederate defenses all the way up to the top of the ridge, doing so without orders. By thus exceeding instructions, Army of the Cumberland soldiers had won the day. Later, the writers described the object lesson. Kimberly and Holloway were the authors who had discussed Hazen so well, noting the fact that this officer's hard training had made the men feel like automatons. But this had been necessary to prepare the soldiers for the demands of service, and, more importantly, the training had not broken the men's spirit, the authors had said. At Missionary Ridge this spirit paid off. Kimberly and Holloway crowed that their regiment's assault represented "the voluntary movement of an intelligent soldiery, without direction from the higher officers of the army." George Lewis of the 124th Ohio agreed. This former major observed that the ridge was "won by the *individual moral force of the volunteer union soldier,* never known before to the history of warfare."[12]

According to the Cumberland authors, this was the secret of the Union's victory in the war and of the nation's power in the world to come. The Cumberland's citizen-soldiers had not simply defeated the Confederacy, they had proved the worth of their breed for the future. In his 1902 history of the Thirty-fourth Illinois, Edwin Payne made the argument by comparing the Civil War to Cuba. Describing his regiment's retreat on the first day of Stones River, he noted that "after the first onslaught, there were heroic rallies of squads, and detachments, only to break and rally again, with a different nucleus and under constantly varying conditions." Overall command had dissolved, but the remnants, under lieutenants, captains, and sergeants, rallied in groups here and there. Payne then made it clear that he was describing something other than a forty-year-old battle. "In the recent military operations at Santiago, in Cuba, the army was accompanied by an officer of the French army, who, in his observations, noted what he termed the 'initiative' in the American soldier." Payne then remarked that "had he been at Stone River, he would have had the opportunity of observing that quality in not only the men in the ranks, but in the officers of all grades and rank."[13]

~

The Cumberland authors' assessment of the war and of the citizen-soldier tradition was certainly optimistic. In their minds, the men had come through a long four years and not only defeated the Confederate rebellion but kept alive the key ingredient for America's military power in the future. Such an upbeat stance seems to require a bit of explaining. By the writers' own admission, the war had dramatically changed course over its term. The eventual victory was gained by means not considered legitimate in 1861. Moreover, it cost 620,000 deaths among the soldiers on both sides, along with a measured but nasty destruction of the South's civil infrastructure. As well, if one considers Republican Reconstruction to be the logical or necessary outcome of the North's hard-won victory, then the battlefield triumph had been betrayed. Over the years several commentators have wondered whether the war was more trauma than triumph, or failure rather than victory. And there are historians writing currently who continue to express such doubts.[14]

The recent literature on Civil War military history provides help in understanding the Cumberland writers' defiant cheerfulness. For many years, historians had assumed that the technological improvements in weaponry—in particular, the rifled musket—had transformed Civil War battlefields into factories of mass-produced death, anticipating the horrors of the Great War's trauma in the trenches or the second war's slaughterhouses at places like Iwo Jima, Stalingrad, or Tarawa. Yet, beginning with Paddy Griffith, doubts about the rule of the rifle and technological mass slaughter have surfaced, culminating in Brent Nosworthy's encyclopedic discussion of the issue. He convincingly argues that several weapons types worked in different combat situations. Soldiers used everything from cavalry sabers to smoothbores to the Christopher Spencer seven-shot repeater, and each effectively in the proper situation. There was no grand technological shift, and, more important, no sense among the soldiers that they were doomed to die in some mechanical meat grinder.[15]

This reworking of the technological question has combined with Earl Hess's excellent work on the Union soldier in combat. As he argues, the men were anything but helpless victims of an inescapable barrage of bullets. Although the Wilderness and Atlanta campaigns would produce new levels of intense and constant fighting, Union soldiers (and Confederates, for that matter) learned that the Civil War battlefield was survivable. Hess details that the men found ways to counteract the chaos of combat. As Mark Neely reminds us, it was no accident that the large majority of soldier deaths came from disease and exposure. More important, Cumberland narrators like Charles Briant made a point of defining attrition in exactly these terms.[16]

As a result of this new literature one can see that the Civil War was certainly cruel, deadly, and even confusing, but it was not a demoralizing carnage machine. Although the soldiers could end up "shook over hell," to use Eric Dean's phrasing, there was no necessary sense of doom, or a view of combat as an inescapable death sentence—a vision that haunts E. B. Sledge's magnificent memoir of the World War II Pacific theater. The process of war making simply did not mandate so pessimistic a reaction. The war was indeed terrible, but that was due to the degenerative, savage nature of the irregular fighting rather than the formal combat, as Michael Fellman has chillingly demonstrated.[17]

As a result, Cumberland veterans writing about it later had reason to feel not only proud but effective. If they went on at length about the conscious responsibility, self-command, and initiative of civilians-as-soldiers, their references were perfectly credible given how the Civil War had actually been fought. Without question, certain battles and situations tested human limits, and the Cumberland authors were hardly unwilling to report as much. Henry Haynie of the Nineteenth Illinois wrote his own description of Snodgrass Hill, noting that on the firing line "every man [was] by now a perfect machine." The soldier was "not to think, but to obey, to cling to his gun, and to aim low."[18] However, when the writers glowed about the men's individuality, assertiveness, and control in the midst of battlefield chaos, their references were legitimate.

This issue of war experience and war remembrance matters because various historians have not only doubted that Union writers like these Cumberlanders were telling the truth, some argue that what they see as the veterans' fabricated memory became an important ingredient in the country's rightward political shift at the turn of the century, and that this shift destroyed the citizen-soldier idea. Cecelia O'Leary argues that the veterans' writings demonstrate that former Union soldiers became social and political reactionaries by the 1880s and 1890s, betraying America's citizen-soldier tradition as a critical part of the bargain. In her view, the men supported a white warrior culture that fused an insistent, belligerent patriotism with an advocacy for military professionalism. Union veterans, she insists, lost their base in the rich diversity and work-a-day world of American civilian life, becoming advocates for a white masculinist militarism expressly divorced from the social and civilian mainstream.[19]

Judging by the Cumberland authors of regimental histories and memoirs, precisely the opposite was true. In his 1905 memoir, *Echoes Of The Civil War As I Hear Them*, Michael Fitch made the case exactly and emphatically. Responding to the famous criticism of American amateurism leveled by German general Helmuth Von Moltke, Fitch acknowledged the power of "scientific warfare" that the new European nation had demonstrated in the Franco-Prussian War. However, the author continued, "the United States is doing an entirely different work for humanity . . . than making a scientific army the end or the means of government." Fitch then quipped that "we are doing this work for the German race itself," because, after all, "so many [Germans] have come to our shores to escape the tyranny of Von Moltke's military discipline." The author went on to admit that the North's Civil War was "unskillfully prosecuted," and that this had probably lengthened the conflict by three or so years beyond what "a strictly disciplined army of sufficient size and commanded by a Bonaparte or a Von Moltke would have required." But, Fitch surmised, it was not necessary "to make a martial machine of the American volunteer." Given the time, he would prevail in war, "but [he] wants to do it in his own way."

Fitch then got to the heart of the issue. A militarized social order would destroy America's particular genius. A large, professionalized, prepared military establishment "would be incompatible with the individual freedom, [and] the commercial and industrial prosperity now so characteristic of the United States." He concluded that "our chief glory and boast consist of these—not in winning battles, especially battles for subduing other peoples with neatness and dispatch."[20]

For Cumberland writers, the war demonstrated that Americans could nurture latent military power in their civilian world while enjoying their peaceful pursuits and freedoms. The authors admitted that war would always demand discipline and rigor, but it also tolerated and even reinforced the individuality and self-reliance that was to these veterans the defining principle of a civilian base and citizen responsibility. In this way, the Civil War had kept Jacksonian individualism and accountability alive. Self-reliant citizens could translate their initiative and self-direction into the middle of a war and then come back home to pursue what Fitch termed "our chief glory and boast."

Worthy to Win

As Cumberland authors enshrined and examined the citizen-soldier ideal, they included the serious issue of moral responsibility in their discussion. If large-scale Napoleonic war had forced the men to learn how to become effective fighters, the conflict had also forced them to learn ethical self-discipline under stress. Specifically, Cumberland recruits had left the restraints of their home communities in 1861 or 1862, but the authors insisted that such a situation provided no reason or excuse for good citizen-soldiers to become licentious. Moreover, the emerging hard war had raised the question of how to define a proper way to deal with noncombatants. The authors agreed that good citizen-soldiers could not become a force of marauders, as had the irregulars and guerillas, but what did that mean? Clearly, discipline had involved much more than learning to obey the commands of officers in combat.

This was a tricky issue for the Cumberland narrators. The men had gone far from home during the war and had entered a wild universe of temptation once they invaded the enemy's country. Moral degeneration had been all too easy to embrace. As well, the war had brought an un-expected level of destruction, and this largely at the insistence of the men themselves. The war was supposed to reveal the civilized state of both sides, but winning required the North to go past the limits established early in the conflict. Even though the men had been the original advocates and practitioners of hard war, the soldiers knew at the time that this could quickly and easily degenerate into mere looting and pillage.

Discussing all this years later, Cumberland writers insisted that moral discipline was absolutely necessary to the legitimacy of the citizen-soldier tradition. True victory hinged on the behavior of the men, not simply the army's ability to defeat the enemy. As such, the authors were certainly tempted to bury inconvenient details as they constructed their written memory, and to some degree they did. But as with the emancipation ques-tion, the interesting fact is that many of the writers were quite frank. Because of the importance of the issue, many authors engaged in self-criticism, picking over the details of Sherman's campaigns, or the behavior of their own units. For victory to be legitimate, the men had to be worthy, and many of the narratives show a refreshing desire to be honest about the subject.

~

In a certain sense, Cumberland soldiers never really left home or the moral restraints that were supposed to govern civilian life. In his study of the recruitment, organization, and campaigns of the original Army of the Ohio, Gerald Prokopowicz discusses the importance of the regiment as a fundamental unit. These organizations connected the men to the home communities they were to leave, or so at least was the intent.

Whether Unionist or Confederate, volunteer recruits did not join a na-tional army; they joined one of these state-mobilized organizations raised from and linked to the civil society. To be sure, the unit that was closest to the men was the company, because these entities were literally enlisted as groupings of neighbors and relatives within a particular county or town. Regiments of ten such companies were then formed by a catch-as-catch-can grouping of units available at the moment. Thus, particular regiments often represented two or more sections of a state. This said, the regiment was nonetheless identified with the civil sector from which it came. Each unit was given its flags (unit colors and the national standard) at a special ceremony. At this event a bond was forged between the community which had crafted these symbols and the men who now carried around as sacred objects these material references to the people they had sworn to defend.

In addition, as Prokopowicz and others have discussed, the experience of war reinforced this regiment-community relationship. Lack of experience and the problems of command and control on the battlefield made larger combat units unwieldy, or better, beyond the soldier's vision or sensibility when it counted on the firing line. To be sure, brigades could be commanded personally and operated at the soldier's scale, but these units were routinely broken up and reconstituted. Once created, regiments were permanent until mustered out and became the army's primary unit of combat and identity as far as the soldier was concerned. As well, they became the primary focus of memory in later years.[21] Thus, however far the men traveled, home in the sense of community responsibility was never farther away than the regimental colors.

But home could seem awfully distant. If physical hardihood and combat discipline were one part of the army's life, too much idle time was another. "Men who never knew one card from another before, here learned to play euchre, and to smoke a pipe," reported Charles Briant of the Sixth Indiana. "Why not?" he asked rhetorically. "Nothing to read, nothing to do, but to think of home and loved ones left behind." The men always wanted "something for amusement, something to kill time," Briant lamented.

Unfortunately, things to kill time were just a bit too available. Writing about it years later, some of the Cumberland authors sighed about the particulars. Robert Rogers observed that several fights occurred in his regiment over gambling debts as the men accumulated IOUs until payday. In a gutsy admission, Ephraim Wilson argued that the winter of 1862–1863 in Nashville produced an enemy worse than combat: the city's notorious Smoky Row. Wilson winced that the prostitutes were "destructive to the morals of the army."[22]

Cumberland authors could be candid about the world of temptation that the soldiers had faced. In attempting to evaluate it later, the writers tried to balance their willingness to admit such problems with their wish to defend the army's reputation. Benjamin Franklin Magee of the Seventy-second Indiana argued that "we are bold to make the assertion that thousands and thousands of soldiers passed through the war with lives and characters just as pure and blameless as any who stayed at home." Magee went on to clarify his statement by noting that it really all depended on the soldier's domestic training. "The war was simply a rigid school for the development of character, the foundation of which had already been laid. If a man's training at home had been correct, his character well formed, and purposes to do right well fixed, like purest gold he came out in the end all the brighter for the rubbing."

In contrast to Magee's effervescence, Frederick Keil sounded more sober, but emphasized the same fundamental issue. Whether or not the men could conquer the problem of license depended on their connection to the civilian world and their ability to return to it. Keil's Thirty-fifth Ohio was hardly "made up of Sunday School boys," the author admitted, but "saints do not fight." Rather, the Thirty-fifth was composed of "orderly, well-behaved citizen soldiers." Critically, he insisted that "we could not afford to acquire habits while in the army, which would place us at a disadvantage with respect to those who were at home." For this reason "we came home better men, better citizens, with an experience which tells us the worth of a nation, and of national honor."[23]

In comments of this type, it is easy to discern a tone of defensiveness. As the veteran writers well knew, the discussion involved more than the soldiers' behavior during the war. As Todd DePastino has observed, Americans during the emerging industrial age began to worry about the rootlessness caused by frequent unemployment. The wandering tramp became a figure of both scorn and fascination. As DePastino details, there was a readiness and eagerness to associate such tramping with Civil War veterans, at least during the Panic of 1873. The men had gotten used to wandering and bumming during the war years, it was believed, and so the temptation to return to a scavenging life on the road was powerful, particularly in times of economic distress. In this view, the Union soldiery may have destroyed the Confederacy, but they had made themselves a dangerous population in the process, as the hard times of the business cycle now revealed.[24]

Army of the Cumberland writers and all Union veterans were insistent to defend themselves against such charges, and so it was vitally impor-

tant in these regimental histories and memoirs to discuss both the temptations of the march and the triumph of character. It was important to illustrate to readers that the men had preserved the home virtues while on
the road. Thus, for the authors of the Eighty-sixth Indiana's history, behavior came down to a matter of personal wisdom versus foolishness. In
a discussion about paydays, the authors observed that smart soldiers had
sent their money home immediately. Others "who were reckless and not
disposed to look ahead," proceeded quickly to lose it all. They "squan-
dered [their pay] in gambling and drink." Thus had the army's invasion of
the Confederacy produced a trial of personal character and wisdom that
mimicked the trial of self-discipline and self-control that one found in the
Darwinist world back home. If the army had produced its share of fools
and cads, the process was no different from civil life.[25]

If tramping became a concern in the midst of the late nineteenth-
century's volatile business cycle, then the issue of excessive or destructive foraging during the war would have been critical for Army of the
Cumberland writers to discuss. After all, drinking, gambling, and dealing
with women of less than sterling virtue were familiar and ancient vices, but
the war's weapon of destructiveness had brought to the fore the new and
controversial matter of bumming. As the narrators readily admitted, the
soldiers had become foragers as soon as they had crossed the Ohio River
into Kentucky, and they had quickly turned this foraging into a method of
war making. Writing about the issue years later, the authors had to distinguish between looting and the legitimate confiscation of supplies and define the difference between vandalism and the use of property destruction
as a weapon of war. It was vitally important to discuss whether or not the
word tramp referred to an orderly march to victory or to a vagabond's excursion into pillage.

In discussing the issue, Cumberland writers could take advantage of
the fact that the North's hard war had been fought within a genuine sense
of limits and restraints. Mark Grimsley, Mark Neely, and others have
demonstrated that Sherman, Grant, and their men retained a sense of
proportion in their destructiveness, however much they had to increase
their pressure on the enemy. To be sure, nineteenth-century Americans
had a vision of unrestricted warfare, but this was applied to Native Americans, as Neely observes. Moreover, a total war did evolve within the Civil
War, but this was developed by guerillas and other irregulars beyond what
the formal armies could control. There had been unrestrained brutality

and vandalism in the great sectional conflict, but one found it in places like Missouri.[26]

For their part, Cumberland authors argued that they had been devoted to a limited concept of hard war and, in various anecdotes and reflections, set about explaining the specifics. In the broadest sense, Cumberlanders distinguished between war against bodies and war against property. The former was nothing less than savagery. George Herr's Fifty-ninth Illinois had served in Missouri before coming east as part of a contingent that joined Buell's army in time for Perryville. While in Missouri the regiment had participated in the Battle of Pea Ridge, and Herr described the aftermath of the fight in which Confederate Native Americans and Texans had participated. The author was infuriated. The Union dead had been "horribly mutilated," he noted, and the Texans had done the work. "The spawn of Caucasian progenitors!" Herr fumed. "Creatures who claimed to be white men, who boasted that they were representatives of Southern chivalry and that each could 'whip five Yankees.'" These were degenerates who had "found a lower level of beastliness than the native savagery of Creeks, Chickasaws, Cherokees and Choctaws." Herr asserted that the Texans had used their Bowie knives to cut through the skulls of men already dead or hopelessly wounded. In his outrage he described them as "jackals [who] safely whetted on the dead their insensate hate, and like jackals they skulked away." Native atrocities did not concern Herr, for "[the Natives] were simply and only hirelings, not having the remotest conception of the principles underlying the war, nor the mental qualifications necessary to an intelligent understanding thereof." The Texans were another matter.[27]

In contrast to such savagery, property war was appropriate. Not only did it grow out of legitimate foraging, it represented an effective method of warring because it did not degenerate into brutality against the body. In particular, women's bodies. White Southern women had received the brunt of the North's invasion during the war. If properly patriotic, Confederate men had been in the army, leaving wives, mothers, and younger sisters to experience the occupation of the blue soldiers. In this situation, taking chickens, horses, and mules represented a real method of war making, but one categorically different both from rape and the burning of houses.[28]

And even such a refined property war included further limits, Cumberland authors insisted. Francis McAdams described an event near Columbia, Tennessee, during the latter part of 1863. A "lady divided a churn of salt among us soldiers, an act of real kindness on her part." However, the author continued, a man from Company E (an individual whom the author names in the text) proceeded to steal meat from her. The provost marshal found out, and the individual "was tied to a tree until the brigade passed. He was afterwards tied to an artillery carriage and labeled with the word, 'Thief,' and marched six miles in that condition." McAdams concluded: "served him right."

Of course, the lady in McAdams's description had not been a defiant Rebel. But, according to the authors of the history of the Eighty-sixth Indiana, this was not necessarily an issue. In one passage the authors described a John Packer (again, the person is named in print for all readers to know). This Packer was a "natural straggler and forager." He was always "looking for and scenting plunder." He would "filch from the dignified country gentleman, or his old decrepit African 'mamma' with equal indifference." The authors sneered that "such was his indifference that it was often a question of whether it arose from a heart devoid of sympathy or from a lack of intelligence."[29]

As with the question of gambling and drinking, Cumberland authors felt most comfortable when they could reduce matters to personal character and individual choice. In their celebration of the citizen-soldier in combat they had turned mass-formation fighting into a war contingent on the initiative and intelligence of individual soldiers: men who could make gutsy moves without waiting for orders. Likewise the issue of vice. John Packer was definitely a bummer, a man who stole without regard for either the context or the person. Obviously, as the authors suggest, this individual lacked either intelligence or the proper training of character that Americans of this generation expected.

But what was one to do with Sherman's march through Georgia and the Carolinas? These campaigns were in part a deliberate and controlled policy of shock against the Confederacy, and in part something close to an invitation for soldiers to roam and steal at will. Current scholarship has noted that Sherman's movements never produced either the devastation or pillage that Lost Cause lore imagined, but these campaigns certainly stretched the rules of war as the soldiers understood them.[30] Thus, Cumberland authors had to measure this stretching against the claims for legitimate Northern victory and the citizen-soldier tradition.

Some narrators headed straight for the results. Alfred Hunter of the Eighty-second Indiana remained forever a hard-war man, insisting thirty years after the conflict that the Confederate leadership should have been hung for treason. To this author, the march to Savannah had been effective enough that "the fighting qualities of the rebel soldier had vanished. Instead of one of them being equal to five 'Yankees,' they would [have] much preferred five on their side to one on ours, and even then I doubt very much if they would have met with success when it came to battle." For his part, David Bittle Floyd stressed the destruction, and the dramatic tone that this gave to invasion. "The whole business portion of [the city] was a roaring, seething mass of flames," he noted in his description of the taking and wasting of Atlanta. "The destruction was complete as far as making the city worthless for military purposes, which was the intention. Some of the magnificent brick business houses, in which were placed the government stores, were no barriers to the onward march of the fire, but only fuel to the resistless fury of the flames." After this opening round of destruction, Floyd continued, Georgians watched "one of the finest armies of the world on the march, as its tide of invasion rolled onward to the sea." This tide provided "a sufficient taste of the bitterness and miseries of war to last [Southerners] for several generations."[31]

Many authors could not quite accept the notion of excessive cruelty justified by its results. William Wirt Calkins of the 104th Illinois described Major General Sherman's famous foraging order in the text of his history, noting categorically that the men were thus prohibited from engaging in any kind of wanton destruction. Judson Bishop of the Second Minnesota made it a point to say that "as far as is known to the writer these instructions were observed by *our* [foraging] details." After his emphasis on the word "our" Bishop went on to admit that "in many cases, no doubt, soldiers who were unrestrained by instructions or discipline were guilty of plundering and cruelty, not to be justified even in war, though such acts could not always be prevented by those in authority."[32]

The march up through South Carolina produced more squeamishness. In that campaign the men had punished the Palmetto State for inaugurating secession and firing on Fort Sumter, and this punishment included looting and the deliberate burning of houses. Up to this point, Cumberland soldiers had not done this save in response to guerilla attack. That changed here. In the 1895 history of the Fifty-eighth Indiana, the author reproduced the wartime journal of Chaplain John Hight, blending the later perspective of historical memory with the chaplain's contemporary observations. From Hight's journal came the pointed admission that "no effort was made to guard property, and the soldiers are permitted to take anything they desire. They are not slow to improve the opportunity offered them." Hight, an abolitionist, then added that "the rebels are now reaping the just reward of their long oppression of the slaves."

In his regimental history, Reverend Floyd tried to add a qualifier. He stated openly that the men had burned private residences alongside cotton gins and other structures. But the author then insisted that all this stopped once the men reached North Carolina. "We were not a horde of Vandals, but one of the very finest types of a disciplined army, composed of intelligent American citizens, volunteered to suppress the rebellion."[33]

There was a good deal of squirming in such remarks, indicating that at least some of the men who had gone with Sherman were a bit sheepish in later years. For their part, the Cumberlanders who had not gone to Savannah and Columbia had no reason to tack or equivocate, and so could develop a more skeptical perspective. The men of the Fourth Corps had gone back to Nashville to fight with Thomas after Atlanta had been taken, and so when their regimental historians sat down later to record their part of the collective memory, their view of the Georgia and Carolina campaigns could be more critical. And it was. Edwin High of the Sixty-eighth Indiana stated directly that the army's conduct in these movements "cannot be justified." The "burning of Atlanta, Milledgeville and Columbia, and the homes of people in the campaign through Georgia and the Carolinas, was cruel in the extreme, and these acts of pillage and arson of property of non-combatants brought opprobrium upon the soldiers." In a damning statement he noted that "it is the chief thing in the history of the war for the preservation of the union that casts a stain upon the fair name of our civilization."

In his 1896 history of the 105th Ohio, Albion Tourgee made the same point. The effect of the great marches was to turn Southerners into "implacable haters of the whole people whose army brought the pillages to their doors." The army completely lost its discipline. Some officers had attempted to prevent excesses, Tourgee noted, but the men had concluded that the top command had given them the license to destroy. The result was vandalism "merely to gratify lawless inclination." The army was simply "turned loose," and the result "cannot be justified or excused." Tourgee then carefully added that this wantonness had happened "not because the volunteer soldier was a pillager or 'bummer' by inclination, but because he was made so by a laxity of discipline, which, whether intentional or unintentional, resulted in putting a slur upon the fair name of this army, which it is useless to deny, and folly to extenuate."[34]

Strong words, surely, and an indication that the Fourteenth Corps that had gone southeast with Sherman had strayed into what Cumberland veterans regarded as dangerous territory. However effective or not as a method of war making, Sherman's campaigns had risked "the fair name of this army," sullying it without justification or excuse if Tourgee's characterization be accepted. The men had been taken to a dark place, in which they might well have gone past the legitimacy of the citizen-soldier into the domain of the brigand. Was all this acceptable because the enemy had cowered at such raiding, as Alfred Hunter insisted, or did the army damage its name beyond excuse or denial? The Cumberland narratives divided on this vitally important question.

As with the issue of how far to pursue the implications of emancipation, Cumberland authors dealt with the divisive matter of hard war by turning back toward home. In this case, they did not suddenly shift the scene to a victory celebration in Peoria or Indianapolis, but argued that the men had kept the home virtues alive by retaining their ties to the women they left behind. This, of course, marked them as proper Victorian men, but it also demonstrated that even when being taken down a path toward a more vindictive and destructive war, the men had nonetheless tried to preserve what they understood to be the heart and soul of true worthiness.

Women, or the sense of their presence, were never far away from the army. Indeed, they were as close as the regimental colors. The original flag presentations had highlighted the women of the community. Various women's groups had made the banners and so their honor was embedded literally in the fabric. Nixon Stewart of the Fifty-second Ohio recorded that the loyal women of Cincinnati had presented the colors to his outfit. The speaker at the presentation told the men that these women "'are here today to cheer you with their presence and smiles, and breathe the prayer that our God may protect you in your lives, and give you victory in the cause of the right.'" Then he got to the point. "'[The flag] is given with the assurance that as long as a drop of blood flows in your veins, it will wave untarnished by infamy, and unstained by dishonor.'"

Women showed up in other ways. John McBride of the Thirty-third Indiana described Caroline Coburn, the wife of his brigade commander. She visited camp often, always with "a hearty greeting" for the soldiers. Other wives visited, McBride recounted, but "none seemed to get so near to the hearts of the boys in the ranks as she whom all called 'Mother Coburn.'"[35]

The feminine presence was definitely appreciated. Of course, not every brigade could have a "Mother Coburn," but the men could long for such a person. The Cumberland authors record that during all their trials, the image of mother, wife, sister, or sweetheart stayed with them. The soldiers had not used the war to escape the society of women and enter some masculine warrior heaven. Quite the reverse. It had been vital to them to remain connected to the domestic sphere.

This was critically important when the inevitable tragedies struck. Lewis Day of the 101st Ohio described a wounded man in hospital. He "called, in his delirium, for his wife and children, appealing to them by name and crying [he insisted] with pain in his feet. Poor fellow! both legs had been amputated at the thigh." Gradually, the cries muted to whimpers and he expired. "I cannot allow myself to think of these sights and scenes, even now, almost a third of a century later."[36]

Because this wish for a womanly presence was so strong, Cumberland men went so far as to feminize themselves. In several of the narratives the authors shifted the imagery from warrior to woman, male to female. In doing so they provided the foundation for the authors to claim that despite the nastiness of hard war the men had kept their composure and their morals. By bringing the ideal of womanhood into themselves, they counterbalanced a cruel and heartless conflict that had threatened to destroy their ethical nature, not simply their bodies.

There are several such references. John McBride discussed his Thirty-third Indiana's early days in Kentucky, noting that sickness ran rampant. As ill soldiers recovered they tended the newly sick ones. These attendants were "untrained, as nurses, but they were unceasing in their vigils by day and by night. They were as tender and sympathetic as women." Thomas Wright of the Eighth Kentucky noted the same phenomenon. In the aftermath of the Stones River battle he observed that "the fierce bloodthirsty lion of our nature gives way to the better and finer promptings of the human heart." The unwounded survivors lifted "the bleeding, mangled forms of our unfortunate comrades . . . [and carried] them into prostrate groups around the fires, made to warm alike friends and now helpless foes." Later these wounded were loaded into ambulances, which caused further suffering. Listening to it caused "the rough, rude appearing soldiers' hearts to soften, and they became as sympathetic as our sisters and mothers."[37]

Here was the antidote to the problem of hard war. The men could not stop the conflict's evolving destructiveness and had no wish to do so. Cruelty had become official army policy, and not just because of Sherman. In response to this evolution the better Cumberland men had looked inward.

They had found in themselves the feminine presence that preserved their individual character and the legitimacy of their army's victory.

George W. Herr certainly argued as much. His Fifty-ninth Illinois had been at Nashville in late 1864, and so he was one of the Cumberland authors who could jab at Sherman and his campaigns. And he did. Herr argued that while Sherman was away wandering across northern Georgia, Thomas had been left to hold off the Army of Tennessee. Had Thomas not been the real hero of the moment, Confederate general Hood's forces would have gone on to "spread death and devastation along the peaceful banks of the Ohio," and this during what was supposed to be "the dying throes of the rebellion."

But Herr was a hard-war man himself. Earlier in his narrative he described Sherman's order removing civilians from Atlanta when this was done as part of the process of capturing the city. The author defended the action. The Union army owed nothing to civilians whose men "were fighting the battles of treason," he said. Critically, however, this hard-war growl softened when Herr then went on to describe how the soldiers as individual men had confronted actual refugees on the road. "It was a curious and touching sight to see the gentleness, the almost womanly delicacy, with which Sherman's soldiers treated the stricken and sorrowing people." Many a "big hulking fellow, who feared neither God, man nor devil, was melted to tears." In particular Herr described "one bearded Hoosier, a corporal was seen trudging along with a family carrying two sick children, one upon each arm." The children's illness had excited the man's sympathy, for "the bearded soldier, endeavoring to soothe and quiet them, cooed as tenderly as a mother." Herr concluded that despite the necessary cruelty of war, "the depopulation [of Atlanta] uncovered the great red heart of the 'Yankee,' and long will the vision be remembered by the Atlantans who witnessed it."[38]

Atlantans would not remember, but Cumberlanders would.

Home Again in God's Country

James Barnes, James Carnahan, and Thomas McCain, the authors of the history of the Eighty-sixth Indiana, commented in 1895 on the demobilization of thirty years earlier. The "grand regiments of all the States" had "melted away." Soldiers in a force "strong enough to conquer a hemisphere" suddenly "merged into the mass of people and were seen no more." According to the authors, this was nothing short of a miracle. The Union army had represented "a consolidation and embodiment of power seldom witnessed" in human history, and yet "it disappeared like a vision, and when one looked for [the former soldiers, one] saw only peaceful citizens engaged in the usual occupations."

In this passage, Barnes, Carnahan, and McCain were like all the Cumberland narrators. Whenever possible, they described the nation's Civil War victory in terms of themselves and their beloved "God's Country." In one way or another, everything circled back to the citizen-soldiery and to the homeland from which the men had been recruited and to which the survivors had returned. To read their regimental histories and memoirs, the veterans did not evaluate the North's triumph in terms of Reconstruction policy, or even in terms of the corporate industrial society that came to dominate the country by the end of the century. It seems as though Cumberland veterans wanted only to celebrate themselves.

Yet the authors were not simply crowing about their achievements. They were using their interpretation of their experience to comment about the homeland and the nation that had grown up in the wake of Confederate surrender. The imagery is indirect, even romanticized, but the writers were making a serious judgment. It mattered, said the authors of the Eighty-sixth, that the army had disappeared when the men came home. Everywhere one looked one saw "[a former soldier] bent over his saw and plane, [while] another swung his scythe in the harvest field, or plied his humble toil along the streets." According to the authors, this was the definition of "the people's war." When the soldiers had finished the job, they "quietly laid aside the instruments with which they accomplished [victory], and again took up those of peaceful industry." In this achievement lay an example and model for the world. "Never did a government on earth exhibit such stability, and assert its superiority over all other forms, as did this Republican Government of ours, in the way its armies disappeared when the struggle was over."[39]

In our own time many commentators have described sentiments like these as fundamentally, even hopelessly nostalgic. In his study of the Grand Army of the Republic, Stuart McConnell argues that Union veterans adopted a "rhetoric of preservation." They saw the nation they had saved as "something maintained intact rather than something greatly changed."[40] According to this reading, veterans like the authors of the Eighty-sixth's history longed for a simpler, more individualistic America. Living in the corporate industrialism of the late nineteenth century, they created images of a pastoral, small-scale, republic of the self-sufficient farm and the roadside shop. And, sure enough, the Eighty-sixth's authors sound like this. After all, they conjured up the saw, the plane, and—of all things—the scythe. Yet during the war the soldiers had been all about organized power and mass organization. They were hardly strangers to the world of large scale; they had helped invent it. And they remembered as much. After all, the historians of the Eighty-sixth insisted that their army had been "strong enough to capture a hemisphere." Despite some of their imagery, Cumberland narrators did not attempt to avoid modern life by act of literary memory. Like the authors of the history of the Eighty-sixth, they were interested in the stability of republican government, and saw their experience as citizens returned home from the war as the model for how to achieve it.

~

Cumberland authors had no problem discussing modern life or organized power. J. Henry Haynie of the Nineteenth Illinois observed in his 1912 history that the United States now boasted a population of ninety-two million and a collective wealth of $117 billion. "It will hardly be denied that this unparalleled prosperity became possible wholly by reason of the patriotism and the sacrifices of those who opposed the armed forces which sought to destroy this Country in the early sixties." Significantly, Haynie went on to add that the mobilization of the North's latent military potential in the 1860s served as warning to would-be opponents of the current age. Union victory "taught the world the advisability, and indeed the absolute necessity, of letting the United States alone, as the one unassailable and defensibly irresistible Power on earth."

On a completely different note Matthew Jamison pointed out that his father's old butchery was nothing like modern meat-packing plants. He called the new system "the American method of slaughtering hogs and curing the pork on a colossal and economic scale."[41]

Cumberland authors made a number of modern connections in their histories. In particular, the Grand Army of the Republic. This was the nation's first true veteran's organization and one of the prime developers of congressional lobbying. The GAR's perennial issue was pensions, and some of the Cumberland writers brought the matter up directly. In his 1894 history, Frederick Keil took a swipe at the Cleveland administration and its hostility to the veterans' cause. When Cumberland soldiers were the thin blue line on Snodgrass Hill on September 20, 1863, Keil remarked, no one "would then have said one word against the soldier." At that moment, "the army stood as a living wall between union[,] defeat, and ruin." Had the soldiers *then* asked that their widows be provided for, or their old age be supported, the country would have granted them anything. But now, said Keil, thirty years later, with the victory safely won, the president whined that "these men are making a raid on the treasury." A former lieutenant contributing a letter to Edwin Payne's history of the Thirty-fourth Illinois made a similar comment. R. J. Heath complained that "after assisting, in my feeble way, in kicking the stuffing out of the institution of slavery in this country—I am compelled to stand on the sunset hills of life and witness the selfishness and greed of those who, [during the war], took advantage of the distress of the Nation [and who are now] . . . still enriching themselves at the expense of the people, and begrudging the defenders of the country the pensions allowed."[42]

Cumberland authors had no desire to turn their war memory into some kind of military pastoral or to run from contemporary life. In so many respects, their narratives were commentaries on the emerging twentieth century rather than a memorial to a nineteenth-century war. As always, the critical issue was the citizen-soldier ideal. In everything they wrote they evaluated the strength of the American military tradition as they understood it. As discussed earlier, they tested it against the strain of combat as they had found it in the Civil War, and argued that the precedent they had established would make the country a military powerhouse in the future. Likewise, they tested it against "God's Country" as they had found it when they had come back home. In this particular situation, the issue was whether or not these citizens made soldiers could dissolve back into the civilian world again.

In both situations, the fundamental issue boiled down to a balance. During the war, the men had found that they could preserve individual initiative and enterprise in a war of mass-formation discipline. Back in the Midwest they attempted to preserve the validity of the qualities of individual character and hard work in the midst of a society dominated by the "American method" of slaughtering hogs. Edwin High of the Sixtyeighth Indiana demonstrated that this latter form of balance was quite possible. In his 1902 regimental history, he created a set of biographical sketches for every member of the regiment he could find, producing quite a list. In so doing, he created a marvelous source on how at least one Cumberland author defined the process of coming home and making a living. It is worth looking at a number of his sketches.

High noted that after rising from the ranks to first lieutenant, James Huffman came back and started a farm in Iowa, "its fertile acres, handsome shrubbery, and stately groves making it one of the finest in the state." It became "an ideal home for the gallant soldier and patriot, and his charming wife and loving children." Huffman died in 1897, having been "faithful to every trust and left to his family a competency honorably acquired, and the priceless legacy of a good name." Richard Leeson had been a first lieutenant in Company C, rising to be brevetted a colonel. He became the owner of "the largest department store in Indiana, the annual sales amounting to over a half million dollars." His great success came by "fidelity and unflinching honesty, and is an example of achievement through strict devotion to duty, and sound business methods." For his part, John Burkhart rose to the rank of captain during the war, went home, and became a builder. He moved to Brookville, Indiana, and constructed there "many of the finest residences in that town." He thereby added considerably "to the architectural beauty" of the place. In addition, he helped remodel the county courthouse and the children's home, and designed and built the city's water works. Francis Sherwood had been a carpenter, but the war had disabled him for that trade. He opened a restaurant in Indianapolis, "which he has followed with success. He is esteemed by all as an upright, reliable man, and well deserves the success he has achieved." John M. Francis had enlisted off the farm at seventeen. He returned home after the war to reside in Sheridan, Indiana, where he "has taken an active interest in the welfare of that city; was one of the first to prospect for oil and gas; was an organizer of the Thistelwaite Bank, served as its first cashier, and is now its vice-president." While "a soldier he did his duty faithfully. As a citizen and neighbor he is held in the highest esteem by those who know him best. Broad minded and generous, he has along his life's journey exerted a wide influence for the good."[43]

No reference here to the old scythe and plane. These returning veterans had embraced a variety of new pursuits, from oil and gas to banking and department stores. At the same time, High carefully noted that the virtues that had distinguished the men in the army had carried over into civilian life. In his postwar career, Leeson had blended "strict devotion to duty" with "unflinching honesty" and "sound business methods." As he had in the war, Huffman had been "faithful to every trust" and so left behind "the priceless legacy of a good name." Despite his disability, Sherwood had proved "upright" and "reliable" in the restaurant business and so deserved "the success he has achieved."

For Cumberland authors, the point was not to preserve an older vision of the nation amid the bustle of the modern era. Their intent was to demonstrate that the values they had inherited during their Jacksonian-age upbringing were still pertinent at the turn of the century. As soldiers they had demonstrated this on the military side. Despite the demands of Napoleonic-scale war and tight discipline, the men had blended initiative, self-consciousness, and individualism into the mix. They did so with such effect that Henry Haynie could claim that the United States was now unassailable despite having no permanent military establishment beyond a navy. In like fashion the soldiers had become citizens again. The values of personal character, individual accountability, attention to duty, a sense of the value of one's good name, all worked quite well in the "God's Country" to which the men had returned. Cumberland veterans had not only prospered but kept their honor besides.

Thus did the authors participate in what Heather Cox Richardson has argued was an attempt by Northerners to extend the ethos of free labor deep into the society of emerging industrialization. According to her, this attempt was serious and deep-seated enough that it proved the most important reason for the North's waning support for political Reconstruction.[44] For their part, Cumberland veterans insisted that they had successfully blended the moral individualism and personal accountability of the Jacksonian era with the organizationalism of the budding twentieth century. They were the example that proved that the country's military tradition had become the base of the society's modern military potential, and likewise that the virtues of personal character could be embedded into the economies of scale of the modern industrial machine. According to the authors, Cumberland soldiers had taught by example.

～

In this way did Army of the Cumberland authors find the North's enduring victory in themselves and in the civilian world that they built when they returned home to Indiana, Illinois, or the other states of the Midwest. As Cumberlanders saw it, the Northern war's enduring legacy was the ability of ordinary men to rise out of the regular pursuits of civil life, become world-class soldiers capable of destroying any foreign enemy, and then return back home to the women and community they had left behind. In that civilian world they then created a peaceful, orderly life, and an enterprising one as well. Northern victory—American victory—was found in a journey: from home into the cruel pit of combat, and then back home to security, peace, and sound business practices.

But focusing exclusively on the good men who won the war would not be sufficient. Albion Tourgee's "fool" could not be disregarded so easily. In *A Fool's Errand* Tourgee had argued that Northerners were guilty of a grand sellout: finding victory in their own prosperity rather than in the moral and political reformation of the former Confederacy. The charge was not without foundation. At the very least it could be said that the North's Civil War victory had been made good only by the sudden emergence of the Chicago–New York City industrial corridor. In some sense, Cumberland authors had to come to terms with what John Neff rightly refers to as the two "alien peoples."[45] Former Confederates and former slaves constituted a real challenge in that how one defined their role in the years after the war defined how one should understand the North's destruction of the Confederacy. Cumberland authors met this challenge not by "reconciling" with their former foes or forgetting that blacks had been part of the war. Rather, regimental historians and memoir writers incorporated both the vanquished and the liberated into their story, but in a way that supported what the writers defined as the North's victory and the nation's destiny.

3
Incorporating Friends and Enemies

War at times has been cruel and unrelenting, and would seem unwar-
ranted amid its devastations and inhuman slaughter of unprotected
and helpless innocents, . . . [but] a new impetus has been given to the
onward march and development of human civilization. . . . Not the
smallest of issues that crowned the war was the emancipation of four
millions of slaves in these United States of America, giving a more
forcible emphasis to the couplet, ours is, "The land of the free and
home of the brave."
> —Rev. Enoch H. Wood, quoted by James Mauzy,
> Sixty-eighth Indiana

Because he had to endure the violent politics of Reconstruction in North
Carolina, Albion Tourgee came to regard the Union's Civil War as a failure. The veteran had defined victory as the opportunity to reform Southern society: to substitute the relations of the market for what he described
as the corrupt forced bargain between master and slave. Other Cumberland veterans were not so disillusioned because they had never tried to
be Carpetbaggers. They saw the prosperity and development of Indiana,
Ohio, or points west and east when they went home to resume their lives,
and saw this peace and growth of the homeland as the just consequence of
their conquest. In a turn-of-the-century America where Southern politics
proved to be a dark and bloody ground, Cumberlanders could readily find
tangible victory in "God's Country" and in themselves as the good men
who won the war.

Yet, locating triumph here and here alone would not be sufficient.
Something had to be said about the liberated slaves and about the Confederates who had been defeated. Said a better way, Cumberlanders had
good reason to incorporate African Americans and Rebels into their master narrative. Depending on how it was done, describing the emancipated
and the vanquished could solidify the army's victory. In particular, the authors used emancipation along with anecdotes about the black charac-

ters they had met during the invasion to demonstrate that the North's war had been humanitarian. As noted earlier, the Union armies had become increasingly destructive during the conflict, transcending the limits established early by generals McClellan and Buell, and breaking the bonds of civilized war according to at least a few of the Cumberland authors. By contrast, emancipation restored decency and selflessness to the North's triumph. Rather like the way Abraham Lincoln was turned into the Great Emancipator, as Kirk Savage has described, Cumberland authors absorbed liberation into the North's war, redeeming what had been a nasty conflict by linking it to a kind of military innocence.[1]

Cumberlanders also tried to firm up the North's elusive victory by using descriptions of the enemy. The authors were always quick to condemn the original Confederate cause, but they also discussed butternut soldiers and civilians in detail. They did this, in part, because Rebels in uniform had represented a formal enemy, and describing combat with them could stand as evidence that Cumberland soldiers had conducted a civilized war under trying circumstances. As the authors were quick to point out, flag-bearing Confederate regiments represented a different kind of foe than did the guerilla or raider. Although the war had been destructive, descriptions of linear or fortification combat with the Confederate army could be used to demonstrate that Cumberlanders had been able to keep the conflict within bounds.

Confederate soldiers and civilians could also testify to the completeness of the North's triumph. The recorded words of butternut infantry and Rebel women could demonstrate that the Union victory had been in some sense total. In contrast to the controversy over Reconstruction and post-Reconstruction politics, testimony from former Confederates could readily be used to prove that the good Cumberland men had indeed won the war.

In any case, the liberated and the vanquished were everywhere in the Cumberland master narrative because these two groups demonstrated that Confederate military surrender in 1865 had indeed ended the war. In contrast to Tourgee's quixotic effort to remake the South and the Southern people during Reconstruction, Cumberland authors located an enduring victory, finding it in the words and actions they recorded in their narratives of wartime experience. Triumph did not depend on some imperative to remake the conquered land and its people, it could be found in the former slaves and former enemies who attested in their own words to the legitimacy and potency of the North's military power.

Humbling Defiant Confederates

In the years when Cumberland narrators put their regimental histories and memoirs together the reunion impulse was certainly present. Indeed, some writers sought to admit the former butternuts into the ranks of the country's citizen-soldiery, thus enlarging the story of America's arrival as a world-class power by adding Confederate bravado into the turn-of-the-century national mix. However, it was far more important to deploy the Confederates—soldiers and civilians—as witnesses to the power and success of the Union's war. If reunion had some claim on the veterans' imagination, solidifying victory had far more.

In the spectrum of the Cumberland narratives two writers created what could be regarded as genuine reunion pieces. Charles Manderson, a Republican senator from Nebraska in the 1880s and early 1890s, wrote *The Twin Seven-Shooters* in 1902. The former colonel of the Nineteenth Ohio produced nothing resembling a regimental history in this work. He never described his regiment's recruiting, the North's outrage over Sumter, or the anger at Southern treason. Nor did he describe the war of invasion that other authors worked through in detail. Manderson reduced the entire conflict to two battles, Stones River and Chattanooga, doing so not to describe combat but to turn the soldiers of the Northern and Southern armies into two important elements of a common Anglo-Saxon race. Discussing Stones River he noted "the dash of the Southerners in attack, the steadiness of Northerners in resistance." The Rebels' aggressiveness, he went on, represented the "impulsive ardor of the one," while the Cumberlanders' steadfastness indicated "the deliberate repose of the other; both so characteristic!"

Nothing here of Southern perfidy, or George W. Herr's sneering at the chivalry. Here was sectional contrast, sure enough, but contrast that created a perfect national synthesis. The "Civil War was waged on both the Federal and Confederate sides with an intensity and manly vigor characteristic of the race that sprang from the loins of the Puritan and the Cavalier." Armies thus drawn from these loins "were never prompted by personal hatred or ill will," Manderson continued. Rather, the common soldiery produced a "mutual respect and common consideration, that led naturally to a reunited country and the placing of the Great Republic in its present position as the Chiefest of Nations."

For Manderson, the story of his narrative was the power of the country produced by merging the former rivals into an unbeatable nation of whiteness. Indeed, his memoir is not about the war at all. It is about his pair of pistols, one of which he lost during the conflict and got back due to the generosity of a former Confederate who had taken it. It should be noted that Manderson included at least a brief reference to Southern war guilt, but he qualified this brief notation with "we have forgiven everything."[2] Clearly, Manderson believed that the emerging power of the United States in the twentieth century had been produced by the fusion of the former Confederacy and the former Union.

Anson Mills of the Eighteenth Infantry, U.S., wrote a far more forceful and credible memoir. Mills had served during the war in a brigade of Regulars that had been assigned to the Army of the Cumberland. He then spent a career in the army, rising eventually to the rank of brigadier general. Toward the end of his long life he composed *My Story*, released in 1918, detailing his views on the Civil War, his service in the West, and his advocacy for international peace in later years.

As part of his lengthy and thoughtful memoir, Mills included an address he had delivered in 1913 to the Society of the Army of the Cumberland, a speech he gave "to inspire just but long-belated honors to the Confederate soldiers in arms." For Mills, the point was not to argue that Confederates and Unionists represented a merger into a common superior race, but to insist that the Civil War itself had been unnecessary. At the time of the war, America was evolving into a more efficient and productive society, the author insisted. "The genius of the ceaseless and tireless mental workers had by mechanical appliances and organized labor in large factories relieved man's brawn and muscle from perhaps 30 percent of its arduous toil in the struggle for existence." But extremists would have none of this progress. "Political fanatics and moral agitators" were intent to ruin the developing workers' paradise. Such people had worked tirelessly to "set up strife between the sections North and South." Their aim was not idealism but pure anarchism: a desire to destroy the government using whatever emotionally charged issue lay around handy, particularly the "recriminating discussion against slavery." As a result, secession and war came, but, insisted Mills, there were "probably not ten per cent of the men North and South who afterward became soldiers for or against the Union who had any sympathy with the fanatical agitators on either side."[3]

In contrast to Manderson and Mills, the overwhelming majority of Cumberland narrators insisted on writing some form of Confederate war guilt into the record. Expressions of this ranged from one or two lines at the beginning of a text to long, chapter-length discussions of the secession process. However composed, the authors made sure that readers put the former Confederacy in its proper historical place. Alfred Hunter of the Eighty-second Indiana took this insistence to the extreme, using his 1893 regimental history to savage the "cowardly heart" of the former Confederate president, Jefferson Davis. This man, captured in "crinoline and female skirts," was "a fit symbol of the cause for which he and the leaders of the South had committed treason to accomplish." Hunter raged that "had a few paid the penalty of treason all would have been well to-day." Thirty years after the war, this author regretted the lack of a group hanging.[4]

Far more typical was the simple argument that secession and the Confederacy be properly remembered as the product of treason. In 1910 S. A. McNeil wrote his *Personal Recollections of Service in The Army of the Cumberland*, a work that appeared rather late in the game—a period when the national reunion movement was presumably sweeping all the older sectionalism aside. McNeil certainly sounded conciliatory in parts of his memoir, writing about picket fraternization and caring for the enemy's wounded, among other things. For example, McNeil noted that during the long Atlanta campaign an Alabama regiment that had been in their front for some weeks was suddenly shifted out of line. "We, who had been so chummy with the Alabama boys, almost regretted their sudden departure. They were jolly good fellows and we carried on quite a business in trading coffee for tobacco."

But such chumminess had its limits. The same McNeil also devoted a whole section of his memoir to attacking the United Daughters of the Confederacy and other cultivators of the Lost Cause. "I deeply deplore the vicious sentiment that has gained prominence in recent years and which has been introduced into some of the school books of our country, that the Southern rebellion was not an act of treason, but a 'War between the states.'" In particular, McNeil objected to the attempt to turn Jefferson Davis into a "martyr of the 'lost cause.'"

McNeil could rage with all the vehemence of a Hunter. "I protest against the erection of monuments to Lee and Davis, because they are not proper object lessons to teach future generations loyalty to the flag and to our country." The author then insisted that "all true Americans who desire to cherish and perpetuate true patriotism" distinguish "between our leader (Abraham Lincoln)" and "the leaders of an unholy cause, who seldom mentioned the name of Lincoln but to revile him as a brute, a gorilla and a monster."[5]

In one way or another, Cumberland authors made sure that their readers understood that the North had been right to win the war. Nothing about the Confederate experiment was ever discussed save to condemn it. Rebel soldiers could be described in certain situations as "jolly good fellows" by at least some of the authors, but no one save Manderson and Mills ever excused or papered over the Rebels' political cause. First and foremost, Cumberland authors insisted on defending their victory.

As it happened, discussions of Confederate soldiers could be quite useful to affirm and further explain this victory. In particular, descriptions of the butternuts could help establish not only the justice of the North's triumph but affirm that the war had been carried on by the rules of civilization. Particularly important here were references to William Tecumseh Sherman's Atlanta campaign. As Earl Hess has rightly noted, the early stages of the war were marked by frustration as well as attrition. The armies entered into battle episodically, producing high casualties but nothing decisive because the forces were both too clumsy and too resilient. With Grant and Sherman's appearance, the strategy changed to one of constant combat—a continuous pressure—that took the form of Grant's Wilderness campaign in the East and Sherman's Atlanta campaign in the West. The result became a version of trench warfare that Hess describes as "eerily prescient of World War I."[6] In the case of Sherman's contest with Confederate general Joe Johnston, the men were not only in close and constant contact, but those instances when straight-ahead assaults were attempted—as at Kennesaw Mountain—produced results not wildly different from the battles of the Somme or Verdun, save in the scale of the combat and the length of the fight.

As it happened, the soldiers on both sides created a kind of regulated and moderated war out of this perpetual contact. Not only picket fraternization but informal truces became a kind of standard practice. As Charles Partridge of the Ninety-sixth Illinois explained it, "the men almost insisted that these amnesties were a necessity, so severe had become the physical strain, and as the officers of the lower rank were as much in need of the respite as were their men these truces were repeated nightly."[7]

Officers at higher levels attempted to keep the pressure on, but the soldiery at the bottom conspired to reduce the pointless sacrifice of life—a practice, it should be noted, that emerged in the Great War as well. Writing about it years later, Cumberland authors took the opportunity to use descriptions of this practice to counteract images of the more savage or brutal elements of the war. In such discussions, combat was reduced to something like a sport. However, these same discussions were also used to establish the Cumberland soldiers and their cause as clearly superior. Ever so nicely, these incidents affirmed the North's victory, and this from the words and actions of the Confederate soldiers themselves.

John McBride's history of the Thirty-third Indiana described a local armistice during the Atlanta campaign. The men exchanged newspapers along with coffee and tobacco. This became the occasion for a comical verbal interchange. "One day a Johnny asked, 'Who commands the army across the river?'" Of course, the reply was Major General Sherman. "'Well, he commands ours, too,' said Johnny, 'for every time you are ordered to move we move too.'" Another Confederate chimed in. "'You'uns don't fight we'uns fair. You'uns go round and fight we'uns on the eend.'"

The authors of the history of the Eighty-sixth Indiana recorded a similar interchange, only this one involved a tussle by words. Union and Confederate soldiers engaged in a debate. During a lull in the fighting, the men started their usual exchange of coffee and tobacco, but then, "slavery pro and con was argued, secession and coercion, and the probable success of the Northern armies finally." The Eighty-sixth's entrant in this contest was one Baker, who held his own quite effectively, judging from the authors' description. This Baker convinced his counterpart "of the utter folly of further fighting on the part of the South. He admitted all was hopeless and declared he intended to abandon the army and the cause upon the first opportunity to desert."[8]

Thus had the war come full circle. A conflict that had emerged out of the populist democracy of the Jacksonian era became a civil contest once again. During this particular truce citizen-soldiers had reverted to their role as a citizenry, and the Eighty-sixth's champion—good old Baker— apparently did his job quite well. All the major issues were debated, and Baker's poor opponent was forced to concede that "all was hopeless." In this as well as McBride's case, the Confederate soldiers affirmed that William Tecumseh Sherman was one hell of a general, or better, that the Union's war in the West had become so efficient and powerful that even an officer with Joe Johnston's undoubted talent could not counteract it. One could hardly wish for better confirmation of the North's military power and the finality of its victory than descriptions of this type.

Charles Partridge of the Ninety-sixth Illinois added outright taunting into his discussion of this process. As with McBride, the reference is comic but the comedy hinges on a dig at the Confederate soldier's manhood. Following an action where a Confederate charge was repulsed, the defeated secessionists asked who had held the line against them. The author's recording of the resulting interchange is worth quoting at length. "'Well, it was a brigade of niggers,'. . . . The Rebels were angry, and fired a volley to show their indignation, following the volley with a torrent of oaths. Quiet was soon restored, when a Yankee called out: 'Oh Johnny! I forgot to say that the niggers were supported by hundred-day men.' In came more bullets and profanity, and then another period of quiet, which was broken by another call from the Yankee: 'Honest, boys, it was the Invalid Corps that you charged.' There was no more talking that night, but lots of ammunition wasted." Partridge went on to note that the general officers frowned on this sort of thing, but could not prevent it because "the soldiers in the ranks felt that it was their war rather than a contest between high officials."[9] Their war, it seems, included the familiar practice of the boasting contest.

Despite the fact that it included the horror of Kennesaw Mountain, the memory of the Atlanta campaign provided the perfect opportunity for Cumberland authors to write a taming of their war into the record. Bullets and canister suddenly became words, terrifying assaults over open ground suddenly became verbal banter, the shouts of men on the charge suddenly became boasting contests or debates. In these instances the world of war became something like homelife again, even though the conflict had actually been transformed into constant contact and trench fighting. Moreover, this domestication of the conflict—unthinkable in "Indian war" or in the Union soldiers' encounters with guerillas—also had the effect of making the Cumberland soldiers clear winners. Such narrations modified the hard war that the authors had to discuss while describing Sherman's March to the Sea and affirmed Northern victory out of the mouths of Confederate soldiers.

It should be noted in this discussion that not all the descriptions of uniformed Confederates ended up so optimistic or defanged. The Cumberland narrators could adopt a tone of outrage and atrocity, depending on the situation. One finds this tone most often in discussions of the looting of Union dead. On rare occasions, Cumberland soldiers had to abandon the field after an encounter with the Army of Tennessee, the most important instance of which was Chickamauga. A few months later, after the victory at Chattanooga, the Cumberlanders returned to the battlefield site. Years later, some writers recalled that the Union dead had been plundered and even mutilated, and they made sure to note the fact into the record. Edwin High of the Sixty-eighth Indiana was one such author. In his 1902 regimental history he copied into the text an official report on the subject, and then commented: "The pitiful side of war is here unfolded. We think of our wounded left weltering in their blood on this field of battle, to die in the jungle, unattended, save by the vampires who rob them of their shoes and clothing and everything of value, and leave them naked, dead and dying." High then concluded that "the bones of our dead at Chickamauga were collected and buried as 'unknown' in the National cemetery at Chattanooga."[10]

Such intense descriptions aside, most Cumberland authors were perfectly willing to show that they had respected those among their Confederate foes who had worn uniforms and fought in organized regiments. Moreover, they were also willing to say that they had treated defeated enemy soldiers with dignity. However, those who engaged in such discussions never failed to add that the North had been right to win the war. The act of emancipation and the country's future power and prosperity demonstrated that the war's verdict had been correct.

In his 1884 memoir, *Sabre Strokes of the Pennsylvania Dragoons*, former sergeant Thomas Dornblaser wrote eloquently about the Confederate soldiers his regiment saw after the surrender. "The paroled prisoners of the South were returning to their homes. Many of them were ragged and barefooted." On their way "these dejected, battle-worn veterans halted in our camps, rested peacefully in our tents, shared our coffee and hard-tack; and, seated around our camp-fires, they spoke freely of their blasted hopes and broken fortunes." In Dornblaser's view these men had gambled everything and lost. "There were many brave men, honest men, sincere men, in the Confederate ranks, who believed firmly in the cause which they were defending." In a language similar to Charles Manderson's, Dornblaser went on to say that these were "true soldiers," who had "met [us] on the bloody field, not in anger, not to avenge themselves, but in sublime devotion to principle." The "human heart," the author continued, was "not capable of a purer, more exalted feeling" than when "he stands before the cannon's mouth for the sake of principle."

Thus the armies had met on several fields over the horrible years of the war, each defending fundamental ideals as they understood them. Here Dornblaser adopted Manderson's sense of the equal dignity of the soldiers of both sides. However, Dornblaser was aiming here for the value of personal character, not the superiority of race. It was, after all, about principle. Moreover, he made sure to add that in the contest between these two groups of good men, the North had been right to win, as the nation's future development had demonstrated and would continue to demonstrate. The future historian, Dornblaser predicted, will someday describe "the wonderful prosperity of our country, and the universal freedom exercised by all classes, without distinction of race or color." The author hoped that the record left by such historians "will yet convince the survivors of the Confederate armies" that had their cause won, the result "would have been a calamity, not only to the North, but also to the South." Dornblaser looked for a day when "the children of the conquered will rise up and thank the armies of the Union for averting the wreck of disunion, and transmitting to posterity, 'One country and one flag.'"[11]

In contrast to the jaunty descriptions of besting the Confederate soldiers in boasting contests and debates, encounters with Confederate civilians were a tricky matter to discuss. The war against civilians had really meant a war against women, for these were the people left behind to defend individual homes and farms against the invaders. During the conflict Northern soldiers had to define a permissible method to violate these women and their property. As Jacqueline Glass Campbell has demonstrated, this necessity provided Confederate women with the opportunity to redefine the nature of the conflict itself. As the butternut armies proved increasingly unable either to control the tempo of the war or keep the Union soldiers out of the South, Confederate women became the soul of resistance. As this occurred the issue of the conflict changed from whether or not the Union army had the power to defeat their military opponents to whether or not the Union's soldiers and officers had exhibited integrity and honor in their invasion. As it became increasingly clear that the Confederacy could not win its independence, Confederate women gained the power to act as judges of the process of defeat. As Campbell has shown, their defiance represented both a necessary yielding to force and an assertion of their moral authority as women.[12] They thus had the power to evaluate the nature of the North's victory. It was no wonder that Cumberland writers like George Herr and Edwin High would later complain about the conduct of Sherman and his troops. Depending on how the soldiers had treated Confederate women and their homes, the North's destructive war might well have been as disreputable as critics like Tourgee later charged.

In their memoirs and regimental histories Cumberland authors thus well understood that making references to Confederate women was a dangerous game. They could hardly be unmindful of what it would mean to their victory if they had gone forth from their homes to defend the virtue of their own communities only to violate the proper women of the South.

Cumberland authors responded to this challenge in two ways. First, they tried to demonstrate that they had deflected the defiance of female Confederates without harming either their opponents' person or their own honor. In addition, they tried whenever possible to turn the actions and words of Confederate women into affirmations of Union victory.

No question about the defiance. Several of the Cumberland authors echoed the sentiments of John Fitch, quoted in the prelude, who had noted the blistering reception the Confederate women of Nashville had visited upon the Army of the Ohio when it entered the city in March 1862. In his 1895 history of the 104th Illinois, William Wirt Calkins observed that when the soldiers crossed from Kentucky into Tennessee the men vanished but women were encountered everywhere. These individuals "used those natural weapons of war, viz.; their tongues, in a most regardless and profane manner."

Cumberland writers tried to demonstrate that they had turned such resistance into some form of harmless repartee. They insisted that they had defused the problem by making it something of a joke. Calkins certainly adopted this pose. When confronted by female intemperate speech, he and his compatriots had remained gentlemen, he insisted, "maintain[ing] the same composure they would have displayed when listening to a curtain lecture at home or a chiding from their sweethearts for some fancied neglect."[13]

Some authors went into detail about such incidents, insisting through their extended commentary that the resistance of Confederate women had been diverted into less incendiary channels. Judson Bishop of the Second Minnesota described being stationed near Franklin, Tennessee, in the late winter of 1863. The men encamped on the estate of Col. John A. Battle of the Twentieth Tennessee, and did so right on the ornamental lawn. The colonel's wife, daughters, and widow of his son were in the house and objected to this intrusion, telling the men that as invaders they deserved no better than the wet fields. The ladies were then told in no uncertain terms that if their unit left it would be replaced by a regiment with a reputation for bad discipline. The Second Minnesota then stayed a month. As the regiment then prepared to move out, Bishop noted that the men said goodbye "to our friends, the ladies of the Battle family," adding that they would be happy to give a message to the colonel "if he would wait somewhere long enough to get it." In reply, the ladies told the men that the Second Minnesota was most cordially "invited to stop and see them as we returned northward, if we had time, 'as we probably wouldn't.'"[14]

Edwin Payne included in his history of the Thirty-fourth Illinois a long journal entry from a Capt. J. M. Myers. Myers described the regiment's stay in Columbia, Tennessee, in the spring of 1862, noting that all the inhabitants were secessionists and the women were "regular fire-eaters." However, he continued, despite "their hostility to our cause, they are very polite and hospitable to us personally." Out of this situation Myers and a brother officer ended up conversing with two young ladies on their porch, which soon turned into an invitation to tea. All went swimmingly. "The casual observer would have taken us for old friends." However the youngest daughter, a girl of sixteen, was one of the most "fiery little rebels" the men had yet encountered. "She first broke out in a tirade of abuse for pulling down the rebel flag from the College [the Columbia Atheneum lady's academy], and said nothing would give her greater pleasure than to see us driven back North at the point of a bayonet."

Here was a fascinating mixture of war and polite civilization. Courtship by proper convention and conversation was integral to what all these parties understood to be refined and elevated living, but here these customs were turned into a form of resistance: a violence of words. At this juncture, the young girl's "aunt cautioned her to be more careful of her language as we might be inclined to resent it." The young officers, in the fashion of proper gentlemen, "laughingly told her to proceed as it was amusing to us as it was gratifying to her." The officers then asked the girl to play the piano, which she did, pounding out "The Bonnie Blue Flag" in insistent tones. The two officers responded by asking her to play "Dixie."

As the entertainment ended, the mood suddenly shifted from this jockeying with courtship ritual. The young girl's mother explained that she had two boys in the Confederate army, "and expressed her fears that she would never see them again." She prayed that God would "'keep and send you safe home,'" but that if the officers ever met her sons to remember to "'treat them as I have treated you, and I shall feel well paid for what I have done for you.'"[15] As this mother well knew, resistance was one thing but war to the bitter end meant a destruction of the most brutal kind. For Edwin Payne, it was important to include this anecdote as a demonstration that Union men and Confederate women were, in a certain sense, allies in a common effort to preserve civilization in the midst of war. The mother's sober wisdom—and her terror of the possibilities—stood in marked contrast to the spit and vinegar of her immature daughter.

Beyond recording such incidents where Cumberland soldiers had successfully deflected female resistance, some authors sought to turn Confederate women into active agents of Northern victory. In some of the most fascinating brief passages in the narratives, certain writers turned banter into downright flirtation. These authors insisted that the Union men had won the hearts of Rebel women, or a certain number of them anyway. In so doing, these Cumberlanders insisted that they had secured the most complete victory that Victorian men could ever win: the moral and emotional allegiance of the South's elevated women.

In his 1896 history of the Thirty-seventh Indiana George Puntenney reported that when his unit went to Huntsville, Alabama, in early 1862, the women had proved incredibly defiant. He even recounted that a soldier, in response to one insult, had knocked the offending woman down. Immediately after relating this stunning information, Puntenney continued that "those ladies soon got over their prejudices, and soon afterwards the best-looking ladies of Huntsville were seen walking the streets escorted by some blue-coated officer or soldier." He then went on to say that many of these Southern ladies married those Union men. In an unmistakable thrust into the legitimacy of the South and its rebellion, Puntenney then concluded that "those ladies were not only good looking, but smart, and knew a good thing when they saw it."

Thomas Dornblaser made the same point. Describing the final Confederate defeat, the Pennsylvania cavalryman observed that "it may seem incredible, and yet it is true, that the ladies of the South felt much more kindly toward the Union soldier after the rebellion was crushed than before." After all, "they had respect for the men who had met and humbled the boasted prowess of Southern chivalry." Dornblaser insisted that these women "went so far as to say that the 'Yankees' must be brave; some admitted that they were handsome, and a precious few even acknowledged that they were lovable."[16]

But the prize comment of this type belongs to Spillard Horrall of the Forty-second Indiana. In his 1892 history of his regiment he jokingly described his regiment's shift to active foraging off Southern civilians. Early in the war, he said, no man from his unit would steal anything except "something to eat or a kiss now and then from a pretty rebel woman, which did not impoverish them; and very few, if *any*, shed tears about the theft."[17]

Horrall dedicated his regimental history to his wife, Jane, and their child. Throughout his narrative he continually connected the Union soldier on campaign to the wives, sweethearts, and mothers left behind. Yet here lies this fascinating little joke, with its dangerous and obvious implications of violation. Horrall's little comment was nothing less than a taunt.

2. Mrs. S. F. (Jane) Horrall with her child, from *History of the Forty-Second Indiana Volunteer Infantry,* Spillard F. Horrall.

Here was both conquest and unconditional surrender wrapped up in a quick phrase. Thus did the author insist that he and his comrades had defeated the rebellion in a way that overwhelmed Southern resistance at its very soul. Of course, the United Daughters of the Confederacy would create a rather different view of such situations.

Our Only Friends

In the course of narrating their invasion of the South, Cumberland authors described many of the African Americans they had met along the way, using a variety of images and stereotypes to do so. At one moment, blacks were described with all the racism that one would expect from men who had been raised in a society whose prime institution of popular culture had been the minstrel show. At other moments, authors described the gallant behavior of the USCT at the Battle of Nashville, or discussed blacks as "our only friends." In one respect it would be accurate to say that Cumberland narrators produced a puzzling and fragmented voice regarding African Americans. At first glance there seems to be no consistency at all.

Yet the Cumberland authors' fundamental theme was victory, including the central corollary that America's citizen-soldiers had delivered the goods. Cumberland narrators fit slaves, refugees, contraband workers, and African American soldiers into this theme. In one way or another, the authors turned their various descriptions of the former slaves into a narrative that legitimated the North's triumph. It is instructive to note that of those Cumberland authors who wrote about the war of invasion in detail, only J. Henry Haynie expressly disconnected soldiers from slaves. Commenting on campaigning in Tennessee, the author of the history of the Nineteenth Illinois noted that "'colored folks' were plentiful," but "as a rule, we were not thus troubled on our marchings down South. Generally speaking, the darkies were faithful to those with whom they had 'grow'ed up,' and remained at home."[18] No other Cumberland narrative features a statement like this. Certainly, some authors ignored the black presence, but only Haynie willingly handed the former slaves over to the enemy. No other writer turned blacks into allies of the Confederates. Simply put, African Americans were far too useful for confirming the Cumberland army's victory to let them fall—rhetorically—into the hands of their former masters.

But in using the slaves' voice the writers created a problem. Without intending it, Cumberland authors necessarily raised the implication that the army or the nation owed something to the slaves who had been so much a part of the Union soldiers' war. Indeed, as will be seen, there were narrators who said as much. Given the twisted fate of Reconstruction, it was a dicey matter to raise the issue of the North's obligation to the former slaves.

~

Some of the Cumberland authors who wrote in the early 1880s harbored a sense of hopefulness close to that of Albion Tourgee. They wanted
a better deal for the former slaves than a segregating America would give
them. Unlike Tourgee, however, they did not write narratives that recorded the failure of Reconstruction policy, nor did they engage in cyni-
cism. Rather, even though they wrote at the same time as *A Fool's Errand* appeared, they retained a heady sense of optimism born of their faith
in the Republican party and their belief in the free-labor ideal, to use
Heather Cox Richardson's definition of the term.[19] As such their histories
stand not as expressions of disappointment but as artifacts of a hope that
proved stillborn.

Benjamin Franklin Magee's history of the Seventy-second Indiana appeared in 1882, the author arguing that he had been a consistent opponent of slavery from a childhood where his mother had raised him to love
freedom. Given such an upbringing he never understood the war as anything but a crusade to end the peculiar institution. In his history he expressed delight that his vision had gradually become official policy. Slaves
became "the steadfast friends of the Union soldiers." Then, said the author, the government had the good sense to reward their allies. "They were
finally armed, and showed themselves worthy of freedom, the ballot, and
civil rights, since the war." Rejecting predictions that emancipation would
produce dire consequences, Magee asserted that former bondpeople were
"pushing their way up from ignorance and base servitude, to the broad,
sunny plains, of general intelligence and lofty freedom." The author then
added that "the Negroes are also producing more than when in slavery, and
their labor is contributing largely to make one grand aggregate of national
wealth and strength."

As far as Magee was concerned the question was simply when the
former Confederates would fully grasp this truth. "We took away slavery,
which cursed their States, and gave them free States." In the former Confederacy "free schools [have] sprung up, larger plantations have been broken up into smaller farms; the miserable negro cabins are giving place to
neat homes of land owners, white and black." In the author's mind at least,
a new day was dawning. "All sectional feelings of bitterness are passing
away; and, in short, they who were 'Johnny Rebs,' are now almost Yanks,
and in a few years will be fully so."[20] In Magee's prose at least, the Cumberlanders' war had paved the way for a genuine free-labor revolution.

Thomas Wright of the Eighth Kentucky was more realistic in that he

saw more of a fight ahead. In his estimation, justice would require a continued political struggle. Yet, in his 1880 history he saw in the Republican
victory of that year the beginning of a final triumph. Arguing that the
youth of the country would grow up Republican so long as the memory
of the Civil War lingered, Wright went straight after the Confederate
Southerners that his Unionist Kentuckians had defeated. "Mourn not over
the death of slavery," he told his former opponents. "Cease your vain re-
grets for the 'lost cause,' stop your efforts to keep alive the once dangerous
but now defunct principles for which Lee and Jackson fought." Wright
counseled the former Rebels to look ahead and "develop the vast hidden
resources of wealth of the sunny South." Critically, he insisted, "declare
that labor shall be respected, instead of despised." Armed with this fundamental principle, the former secessionists could go forth "and be proud
of a government where the humblest laborer can go to his cabin after his
day's labor, and take his little tow-headed boy on his knee and tell him he
has the future and the public schools before him." Thus sustained, Wright
concluded, he "has just as good chances to be President of the United
States as any other boy."[21]

Albion Tourgee's original hopes were not exclusive to him. Other men
who had been in the Cumberland army had sought much the same future.
In the case of Wright and Magee, these two regimental historians wrote
this vision into the record. As a result, their writings became frozen in
time. They represented a wistful dream, a dream that history would soon
destroy. By contrast, other Cumberland writers retained emancipation and
the African American presence, but wove these things into a national victory that would endure into the next century.

~

Outside of the idealistic reflections of Magee and Wright, Cumberland authors incorporated African Americans into their narratives through
anecdotal references and by absorbing the liberation act into the army's
larger mission of redeeming the nation. To begin with the anecdotes, at
first glance these seem to be a contradictory hodge-podge because praise
for slave allies was woven together with racist remarks and humor. Below
the surface paradox, however, a consistent theme emerged. In the end, all
remarks about African Americans in one way or another supported the
claim that the Army of the Cumberland had been powerful, efficient, and
right.

At the negative end were the many camp cook stories. From their earliest days in Kentucky, the regiments had employed refugees as personal

servants and as cooks for the various messes. Many of these individuals became well known to the officers and men because they stayed with the army for some months. In the process, their presumed eccentricities became the fodder for stories. Years later, Cumberland authors were delighted to include these camp servant tales in the record.

David Bittle Floyd produced a particularly good example in his history of the Seventy-fifth Indiana. As Floyd narrated the siege of Chattanooga, he included what he described as a "laughable incident." During a period of constant shelling, their cook had been keeping low. When the cannonading stopped he set about preparing dinner. Then the shelling resumed. "Sambo began to get very nervous. He said, 'It am berry warm heah, massa; I specks a little way back better.'" He was ordered to continue his work. Suddenly, a shell fragment "came whizzing along, and struck the coffee-pot, smashing it, and almost blinding the negro with scalding liquid." Terrified, the cook "started off like a deer, heedless of where he was running to." In his headlong dash he ran into an officer and knocked him down. Furious, the officer then attacked him. "We managed to get the darkey away, but the Captain believed it was a put-up job of the boys." Thus the laughter.

Robert Kimberly and Ephraim Holloway included a similar tale in their regimental study. One of the messes was served by a "little colored boy" who was the pride of his group because "he never failed to come up with his coffee." One morning in the act of boiling the water a "Confederate bullet struck the tin pot, scattered the fire in all directions, and passed between the little darkey's legs." The lad panicked and ran for dear life. "He could be seen for three quarters of a mile, still at full speed, and he may be going yet, for he never returned to the regiment."[22]

The focus of these stories is always the same. Panic. The reader needs little translation. Cumberland authors insisted that the men who had been recruited from the Midwest in 1861 and 1862 represented a normal sampling of the Jacksonian democracy of the region. These novice soldiers then had to learn the ropes in terms of surviving the hardships of army life and standing up to the perils of combat. In particular, the boys had to learn to conquer fear. In the camp cook stories Cumberland narrators confirmed the soldiers' success in this endeavor by invoking the tradition of blackface comic minstrelsy.[23] In the recorded skedaddling of blacks the Cumberlanders testified to their own self-command and self-control. The point in these stories was to contrast the terrified cook or camp servant with the steadiness of the Cumberland soldiers. The good men who won the war laughed when shell fragments hit the coffee pot. Alas, the poor "darkeys" could not.

One finds other disparaging stories. Benjamin Magee, the author eager for free-labor redemption, recorded one. He describes coming across a plantation dance in Alabama, one notable for the fact that a crowd of revelers was packed in a very small space. Thus pressed in, he and his companions undertook an experiment. "We had heard a great deal before the war about the peculiar aroma of the 'nigger' and we determined to see if there really was anything in it." He moved in among the dancers, coming in contact with a "buxom form of a wench that would weigh 200 pounds." Responding to the soldier's attention, she "began to jump up and down on our toes, scrape our shins, blow her slobbers and perspirations into our face." In conclusion of the experiment, Magee stated that "we are well prepared to say there was a peculiar odor . . . our curiosity is entirely satisfied."[24]

There can be no question that Cumberland authors were devoted to the vision of white supremacy that defined their generation. It would have been odd had the case been otherwise. That sense of superiority shows up most plainly here. For a generation of white men who had been born in the society that created the minstrel show, black camp cooks who ran in terror from exploding tin pots were easy to turn into symbols of cowardice. In the same sense, the sexual vulnerability of black women could be readily deflected by sporting references to two-hundred-pound "wenches" at a plantation dance. Cumberland authors certainly knew how to deploy racial imagery both to protect their reputation and to advance their legitimacy.

Other types of anecdotes used racial coding, but did so in a way that presented blacks in a far more sympathetic light. In particular, several stories noted that the Cumberlanders' war of invasion had merged with the slaves' desire for freedom. In effect, the narrators suggested that the Civil War had been two wars: the North's attempt to crush the Confederate rebellion and the slaves' attempt to escape or destroy the peculiar institution. For most Cumberland authors, such stories only added to the army's luster.

From the perspective of the writers, the easiest and safest of these anecdotes were ones that might be termed occasions of blessing and welcome. Cumberlanders proudly recorded incidents along the march when they had been met by individuals or crowds of blacks who received them as liberators. As a later generation of American citizen-soldiers could eagerly affirm, nothing established the legitimacy of one's forceful conquest of an enemy so much as the vocal, ringing endorsement of the captives whom the soldiers would set free.

In his history of the Thirty-first Indiana John Thomas Smith described his unit's entrance into Athens, Alabama, in July 1862. All the whites were gone, he said, but "quite a number of the colored population came out and cheered the old flag." Charles Partridge of the Ninety-sixth Illinois recorded the reaction of local blacks as his unit camped in Lexington, Kentucky. "An old 'aunty' standing by the roadside cried out, 'O Lor bless me, I wish I had some thing to gib 'em.'" An "aged colored man" added to this welcome, "repeating, as rapidly as he could speak it, 'Hurrah for de Union!'"[25]

Significantly, these two citations represent a tight control of circumstances and context. The "colored population" comes out simply to cheer, and they cheer the old flag and the old nation. This is a strict confirmation of the Cumberland army's original mission. For her part, "aunty" thinks only of what food she could provide these good men, while the old man simply cheers the Union. In these two recollections at least, no other agendas seem apparent.

This is not quite the case with George Puntenney's history of the Thirty-seventh Indiana. Here the author recorded his regiment's arrival in Huntsville, Alabama. The "citizens received the soldiers civilly but coldly, while the colored people could not conceal their delight at seeing us, and did not seem to try to do so." One black woman came rushing up, sobbing and crying, and proclaimed, "'Glory to God! Glory to God! I'se been praying for dis dose many years.'"[26] This was a very different kind of welcome. Obviously, this woman had hardly been praying all these years for a war to recement the Union. Clearly, this woman's "glory to God" was all about her and her family's freedom.

For Cumberland authors this desire for deliverance was a welcome and even proud story when it reinforced the justice of the soldiers' war. The writers were particularly enthusiastic in this regard when they included atrocity stories in their narratives. Obviously, such tales dramatically enhanced the Cumberlanders' historical case against the secessionist republic. Exposing the brutalities of slavery confirmed with emphasis that the Confederacy had been illegitimate. The Southern republic could not possibly have produced a viable national mission in an age of humanitarian progress. In the anecdotes that Cumberlanders assembled, the writers demonstrated not only that slavery had been cruel but that the North had been right to crush what Southerners had tried to claim was a second American Revolution.

In Alexis Cope's history of the Fifteenth Ohio, written in 1916, the former captain inserted several diary entries from soldiers in the unit, including an item from Andrew Gleason, a sergeant. While on a foraging detail "a negro woman came out of an adjoining wood with a large bundle on her head, a small babe in her arms, and leading a little mulatto boy." She had been found by some of the men in the unit "in an out-building *chained to the floor.*" The men had quickly "set her free." Upon inquiry the men found out that the owner had wanted "to sell her away from her children and had chained her to prevent her running away." Gleason proudly recorded that "here was a practical and pathetic enforcement of President Lincoln's emancipation proclamation, for we had literally struck the chains of bondage from this poor creature."

In his 1900 record of the Fifty-second Ohio, the Reverend Nixon Stewart recorded a different kind of atrocity. While on Sherman's March to the Sea, the unit entered Milledgeville, Georgia, whereupon "we saw the degrading curse of American slavery." Stewart elaborated that they had entered a local hotel and come upon "a man as white as any Yank" who "said to us: "'Massa's with Gen. M[agruder], Missus and I runs this hotel.'" Stewart added that "the planter saw that humanity was profitable, not always with a black skin." Such planters with their "dogs, horses, and gun[s]," Stewart raged, lived "to perpetuate the foul curse of African servitude, and every true American soldier felt called of God with fire and sword to blot the iniquity from the land."[27]

Anecdotes such as these demonstrate that Cumberland soldiers had every reason to link themselves to the antislavery cause during the war, and every reason to remember the fact later. Such stories help confirm Chandra Manning's argument that Union soldiers went beyond the practical, purely military aspects of using slaves as a weapon to defeat the Confederacy, and embraced liberation as part of a redeemed national mission.[28] Cumberland authors also confirm that the veterans had every reason to remember, preserve, and celebrate this connection later. It reinforced their cause.

But the Cumberland authors' antislavery memory had certain tricky dimensions—dimensions that were revealed when the writers turned from recording atrocity stories and black "hurrahs" on the roadside to exploring how blacks had materially aided the Union's war. As many Cumberland authors liked to say, African Americans had been "our only friends" during the invasion, and while this certainly allowed Union soldiers to incorporate the great humanitarian cause of the age into their victory, it also had other troublesome elements.

In his antislavery memoir, Benjamin Magee was particularly eager to show that slaves had been allies. He included several incidents in which bondpeople became "our friends," one story involving two men from the Seventy-second Indiana, Vance and Montgomery by name. These two were snared by guerillas while the regiment was posted in Tennessee. In describing the details Magee noted the barbarity of what happened next. "Let the reader say, whether in any civilized country its wanton cruelty has been surpassed." The two soldiers were tied to a tree. Despite their protests that they were uniformed prisoners of war, "they were only answered that they were d———d Yankee dogs, and ought to be hanged." Bound securely, the two were shot several times. The bodies were then untied and left "'to rot and be eat by buzzards and hogs,'" according to one of the guerillas. Somehow, Vance survived the shooting. "After a while, a negro came along, and as every negro was the Union Soldier's friend, Vance succeeded in attracting his attention. The wounded soldier was not mistaken. The old negro compassionately and tenderly helped him to the Murfreesboro pike, and there he was taken up, the same day, by the Union cavalry."[29]

In his narrative of the Second Michigan, Marshall Thatcher also included a story about a "faithful negro." Thatcher's cavalry outfit was part of a Union command searching for elements of John Bell Hood's Army of Tennessee as that force prepared to advance on its ill-fated raid into the Volunteer State in November 1864. Thatcher detailed that "an old negro crossed the Muscle shoals on the rocks and fish traps, wading, swimming and stumbling along." His would have been "a perilous undertaking in broad daylight" but "at midnight, at such a season, who can doubt the courage required for such an adventure?" The man brought intelligence of when and where Hood planned to cross the Tennessee. "His story was doubted," but after a close questioning of the individual, the commander ordered his cavalry to "be at the crossing by daylight." Thatcher then crowed: "the enemy appeared, *as advertised*."[30]

Clearly, such anecdotes suggested that the Army of the Cumberland's war against the Confederacy had involved an alliance with slaves. Every incident recorded by writers like Magee about "our only friends" implied that the war had been something of team operation. Contraband workers had provided labor that was absolutely critical. Local slaves had been guides and spies and had rescued Union boys caught behind the lines.

The more that such incidents appeared in the Cumberland memoirs, the more they hinted that African Americans had organized a partisan war against the rebellion, one that was more than critical to winning the victory. Moreover, it was obvious that this partisan war had been waged for a reason other than assisting Northern victory. The man who had maneuvered his way across the Muscle Shoals in the dead of night wanted to do more than help the Union army. Michael Fitch of the Twenty-first Wisconsin certainly got the point. In his 1905 memoir he reprinted a diary entry stating that "the slaves have been our only friends." He continued that "what they have done for the army entitles them to their freedom, or whatever they desire."[31]

Here it was, ever-so-clearly expressed: a profound sense of debt. Cumberland soldiers had used the slaves' active desire for freedom as a weapon to destroy Confederate independence. Black "friendship" behind the lines had been absolutely necessary to Union victory. To his credit, Fitch was not afraid to say it, or to say it in his remembrance of the war—even in 1905. The problem was defining just what it meant to provide "whatever they desire" to those who had been "our only friends."

This was just not a question that most Cumberlanders asked. At least not in print. Instead, the authors circled back, as they always did, to the soldiers who had won the war. Even when the soldiers in question were colored troops. Those Cumberland writers who had been at the Battle of Nashville included remarks describing the deeds of the USCT units who had participated in that action. In doing so, they were full of praise and generous in their discussions for the most part. Yet, these were ironic descriptions. While they certainly remembered African American soldiers and their deeds, the writers necessarily incorporated the soldiers' actions into the Union army's war and its victory.

In his 1916 history of the Fifteenth Ohio, Alexis Cope described the attack of USCT regiments against Peach Orchard Hill on the battle's second day. "A few minutes afterwards we passed over the same ground and saw the dead black men lying side by side with their white comrades." Writing one year after the release of the movie spectacle, *Birth of a Nation,* Cope observed that the sight of these mingled bodies "forever removed from the mind and heart of at least one white soldier all prejudice against the Negro race." In 1900 Isaac Royse of the 115th Illinois described the same assault, noting that the attacking column, composed of both black and white troops, encountered "the most terrific fire of grape, canister and musketry, sufficient to strike terror and dismay into the stoutest hearts." Royse noted that his unit kept up the assault, "keeping abreast of their equally brave colored comrades" until all were compelled to retire.[32]

There was no shortage of praise for black soldiers. George Lewis of the 124th Ohio made the most profuse statement. "I never saw more heroic conduct shown on the field of battle than was exhibited by this body of men *so recently slaves.* I saw a color-bearer of one of these regiments stand on the top of the rebel parapet and shake the flag he bore in the faces of the confederate infantry until he fell, riddled with bullets."[33]

But praise for gallantry in the Union's war was not the same thing as understanding that one had served in a coalition fight and that one owed the partners a substantial share of the victory. The Cumberlanders' view of the USCT was not entirely unlike the Americans' view of *Cuba Libre* in the Spanish-American War. As Louis Perez has demonstrated, Americans lauded the Cuban insurgents before the *Maine* blew up. But, as the author shows, once American soldiers landed near Santiago, the freedom fighters disappeared from the scene.[34] Although absolutely essential to American victory on the island, the Cubans' efforts were either ignored or disparaged. Cumberland authors were hardly so ungracious to the USCT who fought at Nashville. Those who saw blacks in action were obviously struck by the soldiers' performance and were willing to credit their action in the collective memory. However, Cumberland authors never moved from this point to writing a wider history of the North's war as a partnership. Writers might praise "our only friends" but the authors never turned the war into an alliance where Midwestern soldiers cooperated with Southern slaves in the pursuit of distinct, even different, objectives. Cumberland narrators absorbed freedom into their army's rescue of the country's destiny and mission. It was never a coalition war; it was a national victory.

In the end, the sense of obligation to the slaves was expressed on a personal rather than political level. As in everything, Cumberlanders were more comfortable when they could reduce matters to the issue of individual character. In his 1905 history of the Seventy-eighth Pennsylvania, Joseph Gibson recorded that "while in Murfreesboro we saw the first specimen of the great work that the Christian people of the North were destined to do for the colored people who were freed by the Emancipation Proclamation." His unit had employed a cook, one Dudley, who was "like many of the young people who were throwing off the shackles of slavery." Dudley "believed that knowledge was power, and that it was necessary for him to get an education." Gibson continued that the young man was pious, and could be found around the campfire after his duties "with his spelling book and New Testament." Thus, Dudley "seemed the very personification of patience and perseverance, as he struggled with the elementary part of his education." Gibson concluded by noting that the young man had thought of becoming a preacher but changed his mind and became "one of the most prominent colored dentists in the City of Nashville, and became thoroughly trusted by all who knew him, whether white or black."[35]

~

In the end, Cumberland authors incorporated emancipation into their army's legacy by absorbing liberation into the nation's enduring mission. In doing so, the writers removed Reconstruction from the war, save for some incidental asides and hints. After describing invasion, emancipation, and Confederate surrender, they ended their narratives, save for descriptions of their own future as veterans and the nation's future as a great power.

Although readers in the twenty-first century might disparage this as cowardice or betrayal, the Cumberlanders' sense of their legacy had a genuine grit to it. For one thing, the shift from a war to save the Union to a war to incorporate antislavery into the national mission had been an astounding feat during the war. One need only remember George B. McClellan's grand plan for victory. In particular, those memoirs and regimental histories that had been written by Democrats illustrate just how far the soldiers had come. It meant something when the former supporters of Douglas or Breckinridge wrote abolitionism into the war memory.

Robert Rogers of the 125th Illinois was one such author. After describing Robert E. Lee's surrender and the army's demobilization, Rogers observed that the veterans could take stock about what it all meant. For his part, the author reflected that "a great rebellion" had been "crushed, [and] the perpetrators of it allowed to live, through the magnanimity of our government." At the same time, he continued, slavery had been "forever blotted out; removing from our national banner the odium which had rested on it by this foul blot, but which now floats over all our land as the emblem of the free."

In his 1886 history of the western cavalry, Joseph Vale said much the same thing. The war, he insisted, eliminated "the great wrong against humanity, the heinous crime against every right of man, the 'sum of villainies'—the institution of American Slavery." This slavery, Vale continued, had been "the chief pretext for the conspiracy, and declared officially by the chief traitors to be the 'cornerstone of their Confederacy.'"

Union victory, by contrast, brought "freedom to the bondsman, and Nationality, Liberty, and the Union, one and inseparable."[36]

William B. Sipes of the Seventh Pennsylvania cavalry produced the most revealing of these statements. He had edited a Douglas paper in the Keystone State in the years before the war. In his 1905 history, however, he declared that the South had clung to the peculiar institution despite the fact that the North "declared that human slavery was a wrong against civilization and Christianity, that it was a 'relic of barbarism,' and a stain upon the nation's honor." With no less relish than Benjamin Magee, Sipes went on to say that the "rebellious aspirations of the secessionists were crushed, and the blot of slavery had disappeared forever from the face of the nation."

Sipes went even further. With wonderful eloquence he demonstrated how the army's experience in the South had convinced his largely Democratic regiment to convert to the cause of abolition. Not content to leave the emancipation issue to a few general statements, Sipes demonstrated how he and his comrades had been persuaded by the process of invasion. "Seeing, day after day, the hopeless longing for recognition as human beings by old and young; hearing, willingly or unwillingly, the stories of cruelties practiced, wrongs inflicted, and hardships endured—the revolution in sentiment was complete."

What makes Sipes so compelling, though, is where he went next. Given the opportunity to leave the matter at the level of idealistic sentiment, this former Douglas Democrat took the opportunity to jab away at Republican Reconstruction. "Probably the great majority of the men in the ranks would have opposed the elevation of the freed slaves to complete citizenship, but this issue never came before them while in the field." Sipes continued that "the sum of their desire was reached when Lincoln issued his Emancipation Proclamation, and all the slaves were made free." The author then took his shot. "No little trouble was caused by the new status of the negroes," he complained. "They all realized that they were free, and their idea of freedom comprehended a vast amount of idleness and a minimum of labor."[37] Thus did Sipes clearly separate himself from Republican veterans like Magee and Wright, but this same author spoke of emancipation and the nation's destiny and mission in prose that Albion Tourgee would have been happy to claim.

In the end, the meaning of the Cumberlanders' war legacy did not come from such fleeting glances into postwar racial politics positive or negative, or from the refusal of most authors to look at such politics at all.

Rather, it was the fact that the writers incorporated emancipation into the Cumberland army's victory and the nation's destiny secured by it. The issue was not Reconstruction but the kind of war that Cumberlanders—and the Union—had won. The critical fact was the military triumph itself and what had been won, or not won, by it.

Simply stated, the Cumberland soldiers had secured a military victory completely unlike any in the country's history. For all their cultivation of the citizen-soldier tradition, Cumberlanders were actually radical innovators. They did not intend it this way, but history had placed them in a circumstance that no American army had faced before. Put another way, the Cumberlanders had fought America's first foreign war, as such wars would come to be known in the next century. Union forces won a fight using all the destructive power that the mass armies of the twentieth century would employ—with corrections for improvements in technology and infrastructure. At the same time, the North's victory produced an ambiguity and hesitance similar to that created by the next century's wars.

When Cumberland soldiers accepted Confederate surrender, victory simply would not translate into absolute control over the enemy's landscape. Unlike the conquest of the continent accomplished by the defeat of Mexico and the various "Indian" wars, there would be no removal or absolute marginalization of the defeated. There would be no "settlement" process to remake the conquered territory in the victor's image with the victor's institutions, farms, towns, and people. As Albion Tourgee discussed at length, Confederate defeat left the enemy fully in control of his homeland with his ideology intact, and with the means to recreate his institutions. As the Carpetbagger had rightly explained it, Reconstruction fell apart in the face of an enemy determined to succeed and one who had the resources political and otherwise to make that resistance work. However one might condemn or praise Sherman and Grant, the last thing their armies produced was unconditional surrender.

The irony of this was that the North in the Civil War had produced the most powerful formal army the country had ever seen. In mobilization, discipline, logistics, command and control, weapons' technology, and tactical and strategic doctrine, the Union army would readily compare with any the country produced in the twentieth century—again, correcting for evolution in technology and infrastructure. They used this power to decimate their enemy, reducing the Confederate military to utter helplessness by the end. They destroyed the Rebels, invading the enemy in his own home to do it. One can readily note that the army Winfield Scott took with him to Mexico City could not possibly have accomplished anything comparable. Thus, unprecedented military power had produced incomplete or flawed results. The Americans who fought in World Wars I and II could see a similar "incompleteness" in the years following their return home.

As has been seen, Cumberlanders responded to this problem by focusing the victory on the homeland. Triumph lay in the ability to go back to wives, mothers, sweethearts, and the blessed "God's Country." Coincidently, this same "God's Country" became part of the incredibly powerful Chicago–New York City industrial corridor, a society that Cumberlanders seemed perfectly happy to join. Again, later generations of American soldiers could readily relate.

Into this situation of massive destructive power and incomplete effects came emancipation. Here was the first time in American history where the country's soldiers had fought for a group of people not privileged with citizenship or membership in the nation. This was not a war to conquer the west, or a war to keep the British away. Once liberation became part of the Union cause, Cumberland soldiers took on the unprecedented task of fighting for the benefit of an "other." As a result, American war making became a selfless act for the first time. The Union's war did not expand the republic for the benefit of those already privileged. Rather, the destruction of the Confederacy became a humanitarian act.

Thus it happened that the Cumberlanders' war became a fight in which dramatic military power was married to a kind of innocence. The good men who won the war were good not just because they had mastered the hardships of soldiering or preserved personal character under trying circumstances. They were good because they had literally "struck the chains of bondage" from several "poor creatures," to quote Sergeant Gleason. The Cumberlanders who had gone with Sherman had burned the state of South Carolina to the ground, but these were the same men who had come across fugitives and refugees in every Southern county they had visited. And all along the way the men had heard the calls of "glory to God!" Here was a victory very different from Mexico or the various "Indian" wars. Massive power had obliterated the enemy through a hard war, but the men had retained a certain purity because of the people they had liberated. Thus, these soldiers had earned the right to go back home and find victory in their "God's Country" and in the arms of their sweethearts.

Of course, the Americans who entered military service in 1917 or 1942 had no memory of the Army of the Cumberland. They never read any of these memoirs, though the college students among them might have struggled with Ambrose Bierce. Nonetheless, in a certain sense these twentieth-century recruits knew the Cumberland soldiers of old, more than they ever would have suspected. The Cumberland army's war had been in so many ways a war of the American future.

4
Legacies

Probably the greatest single change in American civilization in the war period, directly connected with the conflict, was the replacement of an unorganized nation by a highly organized society—organized, that is, on a national scale.

—Allan Nevins, *Organized War to Victory*

By the turn of the century the legacy of the North's Civil War seemed dead. As America embarked on its imperialistic crusade in 1898, it seemed to betray the great moment of liberation that had happened three decades earlier. After January 1, 1863, the North had used its overwhelming force not only to destroy the Confederacy but also to give freedom a wider meaning. In the process, the American way of war had seemed to become a new thing. In contrast to the Jacksonian generation's use of war as a device to acquire yet more agricultural living space for whites, the North had turned American war making into a selfless and idealistic act. However, by the 1890s all this seemed to unravel.

America reinvigorated imperialism at the turn of the century, not only in the conquest of the Plains Natives but also in the adventure of the Cuban and Philippine war. Furthermore, as a generation of scholarship has demonstrated, this new aggressiveness was about far more than territory (or foreign markets). Late-Victorian America produced a crisis of gender, at least within the privileged classes. Anxious to escape an "overcivilized," feminized society, and fearful of what they termed "race suicide," white males in polite America sought adventure, danger, grime, and sweat. Splendid little war (along with college football and the Boy Scouts) turned out to be just the answer, giving Americans like Theodore Roosevelt their "crowded hour," while seeming to prove that the United States had become an example of the potency of the "Anglo-Saxon race" in the world order. The main prize, as phrased so well by Richard Slotkin, was not territory so much as a desperately craved "regeneration through violence."[1]

Without question, this exuberant masculinity left a legacy. As Max Boot has explored, the squashing of the Philippine "insurrection" gave birth to a twentieth-century succession of "small wars." In particular, the Marine Corps came to specialize in quasi-imperialist interventionism in Latin America, producing a doctrine for prosecuting such limited conflicts along with a tiny group of daring, hell-for-leather heroes led by two-time Congressional Medal of Honor winner Smedley Darlington Butler. America engaged in a number of splendid little wars, and these became an important element of the country's twentieth-century military experience. Yet, as Boot is careful to note, this new legacy never quite caught fire with the army, nor could it rework America's larger citizen-soldier tradition. Indeed, Boot sees this fact as an important ingredient in the country's military failure in Vietnam. The American way of war in the twentieth century never took Smedley Butler *truly* to heart.[2]

Or maybe it is better to say that Americans stayed true to the foundation that Union soldiers prepared in the 1860s. The themes that Cumberland writers developed as vital to their war anticipated what later generations of Americans would use to imagine and describe their own massive conflicts. After all, as Cumberlanders discussed it in their regimental histories and memoirs, the North's Civil War had been a total war not a small one. The nation's integrity and destiny had been at stake. In response to this crisis Unionists produced a mass mobilization that, said the Cumberlanders, was eventually organized into an overwhelming force that destroyed an evil enemy in his own backyard. Moreover, this destructiveness was understood as idealism, not masculine adventure or conquest. However cruel or brutal the devastation, and however incomplete the victory might have been in real terms, Cumberlanders found triumph in the selflessness of the motive and in the enhanced power of the nation. As well, they found ultimate victory in "God's Country" and in the future one could build in a homeland now secure from external danger. Understood in such terms, the Cumberlanders' war memory could travel a long way into the twentieth century.

In this chapter I will focus on two veterans from the Army of the Cumberland, Wilbur Hinman and Joseph Warren Keifer. Hinman became the author of the novel *Corporal Si Klegg and His "Pard,"* a work that very quickly became recognized as an "every-soldier's" story of the Cumberlanders' war. Effectively, it was a master narrative in itself. For his part, Keifer became a Republican congressman from Ohio and served as a general officer in Cuba, translating the North's victory in the 1860s into turn-of-the-century military and naval policy. In each case, the authors represented a bridge from the Civil War into America's twentieth-century future. Each in their way kept the Cumberlanders' war alive and demonstrated how the army's legacy would be both preserved and reworked into an enduring American way of war.

Corporal Si Klegg and His "Pard"

In October 1885 Wilbur Fisk Hinman, former member of the Sixty-fifth Ohio volunteer infantry, began the serialized fictional adventures of one Josiah Klegg. Hinman made his character an underage recruit in a fictitious 200th Indiana, Company Q, using Klegg's adventures to discuss a soldier's coming of age. In writing these pieces Hinman brought to full flower his postwar writing career. After having risen through the ranks to become his regiment's acting lieutenant colonel during the war, he left the army at the demobilization to become a newspaperman. He labored as a reporter for the *Cleveland Herald* and then became city editor for the *Cleveland Leader*. In Washington in 1885 as correspondent for his paper he connected with the editor of the GAR's *National Tribune*. The Si Klegg stories soon followed and in 1887 these appeared as a fully developed war novel.[3]

Hinman's book quickly became famous among veterans for its common soldier's portrait of the war. In this respect it resembles John Billings's *Hardtack and Coffee,* which focused on the eastern army. The two works go beyond the narrow focus of individual regimental histories and the personal memoir and attempt to define a universal experience of Union soldiering. Each narrative dwells on the small, day-to-day things: equipment, rations and foraging, medical practices, drill and marching. In contrast to campaign studies or the works of Sherman, Grant, and other major commanders, Hinman and Billings reported the private's daily war. In this spirit, Hinman would describe the "arch enemy of the soldier," an enemy "more to be dreaded than Gatling guns, Greek fire or breechloading rifles." This horrifying foe was none other than the body louse.[4]

In his introduction to a recent reprinting of Hinman's work, Brian Pohanka observes that *Corporal Si Klegg* was quite a popular book in its time, due to the author's "honest portrayal of soldiering as seen through the eyes of Hinman's protagonist."[5] But the author did more than create a journey into the Union soldier's experience. He described a certain politics of war, or better, he defined the nature of Union victory. The war's meaning and triumph was to be found in Klegg's coming of age. In Hinman's estimation, war created the threat of moral degeneration. In order to dis-

With choking voice Si asked two or three of his comrades to assist him in lifting Shorty's body out of the ditch. They bore it to a grassy spot, under a spreading tree, which Si chose for his companion's resting-place.

"He's mine," said Si, "'n' I'll bury him!"

Procuring a shovel he dug a grave. An unspeakable sadness filled his heart as, with the help of another, he gently wrapped the body in a blanket, and they lowered it into the ground.

"I wish ther' was some preacher here," he said, "to say sich a prayer 's Shorty desarves. 'Tain't a Christian way to kiver him up 'thout nothin' bein' said!"

Si hesitated a moment, and then knelt beside the open grave and reverently repeated the Lord's prayer.

"That's the best I kin do," he said. "My pard wa'n't a saint, 'cordin' as folks jedges 'em, but

"HE WAS MY PARD."

I hope God 'll take him up to heaven. If ther' don't no wuss people 'n' him git thar it 'll be a good 'nuff place fer me!"

Then Si softly covered from sight the body of his comrade. He rudely carved with his knife a piece of board and placed it at the head. It bore the inscription:

> SHORTY
> Co Q 200th Ind.
> HE WAS MY PARD.

3. "He was my Pard." Si Klegg grieving over Shorty, from *Corporal Si Klegg and his "Pard,"* Wilbur F. Hinman.

cuss this, the author made Si into the very embodiment of rural, youthful innocence, which meant that the drama of the novel hinged on what happened to this mere boy as he entered the strange, mean, and deadly world of war making. Si not only experienced combat but hardship, corruption, and temptation. The test was whether the boy could learn the ways of this real world without becoming cynical, hardened, or cruel. With the help of his "pard," Si grew to be a true man. This manliness, in turn, was not about courage under fire (solely), but developing a mature decency and self-control amid the extreme conditions of war.

Hinman also made sure to add a discussion of how war making itself had evolved. Early in the conflict, Si would be tested in the stand-up fight at Stones River in late 1862. Firing calmly in the midst of flying bullets was at that moment the soul of the Northern soldier's war. But things changed. As Hinman argued it, Sherman and Grant had introduced constant pressure and method into the Union's campaigns by 1864, creating a new kind of war making that stressed organization, efficiency, and attrition. As the author freely admitted, this meant that skillful use of power in mass was matched with a certain necessary callousness about individual life. Far from being disillusioned or threatened by this change, Hinman celebrated the shift as the source of military victory.

Out of these two elements came the final triumph. Sherman and Grant found the formula to turn soldiering into a methodical approach to destroying the enemy. For his part, Si Klegg, with the help of his "pard," remained true to his internal values even while learning his harsh trade. As a result, a wise and mature Josiah could go home and claim his real prize: Annabel. He would not only wed the girl he left behind; his efforts in the army had proved that he was worthy of her. Triumph would be found at home with the good women living there. As Hinman stated in the regimental history he wrote—*Story of the Sherman Brigade*—"When the pretty girls 'present arms' after this cruel war is over, won't we 'fall in' and 'salute!' I think after three years or during the war of service, we will still be capable of 'bearing arms'—of that kind."[6] For Wilbur Hinman, this was the priceless trophy of victory.

Poor Si was a hopeless rube. In summer 1862 a recruiting officer came to the little Indiana village that was the hub of the boy's life. This officer seemed impressive. His "step was brisk, and he cultivated a military air with untiring assiduity." But Hinman warned the reader that "he did not want to wade in blood half as badly as people thought he did." This officer "did not get so much as a sniff of powder in a state of violent combustion." The Union recruiter was no gallant but something of a con artist.

Si never saw it coming. "He was a red-cheeked, chubby-faced boy who had some distance yet to go before getting out of his teens." He was a decent lad and a hard worker, but "he had seen nothing of the great world that lay beyond the bounds of his immediate neighborhood." Now, here he was, in town on the day when the recruiter happened to be there. His parents had prevented Si from enlisting in 1861, but now here he was a year later without his folks to protect him. His friends were joining up and were pressuring him, and the recruiting officer looked the very picture of a soldier. Moreover, the recruiter made the army seem so easy. It appeared that "they would be clad in purple and fine linen and fare sumptuously every day, with cream in their coffee and 'soft bread' all year round." And, of course, "none of them would get hurt." All this was too much to resist. "He did not want to enlist without parental consent . . . but the magnet that was drawing him along in spite of himself was irresistible. He couldn't help it; he *had* to go."[7]

In this way did Hinman open his novel. He did not begin with Sumter, Bull Run, or with the threat posed by Bragg's Kentucky invasion in the summer of '62. Antebellum politics and the war's early twists and turns are all placed beyond the view of the reader (at least at this stage). At the center is young Si, a mere boy unable to distinguish reality from fantasy, suddenly put in the position of making the decision of his life. This Civil War recruit was living in the middle of a swirl of events that he could not begin to fathom. Si made this vital choice on blind, youthful impulse.

Critically, the Midwest of Hinman's description was no more aware of the real state of things than was Si himself. Despite the fact that the author uses the recruiting season of 1862 to begin his tale, nothing of the war seems to have caught up with this part of Indiana. The writer's description is an anachronism. It turns the summer of '62 backward into the flush and foolish moment of the spring of '61: a time when no one knew anything of what was coming. In so doing, Hinman makes his protagonist's wide-eyed naivety part of a larger rural innocence.

And, without question, Si's family and friends *are* sweetly unaware. After getting over the shock of her son's enlistment, the boy's mother labors to make sure that he will have everything he needs. "'I s'pose ye'll have to sleep on the ground a good deal o' the time, an' ye'll want plenty o' kivers; so I've got ye an extra blanket an' this heavy quilt—ye must take good care o' that 'cause it's one o' my best ones," the mother insists. More things followed: buttons and a needle case; a "'harnsom' portfolio'" with "'lots o' paper an' envelopes an' pens an' pencils'"; combs and brushes and shoe blacking; a box of medicine; a Bible from the parson; a pair of boots from father because "'they say that the army shoes drops all to pieces in a few days. I 'xpect the contractors gits rich out of 'em.'" It never occurs to his family that Si will have to carry all these things on the march.

And then there was the food. On the day he enlisted the boy's mother and sister "placed upon the table every delicacy that the house afforded. Jars and cans, such as hitherto had only been brought forth on state occasions, were opened and their contents dished out." Si's mother was a "thrifty housewife," so she was "moved by an impulse of no ordinary magnitude when she scatter[ed] her precious jellies and preserves and pickles and things in such reckless profusion." Si loved the meal and found to his delight that the food did not stop coming. As he packed to leave for his enlistment he wondered that "he never had so much in his life before. His mother put in a lot of pies, cookies, etc., that she had baked for him, and Annabel brought over a large fruit-cake."[8]

In this portrait, Hinman's "Injianny" was a land completely unspoiled by war—or any other evil. This was a rural Midwest that did not cultivate corn so much as decency and community. In the author's imagery, the agricultural productivity of the region was domesticated by motherly and womanly love. As the boy prepares to head to a foreign and dangerous land, mother wants to load him to overflowing with the food and "kivers" that represented material prosperity translated into family, good neighbors, and caring. The folks may be unaware of the demands of the march, but they know who they are and what they represent. Truly they symbolize a world apart from war. Si's foolishness stems from the fact that he does not understand that he cannot take this world with him. "Marchin' 'n' campin' won't be nothin' but fun 's long 's a feller's got everythin' he wants. I 'low the boys wouldn't have sich hard times if they all had mothers 'n' sisters like I've got."[9] Nothing here of the real Midwest troubled by political division, resistance to recruiting, emerging Copperhead opposition to the war, anger over rumors of emancipation, or the casualty lists that had been sent home since the opening days of the fight. For Hinman, it was important to have his character start his journey from a world aware of nothing but the maternal love of its women.

Of course, Si had to leave this idyll. As the boy begins his journey, Hinman exposes him first to physical hardship rather than combat. Many of the recruits of summer 1862 were rushed into Kentucky to meet the emergency of Braxton Bragg's invasion of the state. Though training for the rigors of campaigning was lax under the best of circumstances, it was simply nonexistent for many of these "fresh fish." Hinman referenced this fact by making Si's introduction into the real war a trial by marching, not a baptism of fire.

In a lengthy description, Hinman turned the 200th Indiana's first cross-country campaign into a symbolic separation from home. The tramping was hard enough, but what made it worse was the extra baggage that parents, lovers, and friends had loaded on the boys. Hinman includes an extended discussion of poor Si's studied unwillingness to throw his mother's precious gifts away, even though the weight of the burden cut his feet to ribbons. He succumbed, eventually, an event that clearly marked his entrance into a new world that worked by different rules. Things then got worse. Shelter became a casualty as baggage trains lugging the tents never kept up with the men. Then the rations shrank, forcing the new soldiers to cope with the challenging hardtack. Quickly the boys were reduced to basics, and then less. Via these scenes, Hinman removed Si and his fellow recruits from the bounty and shelter of the Indiana they had left and placed them in a new and dangerous world.[10]

As the author details, the men would learn to handle the physical demands. Or the tough fellows would. They would figure out how to travel light, improvise, and preserve their strength. Experience would eventually produce savvy, and Hinman detailed the process.[11] But, for the author, the real issue was not hardship but the threat of moral degeneration. As the march continued, Si encountered varieties of human nature beyond what he had known in quaint, neighborly Indiana. Removed from the prosperous and motherly world of Si's Midwest, men could become something the poor rube could never have imagined. Si ran into nastiness, cruelty, and corruption, and this, moreover, from his comrades in arms rather than the enemy he was supposed to fight.

Early in their first long march, the 200th Indiana was mixed with veteran regiments as the men moved deeper into Kentucky. After one particularly hard marching day the boys were eager to sleep. Too eager. Earlier in the evening, a veteran unit close by had visited the new recruits' camp, seemingly "so kind of heart" as to "proffer their advice and personal services in preparing supper." This advice was "most gratefully received by the sufferers," little suspecting "the real errand of these good Samaritans. This was to reconnoiter and determine the most promising place to strike . . . to replenish their wasted stock of overcoats and blankets." Not long after the supper the exhausted recruits fell fast asleep, allowing the veterans to steal the blankets literally off the bodies of the inexperienced men. Some of the "prowlers" left their own ratted and holed coverings in exchange. Others just stole, "leaving to be settled hereafter whatever moral questions might be involved."

After thus describing the robbery, Hinman made his point. "To take care of number one was a cardinal principle in the mind of the old soldier. If it now and then ran afoul of the Decalogue, the latter had to give way." The next morning Si went to the veterans' camp and found the thief who had stolen his particular blanket, but the robber's comrades made it clear that Si would not be allowed to retrieve it. He returned, "meditating on the depth to which human depravity could reach, and wondering if he would ever be like those terrible veterans."[12]

Graft and sharp dealing were included in this new world of "taking care of number one." Hinman devoted several pages to a discussion of sutlers, arguing that these merchants took advantage of their connection to the army to practice a kind of profiteering that fed off the recruits' ignorance. In particular, there was the matter of "checks." Hinman's "skinners" advanced credit against the soldier's next payday. Si, in his characteristic innocence, "thought the sutler was very kind to 'trust' the boys. Every day or two he bought 'another dollar's worth o' checks, please.' . . . In this way the pickles and cheese and canned peaches did not seem to cost anything." Payday brought reality home as the paymaster—effectively a business partner of the sutler—deducted the provisioner's debts before giving the men their money.

These merchants resorted to downright fraud as well. According to Hinman, the sutlers sold "an endless variety of useless things." In one scene, the author has a "skinner" attempt to sell breastplates to the fledglings "as a protection against bullets," and as a reference to "the armour worn by knights in the olden time." Si was considering the matter until a veteran, a genuine friend in this particular case, told the boy that the thing would not work.

Si was quickly discovering that army life was a game of the survival of the slickest. Food, shelter, coverings, fuel, everything was scarce, and the army seemed to produce no community of shared sacrifice or mutual support. Quite the reverse. In Hinman's description, everyone seemed to be in on the take. He noted, for example, that army contractors provided the men with substandard uniforms. "The clothing of the regiment was already in an advanced stage of demoralization. It was of the 'shoddy' sort, that a good hard wind would blow almost to pieces." For their part, officers took particular advantage of their privilege. They "had the first pick of everything . . . the softest rails to sleep on, the hardtack that was least infected by worms, the bacon that had the fewest maggots, and the biggest trees in a fight." There just seemed to be no end to the corruption.[13]

At its worst this ethos "taking care of number one" produced among the men a kind of delight in being callous. Hard survivalism evolved into a sense of cruel sport. Or so Hinman insisted. For Christmas 1862 Si's family had prepared a box of goodies for him to enjoy for the day's pleasure. After a campaign's worth of hardtack and salt pork, he looked forward to the preserves, pickles, and cakes. Of course, the box did not arrive until long after the holiday. The teamsters had looted it. "A small section of Annabel's cake was left, and the ravagers, with a refinement of cruelty," had written a message on a small piece of paper and wrapped it around the leavings. "This is bully cake. Try it!" The teamsters had been thorough. "[The box] was a sorry mess," as the "broken bottles of pickles and jars of fruit, and the liquids had thoroughly baptized the edibles that the mule drivers had spared."

At this point, it seemed like the thing to do was for Si to get in the game himself. Hinman has Company Q assigned to guard the regimental baggage train, a train that included the colonel's provision wagon. The rutted, horrid roads being what they were, an accident occurred, and the contents of the colonel's vehicle spilled onto the roadway. The "tempting contents [were] exposed to the gloating eyes of the soldiers. There were cans of preserved fruit, and vegetables, and pickles, and lobster, the sight of which drove the boys half crazy." In addition, "there were also some dark looking bottles, but what was contained therein can only be conjecture." The soldiers dove in. For his part, "Si hesitated a moment, while a brief argument was going on between his conscience and his stomach. The latter prevailed, and he went in for his share of the spoils of war."[14] Clearly, Si was learning how to be a veteran.

Taking advantage of a fortuitous circumstance might not represent a dramatic fall from grace, but Hinman was quick to point out that there were deeper dangers. Losing internal arguments with one's conscience— or one's moral common sense—had bigger stakes. In particular, there was gambling. On Si's first payday, he no sooner pocketed his money (after deductions for the sutler) than he came across a game of chuck-a-luck. Here Hinman makes Si the total fool, for the lad thinks he will enter the game just to bet his loose change. He lost the opening rounds, of course, and

then started to succumb to the dangerous logic that he had to keep playing to recoup his losses. Quickly he lost a full dollar.

As authors like Kristin Hoganson and Stuart McConnell have shown,
Union veterans were quick to juxtapose the moral character and honor
that the soldiery had supposedly exhibited during the war against the sor-
didness, materialism, and social conflict of Gilded Age America. Certainly, Hinman's tale of Si's progress reads like a tale of the young bump-
kin fleeced by the industrial city. However, the author's concern was the
army and the experience of war. The issue was not a contrast between the
soldiers' honor and Gilded Age degeneration. Indeed, the problem was
the lack of communalism and comradeship in the army itself. Happily, in
Corporal Si Klegg, the boy is rescued from his foolishness and decline. His
"pard" intervenes. Shorty, described both as an older man and as a soldier
with some experience, saves Si from himself. Shorty puts an immediate
stop to Si's gambling. Seeing the game in progress, Shorty quickly moves
over and pulls the money from the boy's hands. "I ain't goin' ter stan' here
'n' let them fellers skin yer 'live," the "pard" scolded. "Ye won't have a cent
left 'n a half hour. You jest mosey 'long 'th me.'" Si followed and "Shorty
gave him a lecture that lasted him till the war was over, and [Si] never tried
'chuck-a-luck' again."[15]

The point of Hinman's novel is this important partnership. Shorty located the vital moral boundaries, while showing Si the ropes of soldiering. The army had been full of graft and corruption, but the good men had
found a critical counterpoint. According to Hinman, the soldiery had created a vast network of "pards," and this network, as in Si's case, brought
the decent fellows back to their bearings. As will be seen below, Hinman
insisted that this relationship humanized the army and the war in other
ways as well.

~

If, in Hinman's description, raw recruits had to learn how to navigate a
war-world of dangerous immorality, they also had to learn to jettison their
preconceptions of what fighting would be like. Good boys like Si had to
progress from a fundamental innocence to a wise self-control, but they
also had to replace foolish and romantic notions of combat with skilled
expertise, and also had to adjust to the new demands of modern war. As
they found out, soldiering certainly required courage under fire, but when
Grant and Sherman took over these generals produced an organized and
constant war making that stressed individual stoicism. If, on one level,

Hinman's novel was about Victorian moral concerns, it was also a fiction-alized exploration of the coming order of the organized war machine.

Back when he enlisted in Indiana, Si was a rube about combat as about everything else. Hinman described the boy as "burning with desire to fight the rebels." The youth imagined that "he would be charging around on the field of battle, climbing over heaps of slaughtered rebels . . . with a halo of immortal renown." In particular, Si fantasized that the bayonet would be the decisive weapon. Hinman has Si blend a wish for this most personal form of courage with a kind of mock savagery; he pokes and stabs every Confederate in sight, at least in his own mind.[16]

As with everything else, the real war eventually showed up, and came in a form that Si could scarcely have imagined. Hinman spends several pages describing the Battle of Stones River. Here was not only confusion in the Union ranks—an outright Northern skedaddle when the battle began—but a combat that tested the men's nerves in a long, stand-up fight. The author waxed eloquent about Si and Shorty's performance with the 200th Indiana, accrediting their character with being the bedrock of Northern victory. The passage is worth quoting at length. "There, side by side, [Si and Shorty] stand, loading and firing, as coolly as if they were veterans of a hundred battles. Look upon the face of Si and you will see pictured there what it was that conquered the great rebellion. See in those flashing eyes and firmly-set lips the spirit of courage, of unyielding determination, and of patriotic devotion, even to the supreme sacrifice, if need be, of life itself. There were many boys such as he, who were giants in valiant warfare—heroes, indeed, who looked unflinchingly in the face of death on many a well-fought field."[17]

In an instant Hinman's cherubic innocent vanished to reveal the real man underneath. Replacing bayonets with modern ordnance, Si had en-tered a firefight. In that moment the foolish boy suddenly acquired "flash-ing eyes and firmly-set lips." Courage, "unyielding determination," and "patriotic devotion" emerged from this lad who only a few weeks before had known literally nothing about what real war entailed. Without under-standing anything of combat when he enlisted, the boy found that his Indiana family and neighbors had raised him well. Determination, pa-triotism, and devotion came effortlessly to this rube during the hour of maximum danger.

This catharsis, in turn, sobered the lad. If Si replaced his juvenile understanding of combat with a virtuous kind of courage, this produced no bloodlust or delight in fighting. Quite the reverse. The murder appalled him. "Fightin' 's mighty tough business," Si explains to Shorty in the aftermath of the battle. "I ain't much of a ph'los'pher, but I don't b'lieve all this murderin' 'n' manglin' 's right. Ef I sh'd kill a man up in Injianny I'd git hung fer it, 'n' it 'd sarve me right." Si continues that "there's suthin out o' j'int somewhere when people 't pertends to be civilized, 'n' on 'em thinks they's Christians, gits up sich a shootin' match's we had today." The boy concludes that "'there ortn't ter be any war, 'cept 'mong dogs, 'n' tigers, 'n' heathens.'"[18] For Hinman's Si Klegg, war was anything but splendid.

Qualms or not, the conflict continued, and, as Hinman described it, Si found that while determination and personal integrity under fire might be the foundation of the Cumberland army's war, episodic battle was not the winning strategy. Hinman specifically discussed Ulysses S. Grant's reworking of the war in 1864. The author insisted that during the war's first three years the Union had "moved spasmodically, and without concert of action." Occasionally towns or areas were taken, each new trophy being loudly advertised as the "Gibraltar of the South." However, the "rebel armies generally got away when they wanted to." By contrast, Grant understood that victory required "the persistent use of powder and lead." Hinman then described what this persistent use entailed. According to the author, Grant had turned war into a deadly game of checkers: "Having secured a slight numerical advantage over his adversary the player deliberately proceeds to 'man him down,' giving a life for each one he takes, and thus vanquishes him at last. This is the game that was played during the last and bloodiest year of the war, and it succeeded. More men were killed and wounded by lead and iron in the desperate grapple from April, 1864, to April, 1865, than during the previous three years. . . . The price paid was a high one, but the economy of the purchase cannot be questioned."[19]

Sherman contributed to the transformation as well. If, according to Hinman, Grant invented the process of "manning" the enemy down, Sherman combined fighting prowess with forethought and managerial expertise. "It took three years to create such an army," the author crowed, "but when that veteran host moved forward, with perfect mutual confidence between the soldiers and their commanders, it was invincible."

To illustrate his point, Hinman described the challenge of crossing a stream when the enemy proposed to contest it. "Two years earlier the army would have been halted for a week," the author lamented. But in Sherman's army in 1864, what a scene! "Away gallops one of the staff to bring up the train of wagons bearing the pontons—or pontoons as they were universally called." As this was being done, the commanders quickly deployed artillery along with an infantry brigade. "Meantime a thousand men with axes are clearing a road to the point chosen as the point most favorable for the bridge." Then the pontoniers begin a sacrificial work; they begin laying out the boats under fire. "Many of these [men] are stricken down and lie helpless in the boats." But "for every brave pontonier that falls a score of willing volunteers are ready to seize the plank or the oar." The bridge building approaches the far shore at which time the infantry crosses and attacks. "No human power can stay their progress. They throw themselves upon the enemy and break his line. . . . The bridge is quickly finished, and for hours it quivers beneath the marching feet of endless brigades and divisions, and the rumbling wheels of artillery and wagons freighted with material to supply all the enginery of war."[20]

War by attrition and efficiency in this style altered the soldiers' attitudes. If courage had been defined as vertical posture in a firefight in 1862, Hinman argued that the evolution of victory by mathematics suggested another way to think of soldiering. "Experience taught them that it was the part of wisdom, and not inconsistent with the highest courage, to protect themselves when the opportunity afforded." Firing from cover—and eventually from fortifications—produced a more savvy and efficient form of soldiering than standing tall amid the bullets. "They found that it was a good thing to interpose trees and stumps and stone walls between their bodies and the enemy, while loading their pieces."[21] In Hinman's novel, Si and his comrades created a sensible balance between survivalism and stoicism in this new kind of war. Intelligent self-preservation in combat was combined with a willingness to sacrifice all when the circumstances warranted.

War understood in this way was something well beyond the foolishness of bayonet fighting that young Si had imagined back in "Injianny." War had become a cruel efficiency. Hinman could not disguise his thrill at the effectiveness of this new kind of fighting. After all, once armed with this new sense of method and purpose, "no human power" could stop this army that had during the two previous years experienced a mixture of victory and frustration. But the author revealed that he understood the costs as well. War was indeed a cruel economy. In Hinman's phrasing, "the price paid was a high one." Victorious war was anything but the fanciful—and harmless—game of the bayonet that young Si had at first envisioned.

As in the case of the soldier's moral challenges, "pards," according to Hinman, became critical in this new kind of war making. If Shorty was the means through which Si learned discipline and character, the "pard" also became the human counterpoint to organized war. In Hinman's language "pards" became a domestic presence. In the author's description, these pairings introduced home and family into the midst of an alien and destructive world. As Hinman noted in one passage, Si and Shorty had "mated as naturally as birds in springtime." Such twosomes, he continued, "constituted a family, eating and sleeping together." Such partners, he insisted, cared for each other "with all the tenderness of a brother." This brotherliness, in turn, included sleeping together like husband and wife. "There were many times whey they hugged each other like two pieces of sticking-plaster, in the vain effort to generate heat."

For Si, this domestication of the war reached its climax when Shorty died. Hinman makes the "pard" a casualty in the last days of the war, providing a way to transition Si back home to his community, but also to demonstrate that the lad had remained true to the substantive virtues of his home. Si buries Shorty's body himself and memorializes the act by marking the grave. In a war where men fell here and there ignored in the heat of battle, Si devotes individual and tender attention to Shorty's remains. He cares for the body as if he were at home. Hinman then comments: "the sorrow of a bereaved husband or wife was never more sincere and poignant than that of Corporal Klegg for his heroic and helpful pard." Shorty was anything but just a fellow soldier. Si felt the "sorrow" of a "husband or wife." As one would expect in such a situation, Si for some time "was inconsolable."[22]

With this act of burial, Si became a true moral adult. The hopeless rube was long gone. Klegg had come to see the world with more knowing eyes, but this knowing had not made him cynical, disheartened, or callous. After all, he now grieved as a husband or wife. He was no longer a boy, nor had he become some unfeeling soldier. In burying and lamenting Shorty as he did, the young hero returned to the domestic roots he had left behind in Indiana. With this act of burial, Hinman indulged in no preservationist sentimentalism, to use Stuart McConnell's term. Rather, the author sought to humanize a brutal war through the act of what Drew Faust describes as the desire to preserve the good death. Moreover, Hinman likewise avoided reinforcing the sense of disillusionment cultivated by authors like Ambrose Bierce.[23] In individualizing and domesticating Shorty's death, Si preserved his own humanness, while Hinman as an author preserved human character and domestic integrity amid organized, destructive war.

Thus, Si was prepared to go home—to Annabel, of course. "It is scarcely necessary to say that Si Klegg and Annabel were soon 'mustered in.' They fell early victims to the malignant connubial epidemic that devastated the ranks of soldiers and sweethearts for two or three years immediately following the war." Si had gone to the fight with Annabel on his mind. If he had parted with his mother, he began to court Annabel seriously from the moment of enlistment. Now he came home and, as Hinman states, the "pards" of wartime became the "pards" of peace. "Most of the young soldiers began, as soon as they were discharged, to think about getting married." It so happened that "they seemed to have little difficulty in finding 'pards,' and everywhere was heard a joyous chorus of marriage-bells."[24] For Wilbur Hinman, this was the real victory.

~

It can certainly be said that Hinman did little with what a later generation might see as the larger politics of the war. His definition of victory and its resultant obligations was a long way from Albion Tourgee's understanding, or from that of Benjamin Magee and Thomas Wright. Certainly, like most Cumberland veterans, the author happily preserved Confederate war guilt in the record. Hinman creates a scene where Si pronounces his verdict on the war while fraternizing with one of the enemy. "'All I know 'n' all I want ter know is that you rebels 's fightin' agin the flag 'o yer country, 'n' anybody 't does that's goin' ter git walloped mighty bad.'"[25] This, however, was not the issue that Hinman wanted to develop.

As befitting his connection with the *National Tribune*, the author's postwar cause was pension politics. In a brief last chapter the author has Si grow prematurely old, a physical victim of the hard campaigning of his youth. In this, said Hinman, Si was like "nineteen out of every twenty men who endured so much." The once strapping farm boy who had been the sole young male on the family farm quickly lost the ability to keep up with the demands of physical work. "The seeds of disease that were insidiously sown during those months and years of exposure to the elements, sprang up and brought forth a crop of ills that . . . almost unfitted him for manual labor."[26] In response, he applied for a pension and this ran him afoul of the government's bureaucracy.

The problem was the endless red tape, the pointless or contradictory rules, and the meagerness of the reward. In particular, Si lacked a hospital record (he had been incapacitated once, but the army doctor had sent him home on furlough). Years later, as a GAR comrade told him, "'the people at Washington take lots of stock in a good hospital record. It helps mightily in getting a pension. A month in a hospital, even if you wa'n't very sick, counts more 'n three years of trampin' an' fightin',' at the front.'" On another occasion, Si's friend added, "'they think every soldier tells the biggest kind of whoppers, an' every man's affidavit has to be propped up by a lot more or they won't go a cent on it. You've got to prove that you ain't lyin'.'" Si eventually won a meager pension—not worth the trouble of fighting the bureau. Thus, while Si had won the right to wed Annabel during the war, his devotion and honesty had cost him the ability to provide for his family later. Had he malingered in a hospital, he would have gained his wife and children a better pension. As Si's comrade explains: "'If I ever go into another war I'm going to stub my toe or something, if I can't hurt any other way, just to get back to the hospital long enough to make a 'record.'"[27]

With this as the novel's conclusion, Hinman made it clear that he would not venture much beyond the domestic focus of his tale. In the author's mind, his fictional Klegg had proved the worth of the American citizen-soldier. His young Indiana rube had represented the very soul of American rural innocence and had nonetheless survived the indecency, corruption, and cruel efficiency of war. He had come back a physically damaged but morally strengthened man. Si's character was worthy of his Annabel even if he was unable to care for his family as he had hoped.

Little room here for waxing eloquent about emancipation. Indeed, Hinman was distinctly on the conservative side of the Cumberlanders' spectrum on this question. For example, in the verbal encounter with the Confederate soldier quoted above Hinman discusses the subject of liberation war. The Rebel accuses Si and his comrades of coming South "'to steal our niggers.'" Si responds stating that he was no politician, going on to say that "'Abe Lincoln didn't set yer niggers free t'll arter he'd gi'n fair warnin.' Ye mout a-had 'em yet 'f ye'd laid down yer arms 'n' behaved yerselves. Now ye've got ter take the consequences.'"[28] Certainly an accurate enough assessment in its way, and fully in agreement with Major General Sherman's well-publicized point of view on the subject, but hardly a ringing endorsement for the cause of enlarging the nation's mission of freedom.

In the same spirit, Hinman has Si describe contraband labor earlier in the novel. The 200th Indiana was given fatigue duty for the purpose of building fortifications. The boy objects. "'I ain't goin' ter make a nigger o' myself's long's my name's Si Klegg.'" Si continues: "'why don't the Guvyment make [local blacks] do the diggin'?'" He opines that "'there's thousands on 'em lyin' around doin' nothin'.'" Si then brings in the politics of liberation. "'I ain't no statesman, but it looks ter me's though 'f anybody's goin' ter have any good out o' this war the niggers 'llgit the most on it. Ef I had my way I'd make 'em help some way er ruther!'"[29] Again, an accurate enough assessment of many of the soldiers' attitudes at the time, but one could not imagine a more begrudging discussion of the emancipation process.

In addition to this sour perspective, Hinman also had his doubts about the ability of the former slaves to become worthy citizens. In this respect he most closely resembles William Sipes. In his regimental study, *Story of the Sherman Brigade,* the author includes passages doubting the freedpeople's honesty and character.[30] In Hinman's remembered war, emancipation was certainly a result of the fight but hardly a moment of moral triumph.

Given this point of view, it is all the more interesting that Hinman included a story in *Corporal Si Klegg* that referenced "blacks as our only friends." At one point Si and Shorty are taken prisoner, which gives the author the opportunity to discuss the evils of Andersonville. Once the atrocities of this prison camp are properly noted, Hinman has his two characters escape. Whether or not the author intends it, the two men become much like fugitive slaves. "They traveled by night, resting during the daytime in swamps and brakes and thickets, sleeping and watching each in turn." Their hunger became desperate. However, they found "an occasional meal that tasted 'sweeter than honey and the honeycomb,' in the humble cabin of a friendly negro."[31] Even in Wilbur Hinman's novel, the main character cannot get back home—cannot return to his beloved Annabel—without first passing through "the humble cabin of a friendly negro."

From Slave Power Conspiracy to International Empire

In 1900 Joseph Warren Keifer completed his Civil War memoir, *Slavery and Four Years of War.* The author had been the major and then lieutenant colonel of John Beatty's Third Ohio. In this role he had been part of Don Carlos Buell's army, participating in Brig. Gen. Ormsby Mitchel's incursion into northern Alabama, among other operations. Then, shortly before Perryville, he transferred out of the Third to become colonel of the newly raised 110th Ohio, which was sent to the eastern theater. Thus, Keifer was not with the western army for long, but his memoir and career are simply a treasure.[32]

4. President McKinley and Major Generals Keifer, Shafter, Lawton, and Wheeler. (Keifer is the figure standing at left.) From a photograph taken on ship-deck at Savannah, Georgia, December 17, 1898, and reproduced in *Slavery and Four Years of War.*

The intriguing fact about the Ohioan is that he bridged worlds. The former Union colonel released *Slavery and Four Years of War* soon after America's victory over Spain in 1898 and the author devoted an appendix in his memoir to discussing the fact that he had participated in the Cuban war. As he relates, he had been a division commander in the Seventh Army Corps, serving under Fitzhugh Lee, the former Confederate cavalry officer. Moreover, Keifer returned to Congress after this conflict (he had served previously in the 1870s and 1880s), becoming an advocate of protectionism and a world-class navy. Keifer was not simply a Union veteran. He was part of both the great emancipation war and America's embrace of empire.

Keifer saw himself as a consistent, progressive Republican throughout his long life. For one thing, *Slavery and Four Years of War* is hardly a reunion piece. Though he fought in what was billed as a war of sectional reconciliation in 1898, and commanded the First Texas, Second Louisiana, and Second South Carolina within his division in Cuba, the Ohioan used his memoir to reaffirm his original vision of the Civil War.[33] Indeed,

Keifer's two-volume study is the most elaborate political narrative produced by any of the Cumberland writers. The author centered his work on
a meticulous one-hundred-fifty-page chapter that detailed the events that
led the country into secession and war. As such, it is a comprehensive re-
statement of the original Slave Power Conspiracy thesis as this had been
articulated during the original sectional crisis. Then, Keifer added appen-
dicies to his memoir detailing his first political career. He noted that he
served briefly in the Ohio Senate immediately after the war before mov-
ing on to Congress. He then described four terms as representative from
the Springfield district, noting his stint as Speaker of the House during
Chester Arthur's administration (1881–1883). As he portrayed it, he had
been present at the birth of the Republican party, having stumped for Fre-
mont in 1856 despite not being old enough to vote. He then insisted that
he had labored in Congress to protect what he saw as the essentials of
Reconstruction during the Hayes and Arthur administrations.[34] *Slavery
and Four Years of War* is an argument for Keifer's ideological continuity
through a dark and conflicted time.

Moreover, the Ohioan did not stop in 1898. Not only did he participate in the Cuban fight, he went back into Congress during the Roosevelt years, supporting American industrial growth along with the development of a formidable navy. Throughout, he insisted that his career from
first to last was of a piece. Unlike Tourgee, he never described Reconstruction as a failure, nor did he bury the Civil War's original issues in order to
embrace sectional reconciliation, as had Charles Manderson. In his mind,
Keifer found the fulfillment of the North's liberation war in the development of the United States as a world power.

~

If Keifer was a bridge between the Civil War North and imperial
America, the author used *Slavery and Four Years of War* to detail the beginning of the story. Although the Ohioan described his war service and
his advocacy of the Emancipation Proclamation in ringing terms in these
pages, the true heart of his two-volume study is the aforementioned chapter on the antebellum sectional crisis. Here Keifer establishes the North's
war as a liberation crusade and turns the Republican party into a vital
instrument of the cause. The discussion here is rich in particulars and
rhetoric, with the antebellum conflict serving as a clear, unambiguous example of God's judgment working through history. When he focused on
these years, Keifer was eloquent and expansive.

The author began by contextualizing slavery in human history, arguing that the peculiar institution was a thing of ancient lineage born of a human dark side. It represented an unreflective part of humanity where government operated simply from the "power of might." In this guise, one had found slavery everywhere in the past. "Rome had her slaves," he noted, and "the German nations on the shores of the Baltic carried on the desolating traffic." Keifer cited several historical examples. This past, however, was hardly justification. Murder, the author noted, "has existed in the world since Cain and Abel met by the altar of God, yet no sane person for that reason justifies it." More to the point, the institution offended divine justice, and history demonstrated the potency of an angry God. "God's just and retributive judgment has universally been visited on all nations and peoples continuing to maintain and perpetuate [slavery]." The czars of Russia, Keifer insisted, had "listened to the threatened doom, and, to save the empire, put forth decrees to loosen and finally to break the chains of twenty millions of slaves and serfs." The author then added that the British had also "heard the warning cry just in time to save the kingdom from the impending common destiny of slave nations."[35]

Thus, Keifer insisted, the United States flirted with disaster in the early nineteenth century. In defiance of divine progress, the country maintained the sordid institution. Slavery had been "long embedded in our social, political, and commercial relations," and had been "sustained by our prejudices, born of a selfish disposition, common to white people, to esteem themselves superior to others." As a result, while "all the civilized nations of Europe, as well as the nations and even tribes of Asia" abandoned the institution, "it remained for the *United States* to stand alone upholding it in its direst form."[36]

In Keifer's recounting of history, two things saved the country from divinely ordained suicide. First, according to the author, the Northern states abandoned slavery and so developed a free-labor foundation morally insulated from the degenerating effects of the peculiar institution. Second, the South's political leadership in Keifer's description destroyed its system through overreaction and excess. To begin with the first point, the free-labor dynamic became personal in Keifer's hands. He included a brief discussion of his father, who had been born in Maryland but had moved to Ohio. In the latter place he had lived "a quiet, sober, peaceful, contented, studious, moral life . . . always taking a deep interest in public affairs, state and national, his sympathies being with the poor, oppressed, and unfortunate." Such a man would have had no home in Maryland. "His detestation of slavery led him to emigrate from a slave State to one where slavery not only did not and could not exist, but where free labor was well requited and was regarded as highly honorable." Keifer's mother was cut from the same cloth. "With her husband she had ministered to escaped slaves, and [lived to see] slavery (always detested by both) abolished."[37]

Thus did the North's worthy residents escape slavery's evil. However, in Keifer's discussion, escape could not destroy the institution. Divine progress needed the helping hand of Southern folly. "It was Southern madness that hastened the destruction of American slavery," Keifer insisted. Keifer illustrated this argument in detail, first working through John C. Calhoun and the Nullification crisis. As it turned out, Andrew Jackson's staunch and militant Unionism proved "too imminent for Calhoun's nerves." The Carolinian retreated, while his state, said Keifer, waited for the day when a different, more pliant man would come to the presidential chair.[38] From here Keifer discussed the controversy over abolition literature in the mails, Texas annexation, and the Wilmot Proviso, in each case arguing that belligerent Southern extremism caused more and more Northerners to become alarmed. The Kansas crisis and the Dred Scott case proved the culmination of the process, the author stated, because in these controversies Northerners became convinced that the South's leadership intended to nationalize the peculiar institution.

The Lecompton constitution was critical here, according to Keifer, because of the violence and obvious election fraud. This episode, he insisted, convinced many that the "slave power" intended to gain "such domination in the Union as was desired and expected by its leaders." Had the Kansas plot fully succeeded there would have been no need for secession, "no rebellion, but, instead, slavery would have become *national*." Fearful of this the North became increasingly agitated. In Keifer's estimation, the region's residents were "bullied into a frenzy over the demands of those desiring the extension of slavery."

Then came the Dred Scott case, which Keifer spends pages discussing. In the author's view, the Supreme Court radically overreached its jurisdiction, refusing to confine itself to the case at hand. Chief Justice Taney and the majority issued a sweeping proslavery verdict that, in Keifer's eyes, gutted the constitutional powers of Congress to legislate for the territories, or to determine a national policy on slavery at all. Moreover, said the author, the Court's insistence that blacks had no human rights "astonished all civilizations and all Christian people." In reaction, "the North was stunned by the decision." Now even more Northerners "fear[ed] that slavery was soon to become national." Southern pride then added to their dread. "The South exulted boastfully of their cause, loudly proclaiming the paramount, binding force of the supreme judicial tribunal in the Republic. Free labor and free laborers were decried. They were, in speech and press, called *'mud sills of society:'* only negro slavery ennobled the white race."[39]

In this way Keifer constructed a narrative where the South played into God's hands by stimulating the resolve of the North. The arrogance, belligerence, and taunting finally produced the determination to resist. According to the author, this resistance came in the form of the Republican party and its victory of 1860. For their part, the South "had pushed their cause too far to recede," and so secession became inevitable. The result, said Keifer, was the first nation-state created expressly for the purpose of sheltering the peculiar institution. "Never before had it been proposed to establish a nation solely to perpetuate human slavery." The result was both disaster and deliverance. "The effort to establish a slave nation in the afternoon of the nineteenth century resulted in a civil war unparalleled in magnitude, and the bloodiest in the history of the human race." The South destroyed itself and in that act delivered God's divinely ordained progress in the form of emancipation. The war settled "the momentous question, whether or not human slavery should be fundamental as a domestic, social, and political institution."[40]

From this point in *Slavery and Four Years of War,* the Ohioan went on to describe his war service. In keeping with his general focus, Keifer described his time in Kentucky and Virginia in terms of demonstrating how the war shifted to an emancipation crusade once the Proclamation was introduced. The Ohioan's narrative played to its climax. The slave republic, born of miscalculation and arrogance, destroyed both itself and the sinful institution in the crucible of horrid war. God's destiny triumphed. Then, however, the plot began to thin. When discussing his congressional service in his memoir Keifer began to tread lightly and move quickly. When it came time to describe how this emancipation act was preserved and guaranteed after the war, the author turned shifty. To his credit, Keifer did not ignore Reconstruction in contrast to most Cumberland authors. After all, he had been a Republican state legislator and congressman. But compared to his eloquence and elaboration about antebellum affairs, Keifer was both short and disingenuous here.

In particular, he whisked by the Reconstruction amendments in a brief paragraph. He insisted that "in them are no concessions or compromises." They were the "decrees of war, written in the organic law of the United

States." With these the "evil [of slavery] was torn out by the roots," and the "Christian world, the progressive civilization of the age, and consciences of enlightened mankind *now* approve what was done."[41] Keifer's brother officer, Albion Tourgee, would have smirked at such words. The Carpet-bagger well understood that the issue at hand was not the end of slavery but the need to separate the former slave from the violence and vengeance of the former masters. By contrast, Keifer defended his party's political legacy by focusing the amendments backward. In his description, they sealed the verdict of the war, tearing slavery out "by the roots." In a certain sense this was accurate, but the former colonel hardly conveyed the truth of what the amendments had been crafted to accomplish or the context in which they had been composed. Rather, he sought to close this chapter of the country's political life by using the Constitution to seal the doom of slavery.

In like mode did Keifer discuss his tenure as Speaker of the House of Representatives. The author reprinted his farewell address to his fellow members in which he insisted that during his term "sectionalism has been unknown in the enactment of laws." He noted that "in the main a fraternal spirit has prevailed among the members from all portions of the Union." Quite a change from previous legislative sessions. Keifer described the earlier Forty-fifth Congress as bedlam. House Democrats (the majority) refused to pass a budget, hoping to force the president to "approve bills prohibiting the use of troops 'to keep the peace at the polls on election days.'" President Hayes called the next Congress into special session to pass appropriations. Keifer commented that "for the first time in the history of the United States . . . the government should be 'starved to death'" unless the president accepted government-by-blackmail from the House majority. Keifer himself had entered the fray, sticking to his party's guns and the original commitment to voting rights. But then, according to the author, the situation calmed. "The political heresies of the Forty-fifth and Forty-sixth Congresses have generally passed away, and a more patriotic sentiment exists in all parties."[42] Thus describing his time as Speaker of the Forty-seventh Congress, Keifer insisted that the parry and thrust of party politics—and sectional conflict—had moderated. The Ohioan's point was clear enough. The real place to go now was Cuba.

～

For Keifer, the future of an emancipated United States lay in the Pearl of the Antilles and in the legacy produced by the war that, in the Ohioan's judgment, should have brought us the possession of the island. *Slavery and*

Four Years of War includes a recounting of his military service in 1898–1899. In his telling, this new fight was also one for liberation and human progress. Like many Americans at the time, the author recoiled at Governor-General Valeriano Weyler's infamous reconcentrado policy. Keifer described it as an "inhuman" process of "forcing the rural inhabitants from their homes into closely circumscribed so-called military zones, where they were left unprovided with food, and hence to die." This "barbarity . . . excited, throughout the civilized world, deep sympathy for the Cubans." Then, Keifer explained, the destruction of the *Maine* provided the opportunity to rescue this population from Spanish oppression. The author briefly described his service as division commander, noting that his troops saw no action. However, he and his men formed the victory march into Havana. "A city which had been under monarchical rule for four hundred years witnessed the power of freedom, represented by the host of American soldiers." Keifer gushed that "under the flag of a Republic, [the men] mov[ed] triumphantly through the streets, with the avowed purpose of securing freedom to all the people."[43] Yet again had Keifer commanded soldiers in a war of liberation. The resolution of the author's memoir came not with the end of the Forty-seventh Congress but with his participation in this new humanitarian crusade.

Keifer's second political career developed almost seamlessly from this appendix to *Slavery and Four Years of War.* The author had joined a fight that placed the country on the world stage, and this seemed to guarantee that the former colonel and Speaker of the House would return to Congress to be part of the policy making. In any case, this is what happened. Keifer reentered the House in December 1905 and held his seat from the Springfield district until 1912. Judging by his remarks on the floor, he made an easy transition from a defender of emancipation to a Republican of the Roosevelt era. Among other things, he shifted readily from the free-labor ideology of the 1850s to staunch protectionism and also became an advocate for a world-class battleship navy.[44] In this latest political incarnation, Keifer did not shift his fundamental themes so much as his topics of discussion. If his main interest was in the newly created American empire, he looked at these new possessions in terms of the country's national mission—a mission that, in Keifer's mind, was fundamentally unchanged from the 1860s.

The congressman clarified and defined this mission when he compared Cuba and the Philippines. He had been an enthusiastic supporter of the Cuban war but had balked about taking the Philippines as an added trophy. He had noted as much in his Civil War memoir. In *Slavery and Four Years of War* he stated that the Cuban war had been a "friendly usurpation," pursued in "the interest of humanity, civilization, and good government." By contrast, the Pacific islands represented "a new national departure which may prove wise or not, according as we deal justly and mercifully with the people who inhabit [the islands.]"[45] In Keifer's description, the United States acquired the Philippines as an unintended consequence of a humanitarian effort, leaving the country with a set of islands and a precedent it had not really wanted.

During the next decade Keifer continued to develop this theme while in Congress. Discussing a 1907 measure to fortify key points in the archipelago, Keifer stated that all he had wanted from the Spanish was "the complete acquisition of Cuba, and with Cuba I would have been willing to let the Philippine Islands remain Spanish territory, or become independent, or pass into other hands more related to their inhabitants in race, in habits, or conditions." A year earlier he had stated that he had opposed taking anything from Spain at all, "except for the island that we did not get, to wit, Cuba." The island was a "gem" and "Spain wanted to surrender her sovereignty to us" and "the Cuban insurgents wanted, as I know personally, to be annexed to the United States."[46]

If Keifer had shifted over his long career from being an emancipationist to being an imperialist, the Ohioan was careful about the kind of empire he sought. He was no champion of reckless expansionism. He was selective in his advocacy, measuring American growth against his understanding of the country's national mission and destiny. A participant in the nation's move outward, he took care to link his understanding of overseas mission to his vision of an enlightened America. One can find no evidence in Keifer's speeches or writings that he identified with the threatened masculinity that Kristin Hoganson sees as the bedrock of America's imperial expansion. He did not, as Hoganson describes for her subjects, see empire "in chivalrous terms."[47] To the contrary, the former Union colonel defined the issue in terms of human progress and the purity of America's motives, using the same imagery he had employed in discussing the North's mission in the Civil War in his memoir. His careful distinction between Cuba and the Philippines illustrates this.

To be sure, Keifer distinguished between the two territories on the basis of proximity and security interests. Cuba, he said, lay "in the throat of our channel of commerce over the Gulf of Mexico and the Caribbean Sea, and especially to and with the South American republics and Central America." Speaking in 1907 he added that "its importance is to be augmented by the opening of the Panama Canal across the Isthmus." The Philippines had no such geographic importance in Keifer's mind.

However, for the Ohioan, the critical issue was that the Cuban situation highlighted what he saw as the distinction between America as the architect of a new kind of world order and Spain's antiquarianism and brutality. Keifer never tired of insisting that Americans had been pure in their motives when they had entered the Cuban war. In the same 1907 speech the congressman noted that the reconcentrado policy "caused thousands of noncombatants to be starved to death, or to die of incident disease caused thereby, so shocking the sense of civilized people throughout the world, and especially in our own recently redeemed, disenthralled and regenerated Union, that our country demanded that Spain should relinquish Cuba." In a naval appropriations' debate the next year, Keifer added that "the Spanish war was the first and only one ever declared purely on humanitarian grounds in the history of nations." Finally, in 1910, the Ohioan discussed clipping off the exposed portion of the mast of the *Maine*—sticking up above the water in Havana harbor—in order to place it in Arlington National Cemetery (which was done). To Keifer, the mast would symbolize the "beginning of a new epoch in history," and an "epoch in the history of the civilization of this world."[48]

In other words, Keifer hardly saw the Cuban fight as a splendid *little* war. To the contrary, it marked a significant demarcation in the course of human events and the country's history. Because of this, Cuba belonged to American progress just as did the mast of the *Maine* itself. It sanctified our place in world progress. For Keifer, Cuba should be our possession because Spain's brutality tied the local population's suffering to America's destiny in world history.[49] By contrast, the Philippines were an afterthought. No messianic connection existed for Keifer. Nor did the Ohioan refer to the Pacific islands as a necessary American presence in Asia, or as a vital first step into globalism. The archipelago was an unwanted stepchild. In hankering for Cuba while rejecting the Philippines, Keifer had merged expansionism with his concept of the country's humanitarian mission.

But the Philippines were ours after 1898 (or, better, 1902), and Keifer did not propose to abandon the islands. Possession having been mandated by events, the next step, said the Ohioan, was to spread constitutionalism and sound administrative practice to the new territory. In another congressional debate about fortifying the islands Keifer challenged those who went "dribbling" on about how the United States should give up the chain. "We ought to quit this thing of apologizing for having taken them." Now that "they are ours," he continued, the United States should "carry the Constitution there and give the blessings that that carries with it to those people as fast as they can appreciate it." The next year, in another discussion, Keifer further defined these blessings. The American administration had worked to "inculcate a better and higher civilization than was ever known in the islands in all their history." Clarifying, he noted that the governor had "established public schools in the islands." Keifer continued that the administration had reformed the tax structure, "built roads, erected lines of telegraph, built light-houses, and constructed harbor works, erected school-houses, and inaugurated a postal service which largely meets the requirements of business and personal correspondence." As well, reorganized municipal government along with a reformed legal code and judiciary now "protects rich and poor alike." These were dramatic reforms. Given these changes, along with "freedom of speech and the press," Keifer asked "do we not owe it to our Americanism and to our progressive character as a civilized and civilizing nation to maintain and make secure what we have so far accomplished?"[50]

Here Keifer exemplified what Niall Ferguson and Max Boot have each characterized as an imperialism of sound administration. The Ohioan's expansionism had little to do with classical European imperialism, or with military adventurism. Rather, to use Ferguson's expression, Keifer was more interested in "dictating democracy."[51] The congressman was less a colonialist than a man eager to spread method, institutions, and habits of mind. Moreover, to Keifer, this type of expansionism rang true to American history, connecting turn-of-the-century foreign administration to the nation's long-standing sense of exceptionalism. The country had certainly risen to the position of a world power, but it was a power justified because America "should now, in her greatness, stand for all that is good as well as great, and for peace; and in doing this she should be just and generous to all other nations and peoples." For Keifer, the United States might be evolving into an empire, but if so it should become an innocent one. The Ohioan was helping to create what Andrew Bacevich has termed the "myth of the reluctant superpower." As Bacevich describes it, Americans came to believe that the "United States—unlike other nations—achieved preeminence not by consciously seeking it but simply as an unintended consequence of actions taken either in self-defense or on behalf of others."[52] In Keifer's case, the war to save Cuba brought the Philippines along as an afterthought, and this accidental acquisition, in turn, had provided the opportunity to demonstrate our good will by promoting methods of sound and efficient administration as a civilized and civilizing nation.

~

When Keifer returned to Congress he encountered more than an opportunity to link Cuban liberation and Philippine administration to the legacy of the North's victory in the Civil War. In various House debates he ran up against the virulent new racism of the segregation era along with the demand by Lost Cause advocates that the Civil War be redefined. In these discussions the Ohioan was pressed to repudiate his Reconstruction past and bury his understanding of the causes and meaning of the North's war. Keifer would have none of it. He never indulged in what he saw as a politics of false reunionism, though he was a steadfast supporter of cordial relations between the opposing camps of veterans. Moreover, he dealt a small but smarting blow to Southern segregationists. The Ohioan reacted to racial issues and demands for sectional reconciliation in a way that in his mind preserved the consistency of his position. In his view, he remained true to the victory that the North had won.

Keifer could certainly indulge in racism. In yet another congressional debate on the Philippines, Keifer made a point of referring to the fitness of the islands' population for eventual independence. "We can see whether these people are to be civilized or not," he said on this occasion. Continuing, he noted that he had never traveled to the islands but had seen an exhibit at the St. Louis World's Fair a couple of years earlier. "I never was so much amused in my life," he stated, describing an exhibit where "a Negrito, or Igorrote, or a head-hunter in his natural habilaments [was] singing—'My country 'tis of thee, sweet land of liberty; of thee I sing.'" His colleagues joined in laughter, the *Congressional Record* noted.[53]

However, Keifer sounded a different note when discussing Cubans. In his memoir, the author argued that they were "of mixed races," but "they are not to be despised" for this reason. Mixed bloods "mingle freely together," and this seems to produce no stigma, the Ohioan observed. "There do not seem to be any race distinctions where Cubans alone are concerned." The "colored people" of the island, Keifer insisted, "seem to be exceptionally intelligent and energetic, and have a high reputation as brave soldiers." Unlike many Americans who served in the Cuban war, Keifer retained—and expressed—his original high opinion of the insurgents. He may have desired annexation but he remained true to America's initial view of *Cuba Libre*.[54]

Like many of his Army of the Cumberland compatriots, Keifer was quite capable of deploying race and racial imagery selectively. For him, race was not an obsession but a device to use in various contexts. The fundamental concern was Keifer's faith in the sanctity of the American mission and the cause of progressive civilization. In support of this cause, the same Ohioan who chuckled at "tribesmen" singing patriotic hymns could just as readily praise the Cuban insurgency. As well, he could swipe at those who would debase the country by using racial distinctions with what he termed as "cruelty."

In this context one can view Keifer's participation in the congressional debate over a measure by Senator Joseph B. Foraker to create a panel of officers to review the cases of discharged soldiers from the Twenty-fifth U.S. Infantry. The Twenty-fifth was the African American regiment involved in the infamous Brownsville, Texas, incident where, it was alleged, soldiers from the outfit shot up the town. President Roosevelt had dishonorably discharged three companies from the unit because they had refused to provide information to army authorities. Foraker was attempting to provide these discharged soldiers with a way back into the service.[55] On the House floor, Keifer came to the aid of his fellow Ohioan. "These men never had a trial," he stated. They "never have faced a tribunal; never were shown to be guilty before the order for their dismissal was issued, nor since, unless possibly a very few of them on ex parte testimony and without trial." Keifer then slashed at his Southern Democratic colleagues who had insisted that Republicans supported Foraker only because of the party's alleged sentimental affinity for African Americans. Keifer fumed. "Neither in the judgment of civilized man nor in the judgment of Almighty God will the Saxon or white race ever attain, establish, or maintain supremacy in this world by or through acts of cruelty or injustice to an inferior race." The *Record* noted applause.[56]

Keifer was certainly no egalitarian. This reference to Saxon supremacy was perfectly consistent with attitudes he had held from the beginning of his public career. In *Slavery and Four Years of War* he was careful to insist that the peculiar institution had been destroyed by the combination of Southern folly and Northern resolve. Slaves hardly freed themselves. In one passage he noted that America had produced few slave rebellions in its history, because "the African race, the most wronged through the centuries, has been the most docile and the least revengeful of the races of the world."[57] His one reference to a disturbance was to John Brown.

But Keifer's embrace of Saxon supremacy had certain important boundaries. Given Keifer's constant discussion of good government imperialism, superiority was linked to his understanding of American constitutional development and progress. Supremacy entailed forms of order, structure, and system, as opposed to what he described as "cruelty." In this way did Keifer blend his interpretation of the North's victory in the Civil War with the nation's new imperial age, and, in same light, he saw the representatives of the former Confederacy shaming themselves yet again.

Keifer had other arguments with defenders of the former secessionist republic. In his last session in the House the Ohioan responded to an attempt by Georgia representative Charles L. Bartlett to revise the United States judicial code by changing language in those segments relating to war claims. In every instance where it occurred Bartlett wanted to replace the phrase "during the war for the suppression of the rebellion" with "during the Civil War from 1861 to 1865." Keifer rose to ask why, prompting a lengthy exchange. In the course of the discussion Keifer observed that the term rebellion had been used in the Fourteenth Amendment and in subsequent legislation. Bartlett responded that times were different now. The Georgian stated that the war was now past, and the country desired that Keifer and others "join in that spirit that now pervades the whole American people to endeavor, as far as we can, to forget the animosities created by that struggle."

Keifer quickly responded to Bartlett that "if that speech was intended as a lecture to me it comes about 50 years too late." Keifer clarified: "when Lee surrendered at Appomattox, some of us here, with open wounds still running, welcomed the soldier on the other side that we had been fighting against for four years, and laid down our feelings as far as they were concerned, (applause) and I have stood by and had no trouble with them for 50 years since." Thus did the Ohioan show his reconciliationist credentials so far as the former Rebel soldiers were concerned. However, Keifer also left Bartlett in no doubt about the main question. The war would be referred to by its right name. The Georgian stated that Congress in its legislation had avoided the term "War of the Rebellion" for some years. Keifer quickly replied: "That is what it was."[58]

More than anything else Keifer wanted to get on with the project of promoting civilized progress. Like many Republicans with a long standing in Congress, he had let the politics of Reconstruction drift away. The Ohioan had let go of what could not be won, but unlike Albion Tourgee he refused to admit that the cause had been lost or that history had been reversed. The real issue was to shift the theater of action. The nation and world civilization were not going to sit still while old men rehashed old questions. Northern victory had saved the country from the doom of slave nations, and, to hear Keifer tell it, the victory had also created a new era. The important thing was to be part of it. The Ohioan saw himself as the example. The former Union officer had rejoined the service in 1898 to be part of the "redeemed, disenthralled and regenerated Union" that engaged in what he argued was the first military intervention in human history begun solely for humanitarian reasons. Keifer wanted to be up to date. If he so desired, Charles Bartlett could waste his time scouring dusty judicial codes to find every page where the words "war of the rebellion" were used. For his part, Keifer would talk ships, America's international mission, and colonial administration.

And there were more enthralling possibilities. In Keifer's mind, America's move into the great oceans might well produce global peace and stability. Though Keifer was an advocate of naval preparedness, he consistently pointed out that his support for a big navy was predicated on preventing a war not starting one. Strength prevented insult, he insisted. His hope was that from this point world political stability might be the next plateau. Keifer saw the Panama Canal in such terms. The canal should not simply be an American ditch, but rather the occasion for an international demilitarization agreement that, in the congressman's mind, would lead to "a parliament of nations pledged to a perpetual peace on a principal maritime highway of the world." The new canal would produce a new internationalism. "Let there be where the two great American continents meet and where the enterprise of our Republic has constructed an artery of commerce and trade," a canal where all people may pass "in perfect security and peace." Instead of the "insatiable demon of war," humanity would find "the perpetual and busy sound of the battle of industry among the races of the world as they come and go." From such a situation, "a joyous peace [would] reign supreme there for evermore."[59]

This was a vision of progress in history. According to Keifer, John C. Calhoun and other Southern reactionaries had sought to derail America's national mission in their frantic obsession to save the barbaric institution of slavery. Keifer had been part of the crusade to destroy this descent into backwardness. Now, fifty years later, the Ohioan was envisioning "a parliament of nations" and a canal that would act as a template of how the "battle of industry" could replace the "insatiable demons of war." Whatever else might be said, Keifer certainly had a sense of the momentous.

However, the Ohioan also understood that his sense of civilized evolution might well prove wrong. As the congressman noted at one point,

America had entered the Cuban war as "the first and only one ever declared purely on humanitarian grounds in the history of nations." In the same discussion he also warned that "other powers may not prove to be inspired by better or higher international ethics or principles than was the United States in 1898, and a cause for war is easily found by the strong against the weak."[60]

Epilogue

The North's Civil War created a paradox for the victors. In previous conflicts Americans had been able to translate military victory into the absolute control of the conquered (or secured) landscape. By contrast, the
Union's triumph in 1865 simply ended Confederate independence, turning the Southern states into an insurgent territory that congressional Republicans could never master. Surrender of the Rebel armies produced
dangerous tension and perpetual political muddle. This was a fascinating
irony, for the North had organized the society's military power to a degree never before seen in the country's history. In response to Fort Sumter
and the subsequent shame of Bull Run, Union states and regions had recruited men in unprecedented thousands. To this mass of soldiers was
added the U.S. Treasury's financial creativity, women and blacks who insisted on mobilizing themselves, a president who vastly expanded the executive war power, and, above all, a grand promise of freedom. The result
was an American *levée en masse*. When fully organized by various military and civilian leaders, this *levée* was turned into a tremendous destructive force. The Confederacy was crushed by an overwhelming power that
Jefferson Davis—or Edmund Ruffin—could not possibly have imagined
when the first cannon was fired to "reduce" Fort Sumter in April 1861. And
yet the results of it all were so problematic: a victory more in myth than
truth, perhaps.

In this respect, the North's war set the pattern for America's major conflicts in the twentieth century. In each of the great global wars of this
new age, the United States produced massive mobilizations, some type
of military-industrial complex, and millennial expectations. The result
was immense destructive power. Yet frustration, irony, contradiction, and

muddle followed in the wake of military triumph. If the North's victory in the Civil War eventually produced a Fourteenth Amendment (a revolution in words) that proved impossible to turn into any concrete political reality, Woodrow Wilson sought to make the "world safe for democracy" and to create a League of Nations to replace dangerous imperial rivalries. This Virginia-born segregationist even toyed with the idea of a declaration of human rights in order to protect Jews and other ethnic minorities in the newly remade Eastern Europe.[1] However, the United States never joined the League, while economic instability and disappointed hopes stimulated ugly dreams in Germany and Japan. Later, it was argued that World War II would allow the country to use full mobilization to destroy the evil of totalitarianism, but half the victory (at least) belonged to the Soviet Union and the alliance with Stalin turned sour even as the Germans and Japanese still fought. At several points in America's modern military history, we have organized overwhelming power and used it to destroy (or threaten) the immediate enemy, but "real" victory has always remained elusive, fuzzy, or quickly redefined by circumstance.

Cumberland veterans and the men of the other Union armies faced this dilemma for the first time in the country's history and it is intriguing that their response to it amounted to something of a template for America's later wars. Beyond pointing out the obvious fact that they had destroyed their enemy's military power and nationhood, Cumberlanders did not dwell on how surrender changed the former foe. Outside of Albion Tourgee, little or nothing was said about control over the politics of the Southern states. Rather, the veterans shifted the focus to themselves and to the society to which they returned. Cumberlanders found victory in the fact that war had not corrupted them and that they had returned to a land that was both undestroyed and untainted. In Wilbur Hinman's case, his fictional Si Klegg found victory in being worthy to go home to his idyllic "Injianny" and his beloved Annabel. For Joseph Warren Keifer, the America redeemed and purified by emancipation war would now use force only to promote humanitarianism and international good government.

Composed in this way, the Cumberland authors' collective effort did not amount to the memory of a war so much as a way to imagine modern war making. In this respect, they fashioned something entirely different from the Lost Cause. Whether found in such efforts as Laura Martin Rose's UDC history for white Southern schoolchildren or David W. Griffith's spectacle *Birth of a Nation*, the South's Civil War was recast into celebrating the Ku Klux Klan. In this redrafting, racial struggle became the "real war" and the Klan became the valiant Confederate army reborn.[2] By contrast, Cumberland writers turned their experience in the 1860s into a transcendent American military tradition that combined innocence and decency with overwhelming force.

Years later, as Americans absorbed the shock of Pearl Harbor, Frank Capra demonstrated that the themes first developed by these Union veterans remained vibrant, if now reworked to accommodate new circumstances. As the United States entered the Second World War, the Hollywood director put together the famous *Why We Fight* series as a program of required viewing for American servicemen headed overseas. The films sought to respond to the powerful isolationist movement that had so long handicapped Franklin Roosevelt's efforts to involve the country in the struggle. In the first episode, "Prelude to War," a text from George C. Marshall begins the film. The purpose of the series, the quote reads, was to illustrate "the principles for which we are fighting." The text continues that "our flag will be recognized throughout the world as a *symbol of freedom* on the one hand, of *overwhelming power* on the other." Then the vice president, Henry A. Wallace, takes over. A quote from him flashes up on screen. "This is a fight between a free world and a slave world."

Capra then makes clear that this threat to the free world was no fight between abstract political ideologies. According to the film's narrator, fascism worked its way into the very core of the societies that it touched. It perverted childhood into institutionalized militarist indoctrination. Thus, the narrator insisted that if we lost we would lose it all. "Our homes. . . . The hopes we have for our kids. The kids themselves. They won't be ours anymore." As the narrator concludes, "it is us or them." Here was a total war in which the most central of all America's values was at stake: the innocence of children and the peaceable world of childhood.[3]

Several years later NBC television released a documentary that developed similar themes. *Victory at Sea* was shown just as the cold war was rooting itself deep into America. A series of twenty-six episodes shown in 1952 and 1953, the production became a landmark. One episode, "The Turkey Shoot," concerned the Marianas operation that secured what became the B-29 base on Tinian. The episode opens with a long discussion of another one of the Marianas—Guam: the American pick-up from the Spanish in 1898. The island was the "half-forgotten step-child" among American overseas possessions, the narrator says. Under the loose "guardianship" of the navy, "life has remained serene, unruffled." The Japanese interrupted the idyll, taking over the island and subordinating the native inhabitants. It is the Japanese who become colonial masters. In separate scenes, kids during the earlier American occupation play baseball; under Japanese domination frowning children wear headbands and do exercises in disciplined formation.[4]

Fortunately the Americans come back and the episode shows footage of the vicious ground fight in the Marianas, along with the U.S. Navy's famous victory in the Battle of the Philippine Sea (the "Turkey Shoot"). After several scenes of devastation and combat the narrator suddenly asks: "And the people of Guam? The Chammorros?" Civilians suddenly appear. "Down from the hills they come. Out of Japanese concentration camps they come. The weary and the frightened. The sick and the feeble. All are welcomed and helped by the American soldier, who cheerfully abandons the savagery of battle for what is truly in his heart, his nature. Sympathy. Kindness. Compassion." A soldier is shown holding a child. Scenes follow showing medical teams treating the sick and giving vaccines. In these visuals, the very old and very young abound.

After this discussion of Guam the episode continues with a fascinating portrait of the creation of the B-29 base and other facilities. The narrator observes that the Seabees and engineers "take over from those whose job it was to destroy. Destruction gives way to construction, as the fruits of American industry and the know-how of her men transform tropical Guam into a generator for victory in the Pacific." The Navy, the narrator continues, turned the "island into the most potent advanced base anywhere in the world. A Pacific supermarket where the tools of war are stocked." With Guam thus remade into a military grocery store, Tinian deploys the superforts. The episode concludes with several clips of B-29s taking off. "The bases have been established. The mission has been accomplished. Now the B-29s take off, take off for victory." Thus did the true heart of the American soldier and the ingenuity of our industrial "know-how" blend with the great bombers that, of course, were taking off in the firebomb raids (unseen and unmentioned in this episode).

Many years later, Gen. Colin Powell attempted in his own way to preserve—or, better, reestablish—this American way of war. In his case, he sought to blend overwhelming force with carefully calibrated objectives. As he saw it, he wanted to prevent the complications and muddiness of war from distorting American politics and society. A beneficiary of Harry Truman's executive order desegregating the military, Powell had risen from a marginal Bronx neighborhood to command the world's most powerful military force. The Cold War and the military establishment had given him his chance in life. However, he had watched as his cherished army was vilified in the wake of Vietnam by people he defined as extremists. It did not help that this radical movement attempted to incorporate (or co-opt) the substance and rich narrative of the civil rights crusade.[5] In response, Powell hoped to restore the military's power and reputation by reestablishing control of the political context of war. In his tenure as national security advisor and chairman of the joint chiefs, he attempted to use the device of limited and defined objectives to cleanse and simplify the use of overwhelming force.

In this way did the North's emancipation war come to fruition with a West Indian kid from the Bronx. Powell had gotten his opportunity because Truman had desegregated the military in the wake of Hitler's racism and in the face of the new competition with communism. America's military force required a face of decency and human progress. For his part, Powell made the most of his chance. He rose not only to become a part of the institution, he attained a station where he could make policy. Powell not only benefited from American war, he directed and redefined American war making. In this respect, the United States Colored Troops who had served with the Union army at the Battle of Nashville (and other places) had finally won their point.

But it is also the case that Powell's attempt to save the reputation of the American military occurred in a world very different from the one the USCT had known. It can be fairly said that the Union war effort both created and saved a nation. As Cumberland veterans described it later, the war that ended in 1865 freed and made dominant the North's labor system—a tenuous reconciliation between the ideal of agrarian independence and a new industrial productivity—and placed the United States on a path to become a new kind of world power: an empire without the imperialism. Liberated slaves were markers of the power, dignity, and justice of this newly freed nation. Or better, the act of liberating them was. Cumberland veterans were perfectly happy—and perfectly sincere—to remember their war as an emancipation event. However, in celebrating liberation as part of the emergence of this new nation, the interior life and the political condition of the slaves freed by the war (along with the lives of African Americans generally) became a hidden history. When Joseph Gibson beamed with pride at the accomplishments of Dudley the camp cook, the former soldier's words represented a genuine wish that African American labor and character could be folded into the national destiny freed by the war. But the spotlight was on the nation.

It is simply the case that in our time the spotlight has shifted. The civil rights and post–civil rights generation has turned the beam away from the soldiers and toward those liberated by the act of war. We have created a new heroic narrative that highlights the struggle of those trapped by slavery and segregation but who fought against these things nonetheless. These were men and women who were denied any of the "real" weapons of war but found a way to gain eventual victory using faith, intelligence, and a careful calculation of the enemy's strengths and weaknesses. And so we have a second redemption of America. We can contrast the heroism of the self-liberating with the shame and debauchery of their persecutors and thereby release ourselves from our past. But, it must said, this new heroic, redemptive narrative has its own hidden histories and inconvenient truths. What is styled as "black conservatism" along with the cynical manipulation "the race card," among other things, complicate the new master narrative.[6]

In any case, common to the Cumberlanders' vision of a nation freed from slavery and the civil rights generation's vision of a nation freed from racism is the intense wish for innocence and exceptionalism. Many years ago C. Vann Woodward told us that the critical feature of the American character was the desperate desire to be free of history.[7] What we today would call the "real world," with its complexity, interdependence, contradiction, and exploitation, should always happen to someone else. The irony in this is that what Woodward characterizes as the fundamental American fantasy is equally our nation's most redeeming feature and our most dangerous self-delusion.

Appendix: Cumberland Regimental Histories and Personal Memoirs Reviewed for This Study

Aten, Henry J. *History of the Eighty-Fifth Regiment, Illinois Volunteer Infantry* (1901).

Barnes, James A., James R. Carnahan, and Thomas H. B. McCain. *The Eighty-Sixth Regiment, Indiana Volunteer Infantry. A Narrative Of Its Services In The Civil War of 1861–1865* (1895).

Beach, John N. *History of the Fortieth Ohio Volunteer Infantry* (1884).

Bishop, Judson W. *The Story of a Regiment: Being a Narrative of the Service of the Second Regiment, Minnesota Veteran Volunteer Infantry, in the Civil War of 1861–1865* (1890).

Bradt, Hiram H. G. *Third Battery Wisconsin Light Artillery In the Civil War of the United States, 1861–65* (1902).

Briant, Charles C. *History of the Sixth Regiment Indiana Volunteer Infantry. Of Both The Three Months' and Three Years' Services* (1891).

Butler, M[arvin] B. *My Story of the Civil War and the Under-ground Railroad* (1914).

Calkins, William Wirt. *The History of the One Hundred and Fourth Regiment of Illinois Volunteer Infantry. War of the Great Rebellion 1862–1865* (1895).

Canfield, S[ilas] S. *History of the 21st Regiment Ohio Volunteer Infantry, in The War Of The Rebellion* (1893).

Carter, W. R. *History of the First Regiment of Tennessee [Union] Volunteer Cavalry in the Great War of the Rebellion* (1902).

Chase, J[ohn] A. *History of the Fourteenth Ohio Regiment, O.V.V.I. From the beginning of the war in 1861 to its close in 1865* (1881).

Clark, Charles T. *Opdyke Tigers 125th O.V.I. A History of the Regiment and of the Campaigns and Battles of the Army of the Cumberland* (1895).

Cope, Alexis. *The Fifteenth Ohio Volunteers And Its Campaigns. War of 1861–5* (1916).

Crofts, Thomas. *History of the Service of The Third Ohio Veteran Volunteer Cavalry in the War For The Preservation Of The Union From 1861–1865* (1910).

Curry, William L. *Four Years In The Saddle. History of the First Regiment Ohio Volunteer Cavalry* (1898).

Day, L[ewis] W. *Story of the One Hundred and First Ohio Infantry. A Memorial Volume* (1894).

DeVelling, C[harles] T. *History of the Seventeenth Regiment, First Brigade, Third Division, Fourteenth Corps, Army of the Cumberland, War of the Rebellion* (1889).

Doll, William H. *History of the Sixth Regiment Indiana Volunteer Infantry in the Civil War April 25, 1861, To September 22, 1864* (1903).

Dornblaser, T[homas] F. *Sabre Strokes of the Pennsylvania Dragoons, in the War of 1861–1865* (1884).

Erb, William S. S. *Extract from "The Battles of the 19th Ohio" By A Late Acting Assistant Adjutant General, 3rd Brigade, 3rd Division, 4th A.C., Army of the Cumberland* (1893).

Fitch, Michael H. *Echoes Of The Civil War As I Hear Them* (1905).

Floyd, Rev. David Bittle. *History of the Seventy-Fifth Regiment of Indiana Infantry Volunteers, Its Organization Campaigns, and Battles (1862–65)* (1893).

Gibson, J[oseph] T., ed. *History of the Seventy-Eighth Pennsylvania Volunteer Infantry* (1905).

Gillespie, Samuel L. *A History of Company A, First Ohio Cavalry, 1861–1865* (1898).

Haynie, J. Henry. *The Nineteenth Illinois. A Memoir of a Regiment of Volunteer Infantry Famous in the Civil War of Fifty Years Ago for its Drill, Bravery, and Distinguished Services* (1912).

Herr, Geo[rge] W. *Episodes of the Civil War: Nine Campaigns in Nine States* (1890).

H[ewes], F. W. *Outline of the Veteran Service of the Tenth Regiment of Michigan Veteran Volunteer Infantry* (1891).

High, Edwin W. *History of the Sixty-Eighth Regiment Indiana Volunteer Infantry 1862–1865* (1902).

Hinman, Wilbur F. *Corporal Si Klegg and His "Pard": How They Lived and Talked, and What They Did and Suffered, While Fighting for the Flag.* 1887. Reprint, Asburn, VA: J. W. Henry, 1997.

Hinman, Wilbur F. *The Story of the Sherman Brigade. The Camp, The March, The Bivouac, The Battle; And How "The Boys" Lived and Died During Four Years of Active Field Service* (1897).

Horrall, S[pillard] F. *History of the Forty-Second Indiana Volunteer Infantry* (1892).

Hunter, Alf[red] G. *History of the Eighty-Second Indiana Volunteer Infantry, Its Organization, Campaigns and Battles* (1893).

Jamison, Matthew H. *Recollections of Pioneer and Army Life* (1911).

Keifer, Joseph Warren. *Slavery and Four Years of War: A Political History of Slavery in the United States, Together With a Narrative of the Campaigns and Battles of the Civil War in Which the Author Took Part: 1861–1865.* 2 vols. 1900. Reprint, Miami, Fl: Mnemosyne Publishing, 1969.

Keil, F[rederick] W. *Thirty-Fifth Ohio. A Narrative of Service from August, 1861 to 1864* (1894).

Kelly, Welden. *A Historic Sketch Lest We Forget. Company "E" 26th Ohio Infantry In the War for the Union 1861–65* (1909).

Kern, Albert. *History of the First Regiment Ohio Volunteer Infantry in the Civil War 1861–1865* (1918).

Kimberly, Robert L., and Ephraim S. Holloway. *The Forty-First Ohio Veteran Volunteer Infantry in the War of the Rebellion, 1861–1865* (1897).

Kingman, N[ewton] H. *Life Story of Captain Newton H. Kingman. 90th Birthday Revelations* (1928).

Lewis, G[eorge] W. *The Campaigns of the 124th Regiment Ohio Volunteer Infantry with Roster and Roll of Honor* (1894).

[Magee], B[enjamin] F. *History of the 72nd Indiana Volunteer Infantry of the Mounted Lightning Brigade* (1882).

Manderson, Charles F. *The Twin Seven-Shooters* (1902).

Marshall, R[andolph] V. *An Historical Sketch of the Twenty-Second Regiment Indiana Volunteers, From Its Organization To The Close Of The War* (1884).

Mauzy, James H. *Historical Sketch of the Sixty-Eighth Regiment Indiana Volunteers* (1887).

McAdams, F[rancis] M. *Every-Day Soldier Life, or A History of the One Hundred and Thirteenth Ohio Volunteer Infantry* (1884).

McBride, John R. *History of the Thirty-Third Indiana Veteran Volunteer Infantry During the Four Years of Civil War From Sept. 16, 1861, to July 21, 1865* (1900).

McNeil, S. A. *Personal Recollections of Service in The Army of the Cumberland and Sherman's Army From August 17, 1861 to July 20, 1865* (1910).

Mills, Anson. *My Story.* Edited by C. H. Claudy. 1918. Reprint, Mechanicsburg, PA: Stackpole Books, 2003.

Morris, Geo[rge] W. *History of the Eighty-First Regiment of Indiana Volunteer Infantry in the Great War of the Rebellion, 1861 to 1865* (1901).

Owens, Ira S. *Greene County Soldiers in the Late War* (1884).

Partridge, Charles A., ed. *History of the Ninety-Sixth Regiment Illinois Volunteer Infantry* (1887).

Payne, Edwin W. *History of the Thirty-Fourth Regiment of Illinois Volunteer Infantry September 7, 1861—July 12, 1865* (1902).

Peddycord, Will F. *History of the Seventy-Fourth Regiment Indiana Volunteer Infantry. A Three Years' Organization* (1913).

Perry, Henry Fales. *History of the Thirty-Eighth Regiment of Indiana Volunteer Infantry* (1906).

Pickerill, William N. *History of the Third Indiana Cavalry* (1906).

Puntenney, George H. *History of the Thirty-Seventh Regiment of Indiana Volunteers. Its Organization, Campaigns, and Battles—Sept., '61—Oct., '64* (1896).

Record of the Ninety-Fourth Regiment Ohio Volunteer Infantry in the War of the Rebellion (1896?).

Rerick, John H. *The Forty-Fourth Indiana Volunteer Infantry. History Of Its Services in the War Of The Rebellion and A Personal Record Of Its Members* (1880).

Rogers, Robert M. *The 125th Regiment Illinois Volunteer Infantry. Attention Battalion!* (1882).

Royse, Isaac Henry Clay. *History of the 115th Regiment Illinois Volunteer Infantry* (1900).

Schmitt, W[illiam] A. *History of the Twenty-Seventh Illinois Volunteers* (1892).

Scribner, B[enjamin] F. *How Soldiers Were Made; or The War As I Saw It under Buell, Rosecrans, Thomas, Grant and Sherman* (1887).

Shaw, James Birney. *History of the Tenth Regiment Indiana Volunteer Infantry. Three Months and Three Years Organizations* (1912).

Sipes, William B. *The Seventh Pennsylvania Veteran Volunteer Cavalry. Its Record, Reminiscences and Roster* (1905).

Smith, John Thomas. *A History of the Thirty-First Regiment of Indiana Volunteer Infantry in the War of the Rebellion* (1900).

Stewart, Rev. Nixon B. *Dan. McCook's Regiment, 52nd O.V.I. A History of the Regiment, Its Campaigns and Battles From 1862 to 1865* (1900).

Stormont, Gilbert R., compiler. *History of the Fifty-Eighth Regiment of Indiana Volunteer Infantry. Its Organization, Campaigns and Battles from 1861 to 1865, from the manuscript prepared by the late Chaplain John J. Hight* (1895).

Straub, Edward A. *Life and Civil War Services of Edward A. Straub* (1909).

Thatcher, Marshall P. *A Hundred Battles in the West. St. Louis to Atlanta, 1861–65* (1884).

Tourgee, Albion W. *The Story of a Thousand. Being a history of the Service of the 105th Ohio Volunteer Infantry, in the War for the Union from August 21, 1862 to June 6, 1865* (1896).

Vale, Joseph G. *Minty and the Cavalry. A History of Cavalry Campaigns in the Western Armies* (1886).

Waddle, Angus L. *Three Years With the Armies of the Ohio and the Cumberland* (1889).

Wagner, William. *History of the 24th Illinois Volunteer Infantry Regiment (Old Hecker Regiment)* (1911).

Wilson, Ephraim A. *Memoirs of the War* (1893).

Wright, T[homas] J. *History of the Eighth Regiment of Kentucky Vol[unteer] Inf[antry], During Its Three Years Campaigns* (1880).

Wulsin, Lucien. *The Story of the Fourth Regiment Ohio Veteran Volunteer Cavalry From the Organization of the Regiment* (1912).

Notes

Introduction

1. James M. McPherson, *Battle Cry of Freedom: The Civil War Era* (New York: Oxford University Press, 1988); Edward L. Ayers, *What Caused the Civil War? Reflections on the South and Southern History* (New York: W. W. Norton, 2005), 103–30. Also see McPherson's most recent work, an examination of Lincoln as the commander-in-chief who developed (in fact, created) the executive war power as the vital instrument to turn the nation toward a total war against slavery. *Tried by War: Abraham Lincoln as Commander-in-Chief* (New York: Penguin Press, 2008).

2. Aaron Sheehan-Dean has produced an excellent summation of this work. Aaron Sheehan-Dean, ed., *The View from the Ground: Experiences of Civil War Soldiers* (Lexington: University Press of Kentucky, 2007), 1–8. Chandra Manning, *What This Cruel War Was Over: Soldiers, Slavery, and the Civil War* (New York: Alfred A. Knopf, 2007), 113–25.

3. Stuart McConnell, *Glorious Contentment: The Grand Army of the Republic, 1865–1900* (Chapel Hill: University of North Carolina Press, 1992), 177–78. Much of this interpretation derives from the studies of Civil War literature produced by Thomas Leonard and Daniel Aaron. As well, in his classic study of wartime courage Gerald Linderman asserted that Union veterans deliberately misrepresented their war. Thomas C. Leonard, *Above the Battle: War-Making in America from Appomattox to Versailles* (New York: Oxford University Press, 1973); Daniel Aaron, *The Unwritten War: American Writers and the Civil War* (New York: Alfred A. Knopf, 1973); Gerald F. Linderman, *Embattled Courage: The Experience of Combat in the American Civil War* (New York: Free Press, 1987).

4. David W. Blight, *Race and Reunion: The Civil War in American Memory* (Cambridge, MA: Belknap Press of Harvard University Press, 2001), 383–91. Also see a recent inclusion of his thesis in a basic undergraduate reader. David W. Blight, "Quarrel Forgotten or a Revolution Remembered?," in *The Civil War Veteran: A Historical Reader*, ed. Larry M. Logue and Michael Barton (New York: New York University Press, 2007), 407–23. Cecilia Elizabeth O'Leary, *To Die For: The Paradox of American Patriotism* (Princeton, NJ: Princeton University Press, 1999), 29–68.

5. John R. Neff, *Honoring the Civil War Dead: Commemoration and the Problem of Reconciliation* (Lawrence: University Press of Kansas, 2005), 8–9. Also see Andre Fleche, "'Shoulder to Shoulder as Comrades Tried': Black and White Union Veterans and Civil War Memory," *Civil War History* 51, no. 2 (2005): 175–201; M. Keith Harris, "Slavery, Emancipation, and Veterans of the Union Cause: Commemorating Freedom in the Era of Reconciliation, 1885–1915," *Civil War History* 53, no. 3 (2007): 264–90; Joan Waugh, "Ulysses S. Grant, Historian," in *The Memory of the Civil War in American Culture*, ed. Alice Fahs and Joan Waugh (Chapel Hill: University of North Carolina Press, 2004), 5–38; William A. Blair, *Cities of the Dead: Contesting Memory of the Civil War in the South, 1865–1914* (Chapel Hill: University of North Carolina Press, 2004), 1–10.

6. See the excellent discussion of the issue of total war in the exchange of articles found in Stig Förster and Jörg Nagler, eds., *On the Road to Total War: The American Civil War and the German Wars of Unification, 1861–1871* (Cambridge: Cambridge University Press, 1997). Also see John Y. Simon and Michael E. Stevens, eds., *New Perspectives on the Civil War: Myths and Realities of the National Conflict* (Madison, WI: Madison House, 1998); Mark E. Neely Jr., *The Civil War and the Limits of Destruction* (Cambridge, MA: Harvard University Press, 2007).

7. David A. Bell, *The First Total War: Napoleon's Europe and the Birth of Warfare as We Know It* (Boston: Houghton-Mifflin, 2007), 1–20.

8. Kirk Savage, *Standing Soldiers, Kneeling Slaves: Race, War and Monument in Nineteenth-Century America* (Princeton, NJ: Princeton University Press, 1997).

9. I used Charles Dornbusch as my guide for published sources on the individual infantry regiments, artillery batteries, and cavalry units. A complete list of the regimental histories and memoirs consulted is included as an appendix. C[harles] E. Dornbusch, *Regimental Publications and Personal Narratives: Northern States*, vol. 1 of *Military Bibliography of the Civil War* (1961–1962; repr., New York: Arno Press, 1971); and volume 2 of the same series,

Regimental Publications and Personal Narratives: Southern, Border, and Western States and Territories; Federal Troops (1967; repr., New York: New York Public Library, 1994).

10. W[illiam] A. Schmitt, *History of the Twenty-Seventh Illinois Volunteers* (1892); N[ewton] H. Kingman, *Life Story of Captain Newton H. Kingman. 90th Birthday Revelations* (1928); M[arvin] B. Butler, *My Story of the Civil War and the Under-ground Railroad* (1914); Charles A. Partridge, ed., *History of the Ninety-Sixth Regiment Illinois Volunteer Infantry* (1887); Judson W. Bishop, *The Story of a Regiment: Being a Narrative of the Service of the Second Regiment, Minnesota Veteran Volunteer Infantry, in the Civil War of 1861–1865* (1890); Charles F. Manderson, *The Twin Seven-Shooters* (1902).

11. For examples of current analysis on Bierce, see the editors' introduction to S. T. Joshi and David E. Schultz, eds., *A Much Misunderstood Man: Selected Letters of Ambrose Bierce* (Columbus: Ohio State University Press, 2003); and Lawrence I. Berkove, *A Prescription for Adversity: The Moral Art of Ambrose Bierce* (Columbus: Ohio State University Press, 2002); Donald T. Blume, *Ambrose Bierce's Civilians and Soldiers in Context: A Critical Study* (Kent: Kent State University Press, 2004). In particular, review Earl Hess's discussion of Bierce. Hess is one of the few historians to examine both the military history of the war and the memories that were developed later. Earl J. Hess, *The Union Soldier in Battle: Enduring the Ordeal of Combat* (Lawrence: University Press of Kansas, 1997), 171–77.

Prelude

Epigraph. James A. Connolly to Mary Connolly, November 22, 1863, in Paul M. Angle, ed., *Three Years in the Army of the Cumberland: The Letters and Diary of Major James A. Connolly* (Bloomington: Indiana University Press, 1959), 146.

1. Ibid., 27; Mark Grimsley, *The Hard Hand of War: Union Military Policy toward Southern Civilians, 1861–1865* (Cambridge: Cambridge University Press, 1995), 39–46.

2. Gerald J. Prokopowicz, *All for the Regiment: The Army of the Ohio, 1861–1862* (Chapel Hill: University of North Carolina Press, 2001), 35–46; Larry J. Daniel, *Days of Glory: The Army of the Cumberland, 1861–1865* (Baton Rouge: Louisiana State University Press, 2004), 3–56. For the Army of the Ohio's original divisional organization, see Special Orders 19, Department of the Ohio, December 2, 1861, in *The War of the Rebellion: A Compilation of the Official Records of the Union and Confederate Armies,* 70 vols. in 128 parts (Wash-

ington: Government Printing Office, 1880–1901), series 1, vol. 7 (1882), 467–68 (hereinafter OR).

3. Buell's major biographer is Stephen D. Engle, *Don Carlos Buell: Most Promising of All* (Chapel Hill: University of North Carolina Press, 1999). Also see Engle's "Don Carlos Buell: Military Philosophy and Command Problems in the West," *Civil War History* 41, no. 2 (1995): 89–115. Also see Prokopowicz, *All for the Regiment*, 45–46; Ethan S. Rafuse, *McClellan's War: The Failure of Moderation in the Struggle for the Union* (Bloomington: Indiana University Press, 2005), 8–141.

4. See Noel Fisher's discussion of Middle Tennessee's swing vote in the secession crisis of 1861. Noel C. Fisher, *War at Every Door: Partisan Politics and Guerilla Violence in East Tennessee, 1860–1869* (Chapel Hill: University of North Carolina Press, 1997), 22–40. On Nashville's reaction, see Walter Durham, *Nashville: The Occupied City, the First Seventeen Months—February 16, 1862, to June 30, 1863* (Nashville: Tennessee Historical Society, 1985), 1–21.

5. Published originally in 1863, Fitch's *Annals* went through five editions in a year. The volume cited is a reprint of the fifth edition, the original of which included a section on the Chattanooga campaign. John Fitch, *Annals of the Army of the Cumberland: Comprising Biographies, Descriptions of Departments, Accounts of Expeditions, Skirmishes, and Battles*, 5th ed. (1864; repr., Mechanicsburg, PA: Stackpole Books, 2003), 103.

6. On Mitchel and his mission to northern Alabama, see Prokopowicz, *All for the Regiment*, 42–44, 95, 177–18, 122–23; Grimsley, *The Hard Hand of War*, 78–85; Stephen Chicoine, *John Basil Turchin and the Fight to Free the Slaves* (Westport, CT: Praeger, 2003), 44–45. The quotation is from a lieutenant in the Nineteenth Illinois, quoted in Chicoine, page 65.

7. The quotations are from Confederate colonel John S. Scott and from the testimony of an unidentified witness at Turchin's court-martial. These are found in Chicoine, *John Basil Turchin*, 63, 65. See Chicoine's larger discussion of Athens on pages 9–21, 66–73. Also see George C. Bradley and Richard L. Dahlen, *From Conciliation to Conquest: The Sack of Athens and the Court-Martial of Colonel John B. Turchin* (Tuscaloosa: The University of Alabama Press, 2006), 109–25; Grimsley, *Hard Hand of War*, 78–85.

8. Bradley and Dahlen, *From Conciliation to Conquest*, 221–43.

9. John Beatty's war diary was published as *The Citizen-Soldier* in 1879. Citations are from the modern reprint, John Beatty, *The Citizen-Soldier: The Memoirs of a Civil War Volunteer* (1879; repr., Lincoln, NE: Bison Books, 1998), 45.

10. Prokopowicz, *All for the Regiment*, 133.

11. From the moment of Buell's appointment, Lincoln had wanted the Army of the Ohio to liberate East Tennessee. After initially agreeing, the general put the president off, preferring to pursue the line of the Nashville railroad. Because of his soft-war attitudes and his stuffy professionalism, Buell earned the enmity of most of his soldiers, though Henry M. Cist and Thomas Van Horne—two of the army's earliest historians—credited the general's organizational talents. Henry M. Cist, *The Army of the Cumberland* (1882; repr., New York: Blue and Gray Press, n.d.), 75; Thomas B. Van Horne, *The Army of the Cumberland* (1875; repr., New York: Smithmark, 1996), 68. Also see Kenneth W. Noe, *Perryville: This Grand Havoc of Battle* (Lexington: University Press of Kentucky, 2001), 339–43; Prokopowicz, *All for the Regiment*, 185–89; Daniel, *Days of Glory*, 126–77; Rafuse, *McClellan's War*, 118–97.

12. William M. Lamers remains Rosecrans's major biographer. William M. Lamers, *The Edge of Glory: A Biography of General William S. Rosecrans, U.S.A.* (New York: Harcourt, Brace and World, 1961). On Stones River, see Peter Cozzens, *No Better Place to Die: The Battle of Stones River* (Urbana: University of Illinois Press, 1990). When Buell was relieved of command, the Army of the Ohio was redesignated as the Fourteenth Corps, Department of the Cumberland. In January 1863, it became the Army of the Cumberland, which now included three corps: the Fourteenth, the Twentieth, and the Twenty-first. As well, troops from Kentucky under Maj. Gen. Gordon Granger were designated as an additional "Reserve Corps." For the army's order of battle just prior to the Tullahoma campaign, see *OR*, series 1, vol. 23, part 1 (1889), 410–18. On corps and army organization, see General Orders No. 9, Department of the Cumberland, February 2, 1863, *OR*, series 1, vol. 23, part 2 (1889), 36.

13. Edward Hagerman, *The American Civil War and the Origins of Modern Warfare: Ideas, Organization, and Field Command* (Bloomington: Indiana University Press, 1988), 151–230; Brent Nosworthy, *The Bloody Crucible of Courage: Fighting Methods and Combat Experience of the Civil War* (New York: Carroll and Graf, 2003), 617–21. Also see Steven E. Woodworth, *Six Armies in Tennessee: The Chickamauga and Chattanooga Campaigns* (Lincoln: University of Nebraska Press, 1998), 1–78; Lamers, *Edge of Glory*, 244–73; Daniel, *Days of Glory*, 225–358.

14. Rosecrans turned Nashville and Murfreesboro into major supply and refit bases, and this fact turned the countryside of Middle Tennessee into a forage area. Fitch, *Annals of the Army of the Cumberland*, 265–92, 331–56, 626–44. Also see Walter Durham's two works on occupied Nashville. *Nashville: Occupied City*, 267–83; and his *Reluctant Partners: Nashville and the*

Union, July 1, 1863, to June 30, 1865 (Nashville: Tennessee Historical Society, 1987), 116–26, 148–73.

15. Stephen V. Ash, *Middle Tennessee Society Transformed 1860–1870: War and Peace in the Upper South* (Baton Rouge: Louisiana State University Press, 1988), 143–74; John Cimprich, *Slavery's End in Tennessee, 1861–1865* (University: The University of Alabama Press, 1985), 98–117; Peter Maslowski, "'Treason Must Be Made Odious': Military Occupation and Wartime Reconstruction in Nashville, Tennessee" (Ph.D. diss., Ohio State University, 1972).

16. Ash, *Middle Tennessee Society,* 143–74. Also see Stephen V. Ash, *When the Yankees Came: Chaos and Conflict in the Occupied South, 1861–1865* (Chapel Hill: University of North Carolina Press, 1995); Robert R. Mackey, *The Uncivil War: Irregular Warfare in the Upper South, 1861–1865* (Norman: University of Oklahoma Press, 2004), 3–23, 123–54; B. Franklin Cooling, "A People's War: Partisan Conflict in Tennessee and Kentucky," in *Guerillas, Unionists, and Violence on the Confederate Home Front,* ed. Daniel E. Sutherland (Fayetteville: University of Arkansas Press, 1999), 113–32.

17. Ash, *Middle Tennessee Society,* 84–141; Cimprich, *Slavery's End in Tennessee,* 12–80. Slavery's disintegration in Middle Tennessee was aided by the fact that upper-South towns and rural areas had produced a structure of hiring out and other forms of quasi-freedom before the war. Ira Berlin, *Generations of Captivity: A History of African-American Slaves* (Cambridge, MA: Belknap Press of Harvard University Press, 2003), 209–30; John Hope Franklin and Loren Schweninger, *In Search of the Promised Land: A Slave Family in the Old South* (New York: Oxford University Press, 2006); Anita Shafer Goodstein, *Nashville 1780–1860: From Frontier to City* (Gainesville: University Press of Florida, 1989), 136–56.

18. Fitch, *Annals of the Army of the Cumberland,* 665. Also see Ira Berlin, Steven F. Miller, Joseph P. Reidy, and Leslie S. Rowland, eds., *The Wartime Genesis of Free Labor: The Upper South,* series 1, vol. 2 of *Freedom: A Documentary History of Emancipation, 1861–1867* (Cambridge: Cambridge University Press, 1993), 367–86; Lenette S. Taylor, *"The Supply for Tomorrow Must Not Fail": The Civil War of Captain Simon Perkins, Jr., a Union Quartermaster* (Kent: Kent State University Press, 2004); William W. Freehling, *The South vs. the South: How Anti-Confederate Southerners Shaped the Course of the Civil War* (New York: Oxford University Press, 2001), 102–4. However crude his methods, Morton's sense of urgency was genuine and well placed. John Hunt Morgan conducted a major raid against the Louisville and Nashville railroad in August, collapsing the Big South Tunnel near Gallatin, effectively isolating the city. At nearly the same time, Nathan Bedford Forrest was urging Gen.

Braxton Bragg to take Nashville as the Federals evacuated. James A. Ramage, *Rebel Raider: The Life of General John Hunt Morgan* (Lexington: University Press of Kentucky, 1986), 107–18; Brian Steel Wills, *The Confederacy's Greatest Cavalryman, Nathan Bedford Forrest* (1992; repr., Lawrence: University Press of Kansas, 1992), 79–84; Mackey, *The Uncivil War*, 136–39.

19. Maj. Gen. Lovell H. Rousseau to Brig. Gen. W. D. Whipple, *OR,* series 1, vol. 32, part 2 (1891), 268–69.

20. Woodworth, *Six Armies in Tennessee*, 1–78; Peter Cozzens, *This Terrible Sound: The Battle of Chickamauga* (Urbana: University of Illinois Press, 1992), 21–120; Daniel, *Days of Glory*, 285–358.

21. After the disaster at Chickamauga, the Army of the Cumberland was significantly reorganized. Rosecrans was replaced by Thomas, while the War Department merged the Twentieth and Twenty-first corps into a new Fourth Corps, commanded initially by Gordon Granger. The Fourteenth Corps was retained, adding to it the units of the former "Reserve Corps" (John M. Palmer initially placed in command). In addition, brigades and divisions were consolidated, reflecting both the attrition of long campaigning and the casualties of battle. Many brigades would now consist of eight or so regiments, whereas before, four had been common. Finally, after Chattanooga, the Army of the Potomac units under Hooker's command—the Eleventh and Twelfth corps—were placed under Thomas, and thus became part of the Army of the Cumberland. After the Atlanta campaign, the Fourteenth and Fourth corps would be separated, effectively ending the Army of the Cumberland's career as an army. Special Field Orders No. 269, Department of the Cumberland, October 9, 1863, *OR,* series 1, vol. 30, part 4 (1890), 209–13; General Orders 228, Department of the Cumberland, October 9, 1863, *OR,* series 1, vol. 30, part 1 (1890), 1051. For a highly favorable assessment of Thomas, see Thomas C. Buell, *The Warrior Generals: Combat Leadership in the Civil War* (New York: Three Rivers Press, 1997), 188–203, 252–95, 353–411. For a discussion of the Atlanta campaign, see Albert Castel, *Decision in the West: The Atlanta Campaign of 1864* (Lawrence: University Press of Kansas, 1992).

Chapter 1

Epigraph. Thomas Crofts, *History of the Service of The Third Ohio Veteran Volunteer Cavalry in the War For The Preservation Of The Union From 1861–1865* (1910), 207.

1. In particular, see the work of Edward L. Ayers. Edward L. Ayers, *What Caused the Civil War? Reflections on the South and Southern History* (New York:

W. W. Norton, 2005), 131–44; and his *In the Presence of Mine Enemies: The Civil War in the Heart of America, 1859–1863* (New York: W. W. Norton, 2003), 95–187. Also see Michael F. Holt, *The Fate of Their Country: Politicians, Slavery Extension, and the Coming of the Civil War* (New York: Hill and Wang, 2004).

2. Charles C. Briant, *History of the Sixth Regiment Indiana Volunteer Infantry. Of Both The Three Months' and Three Years' Services* (1891), 1.

3. James M. McPherson, *For Cause and Comrades: Why Men Fought in the Civil War* (New York: Oxford University Press, 1997), 16–17. Also see Earl J. Hess, *Liberty, Virtue, and Progress: Northerners and Their War for the Union* (New York: New York University Press, 1988), 22–24; Phillip Shaw Paludan, *"A People's Contest": The Union and Civil War, 1861–1865* (New York: Harper and Row, 1988), 3–18. On volunteer mobilization, see Eugene C. Murdock, *One Million Men: The Civil War Draft in the North* (Westport, CT: Greenwood Press, 1971), 4–6; James W. Geary, *We Need Men: The Union Draft in the Civil War* (DeKalb: Northern Illinois University Press, 1991), 12–35; Fred Albert Shannon, *The Organization and Administration of the Union Army, 1861–1865*, 2 vols. (1928; repr., Gloucester, MA: Peter Smith, 1965), 1: 15–50. On the reemergence of partisan division, see Mark E. Neely Jr., *The Union Divided: Party Conflict in the Civil War North* (Cambridge, MA: Harvard University Press, 2002), 12–17.

4. For the roots of this tradition, see Charles Royster, *A Revolutionary People at War: The Continental Army and American Character, 1775–1783* (Chapel Hill: University of North Carolina Press, 1980); Fred Anderson, *A People's Army: Massachusetts Soldiers and Society in the Seven Years' War* (New York: W. W. Norton, 1984), 26–62, 167–223. For earlier references, see Russell F. Weigley, *Towards an American Army: Military Thought from Washington to Marshall* (New York: Columbia University Press, 1962), 1–9; and his *History of the United States Army* (New York: Macmillan, 1967), 3–94.

5. Robert L. Kimberly and Ephraim S. Holloway, *The Forty-First Ohio Veteran Volunteer Infantry in the War of the Rebellion, 1861–1865* (1897), 7; John N. Beach, *History of the Fortieth Ohio Volunteer Infantry* (1884), 9. In the same spirit, veterans recruited in 1862 in response to the military reverses of that summer argued that they were men with families and established lives, yet were willing to lay it down for the transcendent cause of the nation's life. *Record of the Ninety-Fourth Regiment Ohio Volunteer Infantry in the War of the Rebellion* (1896?), 4–5; Henry J. Aten, *History of the Eighty-Fifth Regiment, Illinois Volunteer Infantry* (1901), 13–16.

6. Rev. David Bittle Floyd, *History of the Seventy-Fifth Regiment of Indiana Infantry Volunteers, Its Organization Campaigns, and Battles (1862–65)*

(1893), 12; S[pillard] F. Horrall, *History of the Forty-Second Indiana Volunteer Infantry* (1892), unpaginated prologue; Judson W. Bishop, *The Story of a Regiment: Being a Narrative of the Service of the Second Regiment, Minnesota Veteran Volunteer Infantry, in the Civil War of 1861–1865* (1890), 22.

7. Geo[rge] W. Morris, *History of the Eighty-First Regiment of Indiana Volunteer Infantry in the Great War of the Rebellion, 1861 to 1865* (1901), 7. See note 5.

8. James D. Richardson, *A Compilation of the Messages and Papers of the Presidents, 1789–1897,* 10 vols. (Washington: Government Printing Office, 1896–1899), 5: 630–32.

9. F[rederick] W. Keil, *Thirty-Fifth Ohio. A Narrative of Service from August, 1861 to 1864* (1894), 212; James A. Barnes, James R. Carnahan, and Thomas H. B. McCain, *The Eighty-Sixth Regiment, Indiana Volunteer Infantry. A Narrative Of Its Services In The Civil War of 1861–1865* (1895), 5–6.

10. Chandra Manning, *What This Cruel War Was Over: Soldiers, Slavery, and the Civil War* (New York: Alfred A. Knopf, 2007), 3–18, 74, 83–102. Also see Mark Grimsley, *The Hard Hand of War: Union Military Policy toward Southern Civilians, 1861–1865* (Cambridge: Cambridge University Press, 1995), 136–37.

11. Susan-Mary Grant, *North over South: Northern Nationalism and American Identity in the Antebellum Era* (Lawrence: University Press of Kansas, 2000). Also see Eric Foner, *Free Soil, Free Labor, Free Men: The Ideology of the Republican Party before the Civil War* (New York: Oxford University Press, 1970); Heather Cox Richardson, *The Greatest Nation of the Earth: Republican Economic Policies during the Civil War* (Cambridge, MA: Harvard University Press, 1997).

12. Geo[rge] W. Herr, *Episodes of the Civil War: Nine Campaigns in Nine States* (1890), 4–5. For a sample of narratives that pursue similar discussions, see Isaac Henry Clay Royse, *History of the 115th Regiment Illinois Volunteer Infantry* (1900), 1–5; Charles A. Partridge, ed., *History of the Ninety-Sixth Regiment Illinois Volunteer Infantry* (1887), 17–26; William Wirt Calkins, *The History of the One Hundred and Fourth Regiment of Illinois Volunteer Infantry. War of the Great Rebellion 1862–1865* (1895), 1–6.

13. Herr, *Episodes of the Civil War,* 6, 15–16. For Herr's full discussion, see pages 3–17.

14. James Birney Shaw, *History of the Tenth Regiment Indiana Volunteer Infantry. Three Months and Three Years Organizations* (1912), 125; Keil, *Thirty-Fifth Ohio,* 1; Robert M. Rogers, *The 125th Regiment Illinois Volunteer Infantry. Attention Battalion!* (1882), 29.

15. Keil, *Thirty-Fifth Ohio,* 3.

16. Manning, *What This Cruel War Was Over*, 71–72. Also see her article, "A 'Vexed Question': White Union Soldiers on Slavery and Race," in *The View from the Ground: Experiences of Civil War Soldiers*, ed. Aaron Sheehan-Dean (Lexington: University Press of Kentucky, 2007), 31–66. William W. Freehling, *The South vs. the South: How Anti-Confederate Southerners Shaped the Course of the Civil War* (New York: Oxford University Press, 2001), 89–114. Also see Ira Berlin, Barbara J. Fields, Thavolia Glymph, Joseph P. Reidy, and Leslie S. Rowland, eds., *The Destruction of Slavery*, series 1, vol. 1 of *Freedom: A Documentary History of Emancipation, 1861–1867* (Cambridge: Cambridge University Press, 1985), 44–54.

17. Michael H. Fitch, *Echoes Of The Civil War As I Hear Them* (1905), 55–56; John R. McBride, *History of the Thirty-Third Indiana Veteran Volunteer Infantry During the Four Years of Civil War From Sept. 16, 1861, to July 21, 1865* (1900), 68, 70.

18. Shaw, *History of the Tenth Regiment*, 137. For similar incidents, see Royse, *History of the 115th Illinois*, 36; Angus L. Waddle, *Three Years With the Armies of the Ohio and the Cumberland* (1889), 64–65; F[rancis] M. McAdams, *Every-Day Soldier Life, or A History of the One Hundred and Thirteenth Ohio Volunteer Infantry* (1884), 21.

19. For examples of particular incidents or general reflections on the quickly developing antagonism between Cumberland soldiers and Confederate civilians, see George H. Puntenney, *History of the Thirty-Seventh Regiment of Indiana Volunteers. Its Organization, Campaigns, and Battles—Sept., '61—Oct., 64* (1896), 21–22; Horrall, *History of the Forty-Second Indiana*, 119; G[eorge] W. Lewis, *The Campaigns of the 124th Regiment Ohio Volunteer Infantry with Roster and Roll of Honor* (1894), 51.

20. Joseph G. Vale, *Minty and the Cavalry. A History of Cavalry Campaigns in the Western Armies* (1886), 52–53.

21. Keil, *Thirty-Fifth Ohio*, 77–78; Bishop, *The Story of a Regiment*, 77–78. For other examples of the shift to hard war, a shift that would include emancipation, see S[ilas] S. Canfield, *History of the 21st Regiment Ohio Volunteer Infantry, in The War Of The Rebellion* (1893), 96; C[harles] T. DeVelling, *History of the Seventeenth Regiment, First Brigade, Third Division, Fourteenth Corps, Army of the Cumberland, War of the Rebellion* (1889), 93; Alf[red] G. Hunter, *History of the Eighty-Second Indiana Volunteer Infantry, Its Organization, Campaigns and Battles* (1893), 26–27, 51; Ephraim A. Wilson, *Memoirs of the War* (1893), 53–54.

22. Note in this regard David Blight's characterization of the North's turn-of-the-century romantic fascination with the Underground Railroad. David W. Blight, *Race and Reunion: The Civil War in American Memory* (Cam-

bridge, MA: Belknap Press of Harvard University Press, 2001), 231–37. Also see the edited collection of essays produced for the National Underground Railroad Freedom Center. David W. Blight, ed., *Passages to Freedom: The Underground Railroad in History and Memory* (2004; repr., New York: Collins, 2006).

23. Partridge, *History of the Ninety-Sixth Regiment*, 101–3. Also see Larry J. Daniel, *Days of Glory: The Army of the Cumberland, 1861–1865* (Baton Rouge: Louisiana State University Press, 2004), 249–57; Jennifer L. Weber, *Copperheads: The Rise and Fall of Lincoln's Opponents in the North* (New York: Oxford University Press, 2006), 43–86; "The Echo From The Army. What Our Soldiers Say About The Copperheads," Loyal Publication Society, Loyal Reprints, No. 2 (1863). For other examples of discussion within the Cumberland regiments, see Shaw, *History of the Tenth Regiment*, 198–200; Aten, *History of the Eighty-Fifth Regiment*, 79–83.

24. Rogers, *The 125th Illinois Volunteer Infantry*, 152. Joseph Glatthaar argues that Union soldiers by this time had developed at least a degree of sympathy for the former slaves, and that many of Sherman's men deplored Davis's action. Joseph T. Glatthaar, *The March to the Sea and Beyond: Sherman's Troops in the Savannah and Carolinas Campaigns* (New York: New York University Press, 1985), 64–65. Also see Anne J. Bailey, *War and Ruin: William T. Sherman and the Savannah Campaign* (Wilmington, DE: Scholarly Resources, 2003), 93–94; Nathaniel Cheairs Hughes Jr. and Gordon D. Whitney, *Jefferson Davis in Blue: The Life of Sherman's Relentless Warrior* (Baton Rouge: Louisiana State University Press, 2002), 304–14.

25. Jay Winik, *April 1865: The Month That Saved America* (New York: HarperCollins, 2001), 123–99, 259–347.

26. T[homas] F. Dornblaser, *Sabre Strokes of the Pennsylvania Dragoons, in the War of 1861–1865* (1884), 243–44.

27. Tourgee's major biographer is Otto H. Olsen. See his *Carpetbagger's Crusade: The Life of Albion Winegar Tourgee* (Baltimore: Johns Hopkins University Press, 1965). The quotation is from a letter to one of Tourgee's fraternity brothers and is found on pages 24–25. For more recent evaluations of Tourgee and his racial politics, see Mark Elliott, "Race, Color Blindness, and the Democratic Public: Albion W. Tourgee's Radical Principles in *Plessy v. Ferguson*," *Journal of Southern History* 67 (May 2001): 287–330; Deborah P. Hamlin, "'Friend of Freedom': Albion Winegar Tourgee and Reconstruction in North Carolina" (Ph.D. diss., Duke University, 2004).

28. Albion W. Tourgee, *A Fool's Errand, By One Of The Fools; The Famous Romance of American History* (New York: Fords, Howard, & Hulbert, 1880). The original edition was released anonymously in 1879. The version quoted

here is the 1880 edition, which included a part 2, entitled *The Invisible Empire: A Concise Review Of The Epoch On Which The Tale Is Based.* Quotes are from page 156. The complete text of the fictional letter comprises pages 153–57.

29. Ibid., 77, 95. Full text of the fictional letter from Exum Davis comprises pages 94–96.

30. Ibid., 126.

31. Ibid., 160–61. The complete text of this fictional letter comprises pages 158–62.

32. Ibid., 110; Albion W. Tourgee, *The Story of a Thousand. Being a history of the Service of the 105th Ohio Volunteer Infantry, in the War for the Union from August 21, 1862 to June 6, 1865* (1896), 353–67.

33. Tourgee, *A Fool's Errand*, 99.

34. Ibid., 161–62.

35. Charles W. Calhoun, *Conceiving a New Republic: The Republican Party and the Southern Question, 1869–1900* (Lawrence: University Press of Kansas, 2006); Heather Cox Richardson, *The Death of Reconstruction: Race, Labor, and Politics in the Post–Civil War North, 1865–1901* (2001; repr., Cambridge, MA: Harvard University Press, 2004). Also see Steven Hahn, *A Nation Under Our Feet: Black Political Struggles in the Rural South from Slavery to the Great Migration* (Cambridge, MA: Belknap Press of Harvard University Press, 2003).

36. Chapter 2 will engage the issue of Jacksonian America's military amateurism.

37. Wolfgang Schivelbusch, *The Culture of Defeat: On National Trauma, Mourning, and Recovery,* trans. Jefferson Chase (2001; repr., New York: Picador, 2004), 1–35. Also see Ayers, *What Caused the Civil War?*, 145–66. The issue of the North's organized military-industrial complex will be treated in chapter 2.

38. Tourgee, *A Fool's Errand*, 161.

Chapter 2

Epigraph. Charles C. Briant, *History of the Sixth Regiment Indiana Volunteer Infantry. Of Both The Three Months' and Three Years' Services* (1891), 332–33, 338.

1. Daniel Walker Howe, *What Hath God Wrought: The Transformation of America, 1815–1848* (New York: Oxford University Press, 2007), 285–327.

2. William Cronon, *Nature's Metropolis: Chicago and the Great West* (New York: W. W. Norton, 1991), 97–340.

3. Robert M. Rogers, *The 125th Regiment Illinois Volunteer Infantry. Atten-*

tion Battalion! (1882), 25; Briant, *History of the Sixth Regiment,* 305; G[eorge] W. Lewis, *The Campaigns of the 124th Regiment Ohio Volunteer Infantry with Roster and Roll of Honor* (1894), 119.

4. For examples of such discussions, see S[pillard] F. Horrall, *History of the Forty-Second Indiana Volunteer Infantry* (1892), 100–101, 109, 136–40; Rev. David Bittle Floyd, *History of the Seventy-Fifth Regiment of Indiana Infantry Volunteers, Its Organizations Campaigns, and Battles (1862–65)* (1893), 38; Geo[rge] W. Morris, *History of the Eighty-First Regiment of Indiana Volunteer Infantry in the Great War of the Rebellion, 1861 to 1865* (1901), 8, 14–15; Alexis Cope, *The Fifteenth Ohio Volunteers And Its Campaigns. War of 1861–5* (1916), 143, 201.

5. Morris, *History of the Eighty-First Regiment,* 15; Henry J. Aten, *History of the Eighty-Fifth Regiment, Illinois Volunteer Infantry* (1901), 296.

6. James A. Barnes, James R. Carnahan, and Thomas H. B. McCain, *The Eighty-Sixth Regiment, Indiana Volunteer Infantry. A Narrative Of Its Services In The Civil War of 1861–1865* (1895), 84. Also see William S. S. Erb, *Extract from "The Battles of the 19th Ohio" By A Late Acting Assistant Adjutant General, 3rd Brigade, 3rd Division, 4th A.C., Army of the Cumberland* (1893), 34.

7. Theodore Crackel, *Mr. Jefferson's Army: Political and Social Reform of the Military Establishment, 1801–1809* (New York: New York University Press, 1987), 36–65; Richard Bruce Winders, *Mr. Polk's Army: The American Military Experience in the Mexican War* (College Station: Texas A&M University Press, 1997), 50–87, 186–201; Marcus Cunliffe, *Soldiers and Civilians: The Martial Spirit in America, 1775–1865,* 2nd ed. (New York: Free Press, 1973), 101–11; Albion W. Tourgee, *The Story of a Thousand. Being a history of the Service of the 105th Ohio Volunteer Infantry, in the War for the Union from August 21, 1862 to June 6, 1865* (1896), 43–44.

8. Winders, *Mr. Polk's Army,* 50–87, 186–201; Amy S. Greenberg, *Manifest Manhood and Antebellum American Empire* (Cambridge: Cambridge University Press, 2005), 18–196.

9. James Birney Shaw, *History of the Tenth Regiment Indiana Volunteer Infantry. Three Months and Three Years Organizations* (1912), 172. On Gilbert, see Gerald J. Prokopowicz, *All for the Regiment: The Army of the Ohio, 1861–1862* (Chapel Hill: University of North Carolina Press, 2001), 155, 182–84. For other discussions of detested officers, see Rev. Nixon B. Stewart, *Dan. McCook's Regiment, 52nd O.V.I. A History of the Regiment, Its Campaigns and Battles From 1862 to 1865* (1900), 60; Aten, *History of the Eighty-Fifth Regiment,* 102.

10. Robert L. Kimberly and Ephraim S. Holloway, *The Forty-First Ohio Veteran Volunteer Infantry in The War of the Rebellion, 1861–1865* (1897), 9–10.

For other descriptions of the process of submitting to drill and officer command, and of descriptions of officers good and bad, see L[ewis] W. Day, *Story of the One Hundred and First Ohio Infantry. A Memorial Volume* (1894), 27; Charles A. Partridge, ed., *History of the Ninety-Sixth Regiment Illinois Volunteer Infantry* (1887), 57; John N. Beach, *History of the Fortieth Ohio Volunteer Infantry* (1884), 27–28; William Wirt Calkins, *The History of the One Hundred and Fourth Regiment of Illinois Volunteer Infantry. War of the Great Rebellion 1862–1865* (1895), 13–16.

11. Barnes et al., *The Eighty-Sixth Regiment*, 184, 198.

12. Kimberly and Holloway, *The Forty-First Ohio*, 73; Lewis, *Campaigns of the 124th Regiment*, 104. References to initiative, enterprise, and independence among the soldiery recur repeatedly. Critically, such descriptions always allude to these traits as characteristics of the American volunteer soldier. For other examples, see R[andolph] V. Marshall, *An Historical Sketch of the Twenty-Second Regiment Indiana Volunteers, From Its Organization To The Close Of The War* (1884), 31–32; Tourgee, *Story of a Thousand*, 43; B[enjamin] F. Scribner, *How Soldiers Were Made; or The War As I Saw It under Buell, Rosecrans, Thomas, Grant and Sherman* (1887), 249–51.

13. Edwin W. Payne, *History of the Thirty-Fourth Regiment of Illinois Volunteer Infantry September 7, 1861–July 12, 1865* (1902), 55.

14. Drew Gilpin Faust, *This Republic of Suffering: Death and the American Civil War* (New York: Alfred A. Knopf, 2008), 266–71.

15. Paddy Griffith, *Battle Tactics of the Civil War* (New Haven, CT: Yale University Press, 1989), 73–90, 137–63; Brent Nosworthy, *The Bloody Crucible of Courage: Fighting Methods and Combat Experience of the Civil War* (New York: Carroll and Graf, 2003).

16. Earl J. Hess, *The Union Soldier in Battle: Enduring the Ordeal of Combat* (Lawrence: University Press of Kansas, 1997), 45–154; Mark E. Neely Jr., *The Civil War and the Limits of Destruction* (Cambridge, MA: Harvard University Press, 2007), 198–219.

17. Eric Dean Jr., *Shook over Hell: Post-Traumatic Stress, Vietnam, and the Civil War* (Cambridge, MA: Harvard University Press, 1997); E[ugene] B. Sledge, *With the Old Breed at Peleliu and Okinawa* (1981; repr., New York: Oxford University Press, 1990); Michael Fellman, *Inside War: The Guerilla Conflict in Missouri during the Civil War* (New York: Oxford University Press, 1989).

18. J. Henry Haynie, *The Nineteenth Illinois. A Memoir of a Regiment of Volunteer Infantry Famous in the Civil War of Fifty Years Ago for its Drill, Bravery, and Distinguished Services* (1912), 224–25.

19. Ceclia Elizabeth O'Leary, *To Die For: The Paradox of American Patriotism* (Princeton, NJ: Princeton University Press, 1999), 29–128.

20. Michael H. Fitch, *Echoes Of The Civil War As I Hear Them* (1905), 346–48. For an example of similar sentiments, see Judson W. Bishop, *The Story of a Regiment: Being a Narrative of the Service of the Second Regiment, Minnesota Veteran Volunteer Infantry, in the Civil War of 1861–1865* (1890), 194–202.

21. Prokopowicz, *All for the Regiment*, 1–34. Also see Hess, *Union Soldier in Battle*, 110–22; Griffith, *Battle Tactics of the Civil War*, 150–58.

22. Briant, *History of the Sixth Regiment*, 86–87; Rogers, *The 125th Illinois Volunteer Infantry*, 70; Ephraim A. Wilson, *Memoirs of the War* (1893), 151–52.

23. B[enjamin] F. [Magee], *History of the 72nd Indiana Volunteer Infantry of the Mounted Lightning Brigade* (1882), 677; F[rederick] W. Keil, *Thirty-Fifth Ohio. A Narrative of Service from August, 1861 to 1864* (1894), 226–27. On the printed title pages of Magee's narrative his name is spelled McGee. However, in the body of the narrative there is a signed photograph of the author with his name spelled as Magee.

24. Todd DePastino, *Citizen Hobo: How a Century of Homelessness Shaped America* (Chicago: University of Chicago Press, 2003), 17–20.

25. Barnes et al., *The Eighty-Sixth Regiment*, 35.

26. Mark Grimsley, *The Hard Hand of War: Union Military Policy toward Southern Civilians, 1861–1865* (Cambridge: Cambridge University Press, 1995); Michael Fellman, "At the Nihilist Edge: Reflections on Guerilla Warfare during the American Civil War," in *On the Road to Total War: The American Civil War and the German Wars of Unification, 1861–1871*, ed. Stig Förster and Jörg Nagler (Cambridge: Cambridge University Press, 1997), 519–40; Mark E. Neely Jr., "'Civilized Belligerents': Abraham Lincoln and the Idea of 'Total War,'" in *New Perspectives on the Civil War: Myths and Realities of the National Conflict*, ed. John Y. Simon and Michael E. Stevens (Madison, WI: Madison House, 1998), 3–24. For Neely's comments on "Indian war," see his *The Civil War and the Limits of Destruction*, 140–69.

27. Geo[rge] W. Herr, *Episodes of the Civil War: Nine Campaigns in Nine States* (1890), 80, 83.

28. Fellman, "At the Nihilist Edge," 527–32; Stephen V. Ash, *When the Yankees Came: Conflict and Chaos in the Occupied South, 1861–1865* (Chapel Hill: University of North Carolina Press, 1995), 200–203; Reid Mitchell, *The Vacant Chair: The Northern Soldier Leaves Home* (New York: Oxford University Press, 1993), 89–112. The Cumberland authors' view of Confederate women will be discussed in the next chapter.

29. F[rancis] M. McAdams, *Every-Day Soldier Life, or A History of the One*

Hundred and Thirteenth Ohio Volunteer Infantry (1884), 55; Barnes et al., *The Eighty-Sixth Regiment,* 288–89.

30. See note 27.

31. Alf[red] G. Hunter, *History of the Eighty-Second Indiana Volunteer Infantry, Its Organization, Campaigns and Battles* (1893), 144–45; Floyd, *History of the Seventy-Fifth Regiment,* 341, 343. For another example, see J[ohn] A. Chase, *History of the Fourteenth Ohio Regiment, O.V.V.I. From the beginning of the war in 1861 to its close in 1865* (1881), 78–80.

32. Calkins, *History of the One Hundred and Fourth,* 256; Bishop, *The Story of a Regiment,* 162.

33. Gilbert R. Stormont, compiler, *History of the Fifty-Eighth Regiment of Indiana Volunteer Infantry. Its Organization, Campaigns and Battles from 1861 to 1865, from the manuscript prepared by the late Chaplain John J. Hight* (1895), 474; Floyd, *History of the Seventy-Fifth Regiment,* 373.

34. Edwin W. High, *History of the Sixty-Eighth Regiment Indiana Volunteer Infantry 1862–1865* (1902), 203–4; Tourgee, *Story of a Thousand,* 355, 366–67. Also see the recorded remarks from the diary of John L. Hostetter in Payne, *History of the Thirty-Fourth Regiment,* 173–74.

35. Stewart, *Dan. McCook's Regiment,* 13; John R. McBride, *History of the Thirty-Third Indiana Veteran Volunteer Infantry During the Four Years of Civil War From Sept. 16, 1861, to July 21, 1865* (1900), 217. For similar references to the importance of or longing for woman's presence, see Morris, *History of the Eighty-First Regiment,* 70; Aten, *History of the Eighty-Fifth Regiment,* 67–68; [Magee], *History of the 72nd Indiana,* 102–3.

36. Day, *Story of the One Hundred and First Ohio,* 187. For similar references, see Charles T. Clark, *Opdycke Tigers 125th O.V.I. A History of the Regiment and of the Campaigns and Battles of the Army of the Cumberland* (1895), 226; Stewart, *Dan. McCook's Regiment,* 30; Ira S. Owens, *Greene County Soldiers in the Late War* (1884), 53–54.

37. McBride, *History of the Thirty-Third Indiana,* 30; T[homas] J. Wright, *History of the Eighth Regiment of Kentucky Vol[unteer] Inf[antry], During Its Three Years Campaigns* (1880), 132. Also see John Thomas Smith, *A History of the Thirty-First Regiment of Indiana Volunteer Infantry in the War of the Rebellion* (1900), 107.

38. Herr, *Episodes of the Civil War,* 292, 299–300, 309.

39. Barnes et al., *The Eighty-Sixth Regiment,* 543–44.

40. Stuart McConnell, *Glorious Contentment: The Grand Army of the Republic, 1865–1900* (Chapel Hill: University of North Carolina Press, 1992), 166–205. The quotation is from page 181.

41. Haynie, *The Nineteenth Illinois,* 16; Matthew H. Jamison, *Recollections of Pioneer and Army Life* (1911), 348.

42. Keil, *Thirty-Fifth Ohio,* 153–54; Payne, *History of the Thirty-Fourth Regiment,* 349–50. See McConnell, *Glorious Contentment,* 125–65.

43. High, *History of the Sixty-Eighth Regiment,* 283, 286, 289, 293–94. For examples of other Cumberland authors who refer to the postwar careers of the veterans, see Calkins, *History of the One Hundred and Fourth,* 366–505; Horrall, *History of the Forty-Second Indiana,* 238–42; John H. Rerick, *The Forty-Fourth Indiana Volunteer Infantry. History Of Its Services in the War Of The Rebellion and A Personal Record Of Its Members* (1880), 138–39.

44. Heather Cox Richardson, *The Death of Reconstruction: Race, Labor, and Politics in the Post–Civil War North, 1865–1901* (2001; repr., Cambridge, MA: Harvard University Press, 2004), 1–5.

45. Albion W. Tourgee, *A Fool's Errand, By One Of The Fools; The Famous Romance of American History* (New York: Fords, Howard & Hulbert, 1880), 158; John R. Neff, *Honoring the Civil War Dead: Commemoration and the Problem of Reconciliation* (Lawrence: University Press of Kansas, 2005), 182.

Chapter 3

Epigraph. James H. Mauzy, *Historical Sketch of the Sixty-Eighth Regiment Indiana Volunteers* (1887), 191.

1. Kirk Savage, *Standing Soldiers, Kneeling Slaves: Race, War and Monument in Nineteenth-Century America* (Princeton, NJ: Princeton University Press, 1997).

2. Charles F. Manderson, *The Twin Seven-Shooters* (1902), iii–iv, 21, 52. By contrast, authors like Edwin High might agree that the sons of Confederate soldiers and the sons of Unionists would combine together in the country's future, but High also made sure to write Southern war guilt into the record and observe that the war had secured the cause of emancipation. Edwin W. High, *History of the Sixty-Eighth Regiment Indiana Volunteer Infantry 1862–1865* (1902), v, 320–21.

3. Anson Mills, *My Story,* ed. C. H. Claudy (1918; repr., Mechanicsburg, PA: Stackpole Books, 2003), 382, 384.

4. Alf[red] G. Hunter, *History of the Eighty-Second Indiana Volunteer Infantry, Its Organization, Campaigns and Battles* (1893), 163–64. For a sense of the variety of the discussions of Confederate war guilt, see Joseph G. Vale, *Minty and the Cavalry. A History of Cavalry Campaigns in the Western Armies* (1886), 492–95; Michael H. Fitch, *Echoes Of The Civil War As I Hear Them*

(1905), 175; William S. S. Erb, *Extract from "The Battles of the 19th Ohio" By A Late Acting Assistant Adjutant General, 3rd Brigade, 3rd Division, 4th A.C., Army of the Cumberland* (1893), preface; Edward A. Straub, *Life and Civil War Services of Edward A. Straub* (1909), 23; Will F. Peddycord, *History of the Seventy-Fourth Regiment Indiana Volunteer Infantry. A Three Years' Organization* (1913), 98–99.

5. S. A. McNeil, *Personal Recollections of Service in The Army of the Cumberland and Sherman's Army From August 17, 1861 to July 20, 1865* (1910), 43, 74, 76. For another example of a direct attack on how Lost Cause advocates were attempting to redefine the war's meaning, see F[rederick] W. Keil, *Thirty-Fifth Ohio. A Narrative of Service from August, 1861 to 1864* (1894), 229–30. One should also observe in this regard that the large majority of memoirs and regimentals published after 1900 preserved a clear and unmistakable sense of Confederate war guilt. Charles Manderson was noteworthy as a dramatic exception. For example, see Geo[rge] W. Morris, *History of the Eighty-First Regiment of Indiana Volunteer Infantry in the Great War of the Rebellion, 1861 to 1865* (1901), 75–79, 156–57; Alexis Cope, *The Fifteenth Ohio Volunteers and Its Campaigns. War of 1861–5* (1916), 10–11; James Birney Shaw, *History of the Tenth Regiment Indiana Volunteer Infantry. Three Months and Three Years Organizations* (1912), 9–10.

6. Earl J. Hess, *The Union Soldier in Battle: Enduring the Ordeal of Combat* (Lawrence: University Press of Kansas, 1997), 45–72. The quote is on page 68.

7. Charles A. Partridge, ed., *History Of The Ninety-Sixth Regiment Illinois Volunteer Infantry* (1887), 369.

8. John R. McBride, *History of the Thirty-Third Indiana Veteran Volunteer Infantry During the Four Years of Civil War From Sept. 16, 1861, to July 21, 1865* (1900), 127; James A. Barnes, James R. Carnahan, and Thomas H. B. McCain, *The Eighty-Sixth Regiment, Indiana Volunteer Infantry. A Narrative Of Its Services In The Civil War of 1861–1865* (1895), 398.

9. Partridge, *History Of The Ninety-Sixth Regiment*, 368. For another example of the use of humor to reinforce Cumberland victory, see S[pillard] F. Horrall, *History of the Forty-Second Indiana Volunteer Infantry* (1892), 124–25.

10. High, *History of the Sixty-Eighth Regiment*, 106. The report referred to is that of Col. William Grose, December 4, 1863, *OR*, series 1, vol. 31, part 2 (1890), 169–73. For other examples, see S[ilas] S. Canfield, *History of the 21st Regiment Ohio Volunteer Infantry, in The War Of The Rebellion* (1893), 163; G[eorge] W. Lewis, *The Campaigns of the 124th Regiment Ohio Volunteer Infantry with Roster and Roll of Honor* (1894), 153–54. On the importance of respecting the bodies of the dead, see John R. Neff, *Honoring the Civil War*

Dead: Commemoration and the Problem of Reconciliation (Lawrence: University Press of Kansas, 2005), 1–65; Drew Gilpin Faust, *This Republic of Suffering: Death and the American Civil War* (New York: Alfred A. Knopf, 2008), 61–101.

11. T[homas] F. Dornblaser, *Sabre Strokes of the Pennsylvania Dragoons, in the War of 1861–1865* (1884), 226–29. Some Cumberland veterans took a swipe or two at their Confederate opponents. Michael Fitch, for instance. Not all Cumberland narrators praised the Rebel soldier's dignity, integrity, or effectiveness. Fitch, *Echoes Of The Civil War As I Hear Them*, 355–61.

12. Jacqueline Glass Campbell, *When Sherman Marched North from the Sea: Resistance on the Confederate Home Front* (Chapel Hill: University of North Carolina Press, 2003), 3–57. Also see Anne Sarah Rubin, *A Shattered Nation: The Rise and Fall of the Confederacy, 1861–1868* (Chapel Hill: University of North Carolina Press, 2005), 208–39.

13. William Wirt Calkins, *The History of the One Hundred and Fourth Regiment of Illinois Volunteer Infantry. War of the Great Rebellion 1862–1865* (1895), 54.

14. Judson W. Bishop, *The Story of a Regiment: Being a Narrative of the Service of the Second Regiment, Minnesota Veteran Volunteer Infantry, in the Civil War of 1861–1865* (1890), 80–83. The quoted material is found on pages 82–83.

15. Edwin W. Payne, *History of the Thirty-Fourth Regiment of Illinois Volunteer Infantry September 7, 1861—July 12, 1865* (1902), 339–41.

16. George H. Puntenney, *History of the Thirty-Seventh Regiment of Indiana Volunteers. Its Organization, Campaigns, and Battles—Sept., '61–Oct., '64* (1896), 22; Dornblaser, *Sabre Strokes of the Pennsylvania Dragoons*, 240. Also see Cope, *The Fifteenth Ohio Volunteers*, 716.

17. Horrall, *History of the Forty-Second Indiana*, 132.

18. J. Henry Haynie, *The Nineteenth Illinois. A Memoir of a Regiment of Volunteer Infantry Famous in the Civil War of Fifty Years Ago for its Drill, Bravery, and Distinguished Services* (1912), 163.

19. Heather Cox Richardson, *The Death of Reconstruction: Race, Labor, and Politics in the Post–Civil War North, 1865–1901* (2001; repr., Cambridge, MA: Harvard University Press, 2004).

20. B[enjamin] F. [Magee], *History of the 72nd Indiana Volunteer Infantry of the Mounted Lightning Brigade* (1882), 697.

21. T[homas] J. Wright, *History of the Eighth Regiment of Kentucky Vol[unteer] Inf[antry], During Its Three Years Campaigns* (1880), 286. For examples of other authors who invoke free-labor ideology, though without the Reconstruction dimension, see Rev. David Bittle Floyd, *History of the Seventy-*

Fifth Regiment of Indiana Infantry Volunteers, Its Organization Campaigns, and Battles (1862–65) (1893), 9–10; Ephraim A. Wilson, *Memoirs of the War* (1893), 152–53; Lewis, *Campaigns of the 124th Regiment,* 105.

22. Floyd, *History of the Seventy-Fifth Regiment,* 203–4; Robert L. Kimberly and Ephraim S. Holloway, *The Forty-First Ohio Veteran Volunteer Infantry in the War of the Rebellion, 1861–1865* (1897), 114–15. Also see Henry J. Aten, *History of the Eighty-Fifth Regiment, Illinois Volunteer Infantry* (1901), 249–50.

23. Robert C. Toll, *Blacking Up: The Minstrel Show in Nineteenth Century America* (New York: Oxford University Press, 1974); Eric Lott, *Love and Theft: Blackface Minstrelsy and the American Working Class* (New York: Oxford University Press, 1993); William Mahar, *Behind the Burnt Cork Mask: Early Blackface Minstrelsy and Antebellum American Popular Culture* (Urbana: University of Illinois Press, 1999).

24. [Magee], *History of the 72nd Indiana,* 573–74. For a similar story, see C[harles] T. DeVelling, *History of the Seventeenth Regiment, First Brigade, Third Division, Fourteenth Corps, Army of the Cumberland, War of the Rebellion* (1889), 114.

25. John Thomas Smith, *A History of the Thirty-First Regiment of Indiana Volunteer Infantry in the War of the Rebellion* (1900), 31; Partridge, *History of the Ninety-Sixth Regiment,* 56. Also see Canfield, *History of the 21st Regiment,* 12.

26. Puntenney, *History of the Thirty-Seventh Regiment,* 20. For another example, see Dornblaser, *Sabre Strokes of the Pennsylvania Dragoons,* 53. For a more sour evaluation, one that refers to the fact that those blacks who looked to the army to free them created a refugee problem, see Kimberly and Holloway, *The Forty-First Ohio,* 116.

27. Cope, *The Fifteenth Ohio Volunteers,* 565; Rev. Nixon B. Stewart, *Dan. McCook's Regiment, 52nd O.V.I. A History of the Regiment, Its Campaigns and Battles From 1862 to 1865* (1900), 147. For other examples, see Puntenney, *History of the Thirty-Seventh Regiment,* 21.

28. Chandra Manning, *What This Cruel War Was Over: Soldiers, Slavery, and the Civil War* (New York: Alfred A. Knopf, 2007), 114–25.

29. [Magee], *History of the 72nd Indiana,* 110–11.

30. Marshall P. Thatcher, *A Hundred Battles in the West. St. Louis to Atlanta, 1861–65* (1884), 192. For other examples of rescue or assistance stories, see Smith, *History of the Thirty-First Regiment,* 52–53; Lucien Wulsin, *The Story of the Fourth Regiment Ohio Veteran Volunteer Cavalry From the Organization of the Regiment* (1912), 94–97; DeVelling, *History of the Seventeenth Regiment,* 114.

31. Fitch, *Echoes Of The Civil War As I Hear Them,* 268.

32. Cope, *The Fifteenth Ohio Volunteers*, 651; Royse, *History of the 115th Regiment*, 241.

33. Lewis, *Campaigns of the 124th Regiment*, 209–10. Also see J[oseph] T. Gibson, ed., *History of the Seventy-Eighth Pennsylvania Volunteer Infantry* (1905), 162. There were dissenters. Robert Kimberly and Ephraim Holloway believed that the USCT aroused too much anger among Confederates, thereby making combat harder than it otherwise would have been. Kimberly and Holloway, *The Forty-First Ohio*, 117.

34. Louis A. Perez Jr., *The War of 1898: The United States and Cuba in History and Historiography* (Chapel Hill: University of North Carolina Press, 1998), 81–107.

35. Gibson, *History of the Seventy-Eighth Pennsylvania*, 69. For similar comments, see Angus L. Waddle, *Three Years With the Armies of the Ohio and the Cumberland* (1889), 64–65; Keil, *Thirty-Fifth Ohio*, 83, 207.

36. Robert M. Rogers, *The 125th Regiment Illinois Volunteer Infantry. Attention Battalion!* (1882), 124; Vale, *Minty and the Cavalry*, 493.

37. William B. Sipes, *The Seventh Pennsylvania Veteran Volunteer Cavalry. Its Record, Reminiscences and Roster* (1905). For the quotations, see pages 1 and 5 in the separately paginated introduction, and pages 166–68 in the regular text.

Chapter 4

Epigraph. Allan Nevins, *The Organized War to Victory, 1864–1865*, vol. 8 of *The Ordeal of the Union* (New York: Charles Scribner's Sons, 1971), 395.

1. On the masculinity crisis the important works include Michael S. Kimmel, *Manhood in America: A Cultural History* (New York: Oxford University Press, 1996), 81–188; E. Anthony Rotundo, *American Manhood: Transformations in Masculinity from the Revolution to the Modern Era* (New York: Basic Books, 1993), 222–83; Gail Bederman, *Manliness and Civilization: A Cultural History of Gender and Race in the United States, 1880–1917* (Chicago: University of Chicago Press, 1995), 1–43, 170–239; John F. Kasson, *Houdini, Tarzan, and the Perfect Man: The White Male Body and the Challenge of Modernity in America* (New York: Hill and Wang, 2001). The reference to Slotkin concerns his brilliant triology of works on the American vision of the west and violence. The appropriate volume for turn-of-the-century militarism is Richard Slotkin, *Gunfighter Nation: The Myth of the Frontier in Twentieth-Century America* (1992; repr., New York: HarperPerennial, 1993), 1–122. Also see footnote 48.

2. Max Boot, *The Savage Wars of Peace: Small Wars and the Rise of American Power* (New York: Basic Books, 2002), 286–317.

3. Hinman published the original of *Si Klegg* in 1887. All references are to the recent J. W. Henry reprint edition. Wilbur F. Hinman, *Corporal Si Klegg and His "Pard": How They Lived and Talked, and What They Did and Suffered, While Fighting for the Flag* (1887; repr., Asburn, VA: J. W. Henry, 1997). For biographical details, see Brian Pohanka's introduction to this volume, i–xiii. Klegg should be read together with Hinman's history of his Ohio outfit. Wilbur F. Hinman, *The Story of the Sherman Brigade. The Camp, The March, The Bivouac, The Battle; And How "The Boys" Lived and Died During Four Years of Active Field Service* (1897). Also see his compilation of sketches entitled *Camp and Field. Sketches of Army Life written by those who followed the flag* (1892).

4. John D. Billings, *Hardtack and Coffee, Or The Unwritten Story of Army Life* (1887; repr., Lincoln, NE: Bison Books, 1993). Hinman, *Corporal Si Klegg*, 254.

5. Hinman, *Corporal Si Klegg*, viii.

6. Hinman, *Story of the Sherman Brigade*, 380.

7. Hinman, *Corporal Si Klegg*, 1, 3–4, 8. For his part, Billings makes a similar assessment, describing the recruiting process as a religious exercise disconnected from the issues that had begun the war. Billings, *Hardtack and Coffee*, 38–41.

8. Hinman, *Corporal Si Klegg*, 21, 30–31, 39. By contrast, Billings writes a first chapter on Southern treason, along with the evolution of the Union war effort toward antislavery. Billings, *Hardtack and Coffee*, 15–33. In his regimental study, Hinman certainly referenced and discussed the response to Sumter, and provided a detailed discussion of Democratic resistance to recruiting. Hinman, *Story of the Sherman Brigade*, 33–35, 38–40.

9. Hinman, *Corporal Si Klegg*, 30.

10. Ibid., 134–63.

11. Note, in this regard, Hinman's discussion of the evolution of tents and the uses that soldiers found for the canteen. Ibid., 56, 574–90. This evolution figures large in Billings's work as well. Indeed, the shift from raw recruit to expert soldier is this author's basic plot. Billings, *Hardtack and Coffee*, 43–142, 198–278, 316–49.

12. Hinman, *Corporal Si Klegg*, 175–76, 185.

13. Ibid., 97–99, 263, 307, 348. Billings creates nothing like this sinister atmosphere. Indeed, he had no problem with sutlers. Billings, *Hardtack and Coffee*, 224–25.

14. Hinman, *Corporal Si Klegg*, 326–27, 381.

15. Ibid., 359. For his part, Billings recognized the problem of moral degeneration in camp, gambling included. However, Billings focused more on the temptations that came with widespread foraging. Finally, Billings, too, stressed the role of "pards." Billings, *Hardtack and Coffee*, 144–63, 223–24, 231–49. Kristin L. Hoganson, *Fighting for American Manhood: How Gender Politics Provoked the Spanish-American and Philippine-American Wars* (New Haven, CT: Yale University Press, 1998), 28; Stuart McConnell, *Glorious Contentment: The Grand Army of the Republic, 1865–1900* (Chapel Hill: University of North Carolina Press, 1992), 206–38.

16. Hinman, *Corporal Si Klegg*, 43, 88–93. In his regimental study, Hinman includes a real story about Bowie knives that were given as gifts to wet-behind-the-ear recruits. Hinman, *Story of the Sherman Brigade*, 37.

17. Hinman, *Corporal Si Klegg*, 407. For his part, Billings makes only indirect references to combat. His focus is on the army's increasing organizational efficiency.

18. Ibid., 416–17.

19. Ibid., 591–93.

20. Ibid., 599–603. Hinman might have added that he believed that the Union army had also improved in efficiency under fire. He makes exactly this point in his description of Charles Harker's brigade (of which Hinman's regiment was a part) on Snodgrass Hill. Hinman, *Story of the Sherman Brigade*, 429–30.

21. Hinman, *Corporal Si Klegg*, 409.

22. Ibid., 75–76, 664. Observe that Billings includes a war poem—"We Drank From the Same Canteen"—that creates a similar image to Hinman's. Billings, *Hardtack and Coffee*, 223–24.

23. McConnell, *Glorious Contentment*, 177–78. Drew Gilpin Faust, *This Republic of Suffering: Death and the American Civil War* (New York: Alfred A. Knopf, 2008), 3–24, 61–63. Also see Faust's comments on Bierce and what she sees as his contempt for the impulse to sentimentalize and romanticize war death. See pages 196–200. Also see Mark S. Schantz, *Awaiting the Heavenly Country: The Civil War and America's Culture of Death* (Ithaca, NY: Cornell University Press, 2008), 163–206.

24. Hinman, *Corporal Si Klegg*, 676.

25. Ibid., 467–68. Also see Hinman, *Story of the Sherman Brigade*, 714.

26. Hinman, *Corporal Si Klegg*, 680–81. Also see McConnell, *Glorious Contentment*, 166–205.

27. Ibid., 683–85.

28. Ibid., 468.

29. Ibid., 429.

30. Hinman, *Story of the Sherman Brigade*, 244–45.

31. Hinman, *Corporal Si Klegg*, 645. In his regimental study, Hinman certainly discusses the links between the Union war and emancipation. Hinman, *Story of the Sherman Brigade*, 79, 209, 221, 260.

32. John Beatty mentions Keifer several times in his 1879 war diary. John Beatty, *The Citizen Soldier: The Memoirs of a Civil War Volunteer* (1879; repr., Lincoln, NE: Bison Books, 1998). In addition to his speeches in the *Congressional Record*, there is a large collection of the former colonel's letters to his wife, written during the war. See The Papers of Joseph W. Keifer, Library of Congress, MSS 18,764. For Keifer's war service in Virginia, see Thomas E. Pope, *The Weary Boys: Colonel J. Warren Keifer and the 110th Ohio Volunteer Infantry* (Kent: Kent State University Press, 2002).

33. Joseph Warren Keifer, *Slavery and Four Years of War: A Political History of Slavery in the United States, Together With a Narrative of the Campaigns and Battles of the Civil War in Which the Author Took Part: 1861–1865*, 2 vols. (1900; repr., Miami, FL: Mnemosyne Publishing, 1969). For the order of battle of Keifer's division, see Center of Military History, United States Army, *Correspondence Relating to The War With Spain, including the Insurrection in the Philippine Islands and the China Relief Expedition, April 15, 1898, to July 30, 1902*, CD-ROM (Washington: Government Printing Office, 1993), 1: 547–55.

34. The first volume starts with the huge chapter on antebellum politics and then presents Keifer's war service up to 1863. Volume 2 details the latter two years of the war and then adds a long appendix "A," detailing Keifer's personal life, congressional service, and Cuban war service. He then adds other appendices, which are composed of documents.

35. Keifer, *Slavery and Four Years of War*, 1: 6, 8–9.

36. Ibid., 1: 9, 145.

37. Ibid., 2: 238, 246–47.

38. Ibid., 1: 54, 60. See William W. Freehling, *Secessionists at Bay, 1776–1854*, vol. 1 of *The Road to Disunion* (New York: Oxford University Press, 1990), 253–86.

39. Keifer, *Slavery and Four Years of War*, 1: 98, 110.

40. Ibid., 1: 125, 156–57.

41. Ibid., 1: 145. At the time Keifer was hardly satisfied that the amendments had resolved the slavery question. In reaction to the Supreme Court's invalidation of the Civil Rights Act of 1875, Keifer responded by drafting an-

other potential amendment, this one to "secure the equality of citizenship." See 48th Cong., 1st sess., *Congressional Record* (December 11, 1883): 107.

42. Keifer, *Slavery and Four Years of War*, 2: 262–63, 266, 283. Also see Charles W. Calhoun, *Conceiving a New Republic: The Republican Party and the Southern Question, 1869–1900* (Lawrence: University Press of Kansas, 2006), 160–68.

43. Keifer, *Slavery and Four Years of War*, 2: 286, 293. For basic discussions of American intervention, see David F. Trask, *The War With Spain in 1898* (New York: Macmillan, 1981), 1–29; Hugh Thomas, *Cuba: The Pursuit of Freedom* (New York: Harper and Row, 1971), 417–93. In particular, see Louis A. Perez Jr., *The War of 1898: The United States and Cuba in History and Historiography* (Chapel Hill: University of North Carolina Press, 1998), 23–56.

44. For samples of his remarks on these subjects, see U.S. Congress, House, Representative Keifer speaking on a proposed revision of the Dingley Tariff, 61st Cong., 1st sess., *Congressional Record* (March 27, 1909): 429–33; U.S. Congress, House, Representative Keifer on the naval appropriations bill, 59th Cong., 1st sess., *Congressional Record* (June 21, 1906): 8886.

45. Keifer, *Slavery and Four Years of War*, 2: 299. Keifer also included Puerto Rico as an unintended acquisition.

46. U.S. Congress, House, Representative Keifer on the army fortification bill, 59th Cong., 2nd sess., *Congressional Record* (January 14, 1907): 1104; U.S. Congress, House, Representative Keifer on fortifications for the Philippines, 59th Cong., 1st sess., *Congressional Record* (February 14, 1906): 2565.

47. Hoganson, *Fighting for American Manhood*, 44.

48. U.S. Congress, House, Representative Keifer on the army fortification bill, 59th Cong., 2nd sess., *Congressional Record* (January 14, 1907): 1103–4; U.S. Congress, House, Representative Keifer on the naval appropriations bill, 60th Cong., 1st sess., *Congressional Record* (April 15, 1908): 4797; U.S. Congress, House, Representative Keifer on bill to raise the battleship *Maine*, 61st Cong., 2nd sess., *Congressional Record* (March 23, 1910): 3625.

49. Of course, Americans had eyed Cuba for decades. Ironically, during the antebellum period visions of Cuban expansionism had been the dream of Southern extremists, as Keifer well knew. Robert E. May, *The Southern Dream of a Caribbean Empire, 1854–1861* (Gainesville: University Press of Florida, 2002), 46–76; Perez, *The War of 1898*, 23–56; Keifer, *Slavery and Four Years of War*, 1: 125.

50. U.S. Congress, House, Representative Keifer on fortifications for the Philippines, 59th Cong., 1st sess., *Congressional Record* (February 14, 1906):

2565; U.S. Congress, House, Representative Keifer on the army fortification bill, 59th Cong., 2nd sess., *Congressional Record* (January 14, 1907): 1103. Also see Brian McAllister Linn, *Guardians of Empire: The U.S. Army and the Pacific, 1902–1940* (Chapel Hill: University of North Carolina Press, 1997), 5–22.

51. Niall Ferguson, *Colossus: The Price of America's Empire* (New York: Penguin, 2004), 41–45, 52–60; Boot, *The Savage Wars of Peace*, 129–55.

52. U.S. Congress, House, Representative Keifer on the army fortification bill, 59th Cong., 1st sess., *Congressional Record* (January 14, 1907): 1106; Andrew J. Bacevich, *American Empire: The Realities and Consequences of U.S. Diplomacy* (Cambridge, MA: Harvard University Press, 2002), 7.

53. U.S. Congress, House, Representative Keifer on the tariff, 59th Cong., 1st sess., *Congressional Record* (January 10, 1906): 927. In this regard, note Eric Love's recent argument identifying racism as a powerful force opposing American imperialism. Eric T. L. Love, *Race over Empire: Racism and U.S. Imperialism, 1865–1900* (Chapel Hill: University of North Carolina Press, 2004), x–xvi.

54. Keifer, *Slavery and Four Years of War*, 2: 293–94; Perez, *The War of 1898*, 81–107. Also see Graham E. Cosmas, *An Army for Empire: The United States Army in the Spanish-American War* (Columbia: University of Missouri Press, 1971).

55. According to Edmund Morris, Foraker introduced his measure as part of a plan to secure the 1908 presidential nomination. Edmund Morris, *Theodore Rex* (2001; repr., New York: Modern Library, 2002), 462–63, 467, 471–72, 477–78, 511. For the critical studies of the incident, see John D. Weaver, *The Brownsville Raid* (New York: W. W. Norton, 1970), 102–223; James N. Leiker, *Racial Borders: Black Soldiers along the Rio Grande* (College Station: Texas A&M University Press, 2002), 118–45.

56. U.S. Congress, House, Representative Keifer's remarks in favor of S. 5729, a measure to create a board of officers to review the cases of the men discharged from the Twenty-fifth Infantry, 60th Cong., 2nd sess., *Congressional Record* (February 27, 1909): 3397–98.

57. Keifer, *Slavery and Four Years of War*, 1: 62.

58. U.S. Congress, House, Representative Keifer's reply to Representative Bartlett of Georgia, 61st Cong., 3rd sess., *Congressional Record* (February 1, 1911): 1788. For similar sentiments expressed in Keifer's memoir, see Keifer, *Slavery and Four Years of War*, 1: 167–70; 2: 288–90.

59. U.S. Congress, House, Representative Keifer on the resolution to seek international treaty demilitarizing the Panama Canal, 61st Cong., 2nd sess., *Congressional Record* (May 17, 1910): 6435.

60. U.S. Congress, House, Representative Keifer on the naval appropriations bill, 60th Cong., 1st sess., *Congressional Record* (April 15, 1908): 4797.

Epilogue

1. Arthur Walworth, *Wilson and His Peacemakers: American Diplomacy at the Paris Peace Conference, 1919* (New York: W. W. Norton, 1986), 472–84.

2. Karen L. Cox, *Dixie's Daughters: The United Daughters of the Confederacy and the Preservation of Confederate Culture* (Gainesville: University Press of Florida, 2003), 107–10.

3. "Prelude to War" was the first installment of seven episodes, the separate installments were produced between 1942 and 1945.

4. For a critical examination of the series, see Peter C. Rollins, "*Victory at Sea*: Cold War Epic," in *Television Histories: Shaping Collective Memory in the Media Age*, ed. Peter C. Rollins and Gary R. Edgerton (Lexington: University Press of Kentucky, 2001), 103–22.

5. Colin L. Powell with Joseph E. Persico, *My American Journey* (New York: Random House, 1995), 122–25, 154, 453.

6. Christopher Alan Bracey, *Saviors and Sellouts: The Promise and Peril of Black Conservatism, from Booker T. Washington to Condoleeza Rice* (Boston: Beacon Press, 2008).

7. C. Vann Woodward, *The Burden of Southern History*, rev. ed. (1960; repr., New York: Mentor Books, 1969), 134–36.

Index